WISDOM
AND SPIRITUAL
TRANSCENDENCE
AT CORINTH

WISDOM AND SPIRITUAL TRANSCENDENCE AT CORINTH

Studies in First Corinthians

Richard A. Horsley

CASCADE *Books* • Eugene, Oregon

WISDOM AND SPIRITUAL TRANSCENDENCE AT CORINTH
Studies in First Corinthians

Copyright © 2008 Richard A. Horsley. All rights reserved. Except for brief quotations in critical publications or reviews, no part of this book may be reproduced in any manner without prior written permission from the publisher. Write: Permissions, Wipf and Stock Publishers, 199 W. 8th Ave., Suite 3, Eugene, OR 97401.

Cascade Books
A Division of Wipf and Stock Publishers
199 W. 8th Ave., Suite 3
Eugene, OR 97401

ISBN 13: 978-1-59752-844-3

Cataloging-in-Publication data:

Horsley, Richard A.
    Wisdom and spiritual transcendence at Corinth : studies in First Corinthians / Richard A. Horsley.

    xiv + 168 p.; 23 cm.

    Includes bibliographical references (p. 161–168).

    ISBN 13: 978-1-59752-844-3 (alk. paper)

    1. Bible. N.T. Corinthians, 1st—Criticism, interpretation, etc. 2. Bible. N.T. Epistles of Paul—Criticism, interpretation, etc. 3. Wisdom literature—Criticism, interpretation, etc. 4. Philo of Alexandria. 5. Bible. O.T. Apocrypha. Wisdom of Solomon—Criticism, interpretation, etc. 6. Gnosticism. I. Title.

BS2675 H65 2008

Manufactured in the U.S.A.

Contents

Acknowledgments • vii

Preface • ix

1 Spiritual Status among the Corinthians • 1

2 Wisdom of Word and Words of Wisdom • 21

3 Spiritual Marriage with Sophia • 39

4 Gnosis in Corinth • 65

5 The Confessional Formula in 1 Corinthians 8:6 • 89

6 Consciousness and Freedom • 97

7 Ecstatic Prophecy in Corinth • 115

8 No Resurrection of the Dead? • 128

Abbreviations • 157

Bibliography • 161

Acknowledgments

Seven of the chapters in this volume originally appeared in the following journals and are used with permission. The author and publisher are grateful for the cooperation of these journals and their editors.

Chapter 1: "Pneumatikos vs. Psychikos: Distinctions of Spiritual Status among the Corinthians." *Harvard Theological Review* 69 (1976) 269–88. Published under the auspices of the President and Fellows of Harvard College.

Chapter 2: "Wisdom of Word and Words of Wisdom in Corinth." *Catholic Biblical Quarterly* 39 (1977) 224–39. Published by the Catholic Biblical Association of America.

Chapter 3: "Spiritual Marriage with Sophia." *Vigiliae Christianae* 33 (1979) 30–54. Published by E. J. Brill (Koninklijke Brill N.V.).

Chapter 4: "Gnosis in Corinth: I Corinthians 8. 1–6." *New Testament Studies* 27 (1979) 32–51. Published by Cambridge University Press under the auspices of the Studiorum Novi Testamenti Societas.

Chapter 5: "The Background of the Confessional Formula in 1 Kor 8.6." *Zeitschrift für die neutestamentliche Wissenschaft und die Kunde der älteren Kirche* 69 (1978) 130–35. Published by Verlag Walter de Gruyter & Co. GmbH.

Chapter 6: "Consciousness and Freedom among the Corinthians: 1 Corinthians 8–10." *Catholic Biblical Quarterly* 40 (1978) 574–89. Published by the Catholic Biblical Association of America.

Chapter 7:   This essay has not been previously published.

Chapter 8:   "'How Can Some of You Say that There Is No Resurrection of the Dead?' Spiritual Elitism in Corinth." *Novum Testamentum* 20 (1978) 203–31. Published by E. J. Brill (Koninklijke Brill N.V.).

Preface

Collected here are several closely interrelated essays on the religious worldview and excitement of the Corinthian "spirituals" and Paul's response to them, originally published in the late 1970s. The research on which these articles is based was done in preparation for a dissertation accepted in 1971. The research appeared reworked into separate articles many years later because of the pressures to "publish or perish." Attempting to be an egalitarian parent of small children and develop a small Study of Religion program at the University of Massachusetts Boston had left no time to make the dissertation into a book. Ironic to have carved it up into separate articles.

In a field heavily oriented to philology and in a time when professors encouraged graduate students to do a carefully focused "word-study" for a dissertation (the heyday of Kittel's *Theologische Wörterbuch des Neuen Testaments*), I was determined to do virtually the opposite. I had become convinced that particular words and symbols were integral components of broader patterns of meaning or whole worldviews and, more significantly, in a pluralistic cultural situation, could have very different meanings, connotations, and overtones in different worldviews. Thus in study of New Testament literature in the context of the communities in which it was rooted in a pluralistic cultural situation, it was essential to consider a complete epistle of Paul or a complete Gospel, not separate words or passages. The corollary, moreover, was that comparative material should be considered not word by word but complete text by complete text, author-thinker by author-thinker. At the most fundamental level, that was both the fundamental premise and the basic contention of the dissertation.

Readers of these essays will find a certain amount of overlap among them. That is because it was necessary, following my premise and contention, to show in each one how the key symbols and slogans of the Corinthian spirituals to which Paul responds in each section of 1 Corinthians fit together with those in other sections of the letter—as evidenced by the appearance of the same language in multiple passages of Philo and Wisdom of Solomon. This volume of collected essays offers the opportunity to attempt to "put the pieces back together again" in the way originally intended in the dissertation. The resulting picture is incomplete since I never did develop the material on 1 Cor 10:1–13 and chapters 12–14 into articles. To partly fill in the missing pieces, I have supplemented the seven articles with a short chapter on the Corinthians' ecstatic prophecy to which Paul appears to be responding particularly in 1 Cor 14.

Conceptualization and Approaches Operative in the Analysis and Argument

In retrospect, as a first step in analysis of the conflict between Paul and some of the Corinthians, I was practicing a sort of elementary rhetorical criticism on key sections of 1 Corinthians. At the time, well before the rediscovery of rhetoric and rhetorical criticism there was no name for it, much less a well-defined method. In the 1960s we were already aware that Paul's letters were each addressed to a particular community and situation, hence often had different concerns. A comparison of the occurrence of key terms letter by letter, using a concordance, indicated that most of the key terms in 1 Corinthians appeared only or mainly there. That suggested that those terms were clues to particular issues that came up in the Corinthian assembly. A little elementary rhetorical criticism then indicated that Paul almost always disagreed with or seriously qualified those key terms, phrases, or slogans. This suggested that they were language of certain Corinthians that Paul was attempting to argue against or refute. The sophisticated rhetorical criticism practiced on 1 Corinthians by my collegial friends and mentors Anne Wire, Elisabeth Schüssler Fiorenza, and Margaret Mitchell basically confirm my hunches about the position Paul was arguing against, as I found then working on the commentary on 1 Corinthians for the Abingdon New Testament Commentary series. The use of such sophisticated rhetorical criticism now, decades later, could refine considerably the discernment of the Corinthians' viewpoint Paul is arguing against. Indeed such sophisticated rhetorical criticism of 1 Corinthians is still needed insofar as many interpreters of 1 Corinthians ignore its implications and avoid recognition of the strange and awkward formulations that result in Paul's "teachings" and "theology."

In both the dissertation and the derivative articles I found it extremely difficult to find a satisfactory conceptualization for how sets of language express whole structures of meaning in and by which people live—to conceptualize how the Corinthians' language all fit together into a distinctive understanding of existence, and correspondingly how Paul's expressed a different one. "Worldview"/*Weltanschauung* seemed too wooden at the time. Certainly nothing even approaching such a concept was even entertained in the field of New Testament studies. The concept "theology" was too narrow and modern and imposed too much theological freight onto ancient texts and people. "Christology" and "soteriology" were too narrow and fragmenting, and again imposed too much Christian theological freight. I remember reading widely in such suggestive and stimulating works as Ernst Cassirer, *The Philosophy of Symbolic Forms* looking for help. I thought that existentialist philosophical concepts such as "existence" were too "modern" and simply too vague. Despite the title, John Cobb's recently published *The Structure of Christian Existence* was also suggestive. (One term Wayne Proudfoot, in the field of philosophy of religion, and I conned thirty-five or so other grad students in the various sub-fields of Study of Religion to attend an interdisciplinary seminar—non-credit, of course, since none of the faculty was interested even in attending—discussing this book comparing many different "structures of existence.") This was well before the conceptualization of religion as a "symbol system" by Clifford Geertz and the similar conceptualization of "the social construction of reality" by Peter Berger and Thomas Luckmann caught on among many struggling to find an alternative to traditional Christian theological conceptualization. At the time I settled on the even then unsatisfactory "structures of consciousness" in order to indicate that patterns of meaning and expression are embedded in consciousness and that language is inseparable from the meaning/thought it expresses. In the articles, for want of a more satisfactory alternative, I reverted to the hackneyed "worldview," which hopefully points in the right direction.

Among other things, again in retrospect, these articles are essays in the sociology of knowledge. When Berger and Luckmann's *Social*

Construction of Reality first appeared I lapped it up. Here finally was a way of conceptualizing what I was finding evidence for in 1 Corinthians and (what I considered) related texts. Their reflections on socialization and "secondary socialization were particularly pertinent to the pluralistic cultural context in which Paul and other "apostles of Christ" carried out their mission. Paul, Peter, and others whose understanding of reality had been shaped by experience in Palestinian Jewish or Diaspora Jewish culture went to towns and countries with very different cultures to preach the gospel and organize communities of Christ-believers. It should not have been surprising that the latter would have difficulty understanding what the former were talking about, that there would be misunderstandings and different understandings of what the gospel and communities were all about.

Berger and Luckmann saw that religious conversion is a paradigmatic illustration of what can happen when people embedded in one culture/religion suddenly identify with another. The "secondary socialization" of learning to think and feel and identify in a new culture is a difficult process for which the concept of a sudden "conversion" is a gross oversimplification. And especially if the "conversion" situation is not one person entering a new culture and community but a missionary going into a culture and community where the converts think and feel alike, but differently from the missionary. In such circumstances the result will hardly be the converts' simple assimilation of the missionary's worldview. On the contrary, the original "socialization" will be likely to prevail. The situation in the Corinthian assembly that Paul and others catalyzed, however, would have been even more complex in having a mix of cultural influences and people who were seeking for and eager to construct a new identity. Moreover, Paul was not the only "missionary" to work in the community. Apollos had clearly become a rival with a different message. And his message was closer to the general culture in which they were embedded. That is the fluid and volatile contact of cultures that we find reflected in the arguments of 1 Corinthians.

The Changing Landscape of Studies of Paul and of 1 Corinthians

These articles, and the dissertation behind them, were attempts to read Paul's letters not verse by verse or as statements of theology, but argument by argument and issue by issue as addressed to a particular situation. With the development of rhetorical criticism this has caught on a bit more. Paul's arguments are much more complex in addressing particular situations than appears on the surface when taken at face value. They are one side of a conversation, sometimes more than a two-way conversation. This means, moreover, that language can be used in other ways than literal, whether by Paul or by the people to whom he may be responding. An example that makes a great deal of difference for interpretation of Paul and his assemblies is 1 Cor 1:25–30. Interpreters hungry for information on the social standing of "early/the first urban Christians" have generally taken these statements/terms literally. I argue that the terms refer (metaphorically) to spiritual status, as in most ancient philosophical as well as Hellenistic Jewish texts, which changes the way we use them as evidence for social status. Paul can even indulge in sarcasm, as in 1 Cor 2:6–16, which is misunderstood if not read in the context of the argument of 1 Cor 1–4, especially 1:18—3:5.

In locating Paul and the Corinthian spirituals he is addressing in relation to the broader cultural context of the Hellenistic-Roman world, these investigations shift attention from the "history of religions" background and Gnosticism broadly conceived to Hellenistic Jewish religiosity and the Wisdom of Solomon and Philo of Alexandria in particular. This has proven to be a much more proximate cultural comparison, both chronologically and in terms of the ethos from which "early Christianity" emerged.

Nevertheless these articles were written when we were still working with only the broadest synthetic picture of the Greek cities and Hellenistic culture as the ethos in which Paul carried out his mission. That broad picture continues in the influential sociological analysis of the *First Urban Christians* by Wayne Meeks. In recent years, however, with more focused studies of particular cities and areas of the Roman empire available and more precise analysis of philosophy, diaspora Jewish communities, and regional cultures, it should be possible to move toward more precise contextual reading of Paul's letters and through them via rhetorical criticism, of the mission in particular places such as Philippi and Corinth. But since Corinth was a highly fluid mixture of cultural influences located at a major intersection of trade routes, investigations of distinctive particular cultural expressions such as Philo's treatises may come together all the more suggestively with a fuller picture of culture in Corinth.

One of the most important developments in biblical studies, as in many fields, had been the emergence of sophisticated feminist analysis over the last three decades. This has made as great or greater an impact on our understanding of Paul in general and 1 Corinthians in particular as any development in the field. Elisabeth Schüssler Fiorenza's work in general and particularly Anne Wire's *Corinthian Women Prophets* have dramatically changed the way we approach Paul and 1 Corinthians and the ways we analyze, read, and interpret. Although they have some minimal inclusive language, one of the serious deficiencies of these articles from the late 1970s is their lack of feminist analysis that emerged in the next decade or so. These articles and Wire's analysis would seriously affect each other if brought together, with some serious qualification here and there. Yet in general they are compatible in their sketches of the Corinthian spirituals/women prophets.

Finally, the location of Paul's mission and letters in the context of the Roman empire and the recognition of its anti-imperial stance and implication offers yet another dimension in which the comparison and contrast between Paul's and the Corinthians' (and Philo's and Wisdom of Solomon's) views and expressions may prove useful. Considered in the context of the domination of Roman imperial rule and culture, both are ways, however different, of refusing to be defined by and controlled by Empire. The Corinthian spirituals' and Philo sought personal spiritual transcendence, which, ironically, was a more realistic route than Paul's drive to build an international alternative society based in local communities awaiting the concrete realization of the kingdom of God. But of course the latter has proven to be the most lasting long-range vision.

I would like to dedicate this volume to the memory of George MacRae. He had recently joined the Harvard Divinity School faculty when I completed the dissertation. When I went to him for advice about articles that might be based on the dissertation, he was most generous with his time and counsel. He became my mentor during the process of writing these essays. He read all of them carefully, then made suggestions about journals to which they could be submitted. Thanks to his mentoring and suggestions for revision and submission each article was quickly accepted for publication, so that all appeared within two or three years. George MacRae was a most generous, gentle, and wise man. I have missed him deeply and honor what a fine teacher and mentor he was to many students.

1

Spiritual Status among the Corinthians

In 1 Corinthians the apostle Paul is attempting to straighten out some people in his newly founded community who, by virtue of their possession of wisdom, were claiming a special spiritual status. Apparently they designated themselves as πνευματικοί (*pneumatikoi*) in contrast with the ψυχικοί (*psychikoi*), or those of lesser religious achievement. By a careful reading of Paul's arguments in 1 Corinthians we can discern some of their key religious terminology and principles.[1] On the basis of pertinent parallels to these terms and principles, especially in Hellenistic philosophical sources and Hellenistic-Jewish texts, it is then possible to draw certain conclusions regarding the religious viewpoint of these Corinthians.[2]

With regard to the *pneumatikos/psychikos* terminology, however, we are in an awkward situation. This is perhaps the most distinctive part of the language of these Corinthians. The *pneumatikos/psychikos* terminology runs like a red thread through most of the main sections of Paul's argument directed at the Corinthians (i.e., in the major sections of the letter: chapters 1-4; 8-10; 12-14; 15). In 1 Cor 2:13-15, *pneumatikoi* refers to those capable of possessing special spiritual revelation or wis-

---

1. Paul's negative reaction to certain aspects of these Corinthians' language and behavior enables us to reconstruct at least some of the Corinthians' viewpoint. Thus it is possible, for example, to determine the self-designations of the Corinthians from 1 Cor 1:26-27; 2:6—3:4; and 4:8-10: wise, powerful, of noble birth, perfect (vs. babes), rich, kings, etc. For a complete and systematic analysis and reconstruction, see Hurd, *Origin*.

2. Conzelmann, *1 Corinthians*, says that the background of Paul's "opponents" in 1 Corinthians cannot be established on the basis of the material available. Like previous commentators on the letter, however, he does not deem it of primary importance to pursue more *systematically* the potential pertinence of the rich literature he cites.

dom, in contrast to the *psychikoi* who do not have this ability. The same terms in 15:46–47 seem to refer to two different human beings or types of humanity which are respectively also "heavenly" (ἐπουράνιος) and "earthly" (χοϊκός), the former having some sort of priority over the latter. In chapters 12–14 the *pneumatika* are clearly the special spiritual gifts such as glossolalia and ecstatic prophecy, and *pneumatikos* refers to the special standing of one who enjoys such spiritual gifts (14:37). In 10:1–4 the same term refers to the spiritual nourishment and benefits derived from key soteriological scriptural symbols spiritually understood. For this distinctive language so important for understanding the Corinthian situation, however, there is no convincing terminological parallel whatsoever in contemporary comparative material. Hence it has been difficult to determine the background of this language and its meaning for the Corinthians' self-understanding.

Previous Hypotheses

The presence of the *pneumatikos/psychikos* terminology in 1 Cor 2 and 15 has been one of the main bases for arguing the Gnostic character of the "opponents" (or of Paul himself) in 1 Corinthians. Wilckens, following the lead of Reitzenstein, made such a case with the aid of Hermetic and Valentinian material.[3] But the terms *pneumatikos* and *psychikos* do not even occur in the *Poimandres*. Nor does this "Gnostic" document maintain any anthropological distinction between "mind" (νοῦς; or "spirit" πνεῦμα) and "soul" (ψυχή) on the basis of which the adjectival usage could have developed. Indeed, "mind" and "soul" stand more in a parallel relationship than in a superior–inferior one.[4]

Pearson has recently revived a proposal made previously by Dupont, namely that the pneumatic/psychic distinction developed out of the interpretation of Gen 2:7 in Hellenistic Judaism.[5] Pearson's form of the proposal finds in this Hellenistic-Jewish interpretation of Gen 2:7 both the origins of the *pneumatikos/psychikos* terminology and the theological background and context for this basic contrast found in 1 Cor 2:13–15

---

3. Wilckens, *Weisheit und Torheit*, 89–90; Reitzenstein, *Mysterienreligionen*, 342–45.

4. Note the sharp critique of Wilckens in Pearson, *Pneumatikos–Psychikos*, 8–9.

5. Pearson, *Pneumatikos–Psychikos*, esp. 11–12, 17–21; Dupont, *Gnosis*, 172–80; see also the important review of Dupont by Bultmann, esp. 14–16.

and 15:44–50. This argument, however, is based on some questionable contentions.

The specific terminology, the *pneumatikos/psychikos* contrast, does not occur in Philo or other Hellenistic-Jewish writings.[6] Similarly, neither Philo nor the Wisdom of Solomon makes any fundamental anthropological distinction between the "soul" (ψυχή) and the "spirit" (πνεῦμα), as the higher part of the soul, on the basis of which the adjectival usage might have developed.[7] Nor is there any evidence in Philo and Wisdom that there is among Hellenistic Jews a preference for the term "spirit" (πνεῦμα) instead of "mind" (νοῦς) for the higher, rational part of the soul.[8] Actually the terms "soul" (ψυχή), "spirit" (πνεῦμα), "mind" (νοῦς

---

6. The term *pneumatikos* occurs by itself a very few times in Philo, and then with little or no religious significance: "pneumatic sinews" or "nerves" in *Her.* 242; *Praem.* 48; *Aet.* 125; in *Op.* 67 nature provides a "pneumatic" substance for the soul's powers of sense-perception. Of greater interest here is *Abr.* 113: Sarah thinks the appearance of the visiting strangers is like "prophets or angels transferred from 'spiritual' and soul-like essence into human form" (note the parallel of "spiritual" and "soul"). It may be significant, however, that elsewhere Philo speaks of prophets and angels not as "spiritual" but as "ethereal" or "heavenly" beings. The term *psychikos* Philo uses dozens of times, almost always in a way that makes a metaphor or trope of the term it modifies. Thus food, death, light, house, wealth, passover, etc., are applied to the inner life of the soul—a meaning hardly helpful to Dupont's and Pearson's thesis. The usage is consistent and it is neutral in the sense that "psychic" never carries any pejorative connotations and there is no comparison with any higher aspect such as "spiritual" or "divine." In other Greek-Jewish literature, the writings of the Septuagint in particular, *pneumatikos* and *psychikos* appear neither in paired contrast nor separately—with the one exception of the *psychikos/somatikos* pair in 4 Macc 1:32.

7. Pearson's method here is formally the same as that of Reitzenstein and Wilckens: attempting to explain the meaning of the *pneumatikos/psychikos* contrast on the basis of a contrast between the nouns *pneuma* and *psychē*, but he substitutes Hellenistic Judaism for Gnosticism.

8. Indeed, no evidence is provided (Pearson, *Pneumatikos-Psychikos*, 11) for this contention on which the rest of the argument depends. Eduard Schweizer's comments ("πνεῦμα," 396) hardly support this contention. As Pearson contends, the use of *pneumatikos* for the highest religious status or the highest part of the self would be more understandable if πνεῦμα were used for the highest part of a person, in contrast to ψυχή as a lower part. However, Philo uses πνεῦμα very rarely with respect to the higher soul (a dozen times, vs. hundreds for νοῦς and διάνοια), and then it is not instead of, but in close connection with the other terms and usually as the *essence* of the rational soul. Wisdom uses πνεῦμα interchangeably with ψυχή. In Wis 15:11 this is in an allusion to Gen 2:7. But this usage of πνεῦμα is not necessarily related to interpretation of Gen 2:7. The translation of the Hebrew *ruaḥ* surely provides one of the roots of this usage. Psalms 77:3, 6 and Job 32:8, 18 are two examples where the context is contemplation of God or the possession of wisdom. Philo's use of Stoic philosophical language accords with his

or διάνοια), "rational soul" (λογικὴ ψυχή), etc. are largely parallel or interchangeable in Philo and Wisdom.

In Wis 15:11 (cf. 15:8 and 16) "soul" and "spirit" are parallel, without distinction in meaning. In 2:22—3:1 it is "soul," not "spirit," used in reference to man as created for incorruption, as an "image" (εἰκών) of God's own eternity. In 9:15 *psychē* and *pneuma* are parallel, synonymous terms for the soul that the corruptible, earthly body weighs down. There is no indication in Wisdom of any distinction between these terms in use and meaning, let alone between higher and lower parts of the soul expressed in these terms. In Wisdom the basic anthropological and soteriological divisions lie between the soul and the body, and between the wise, righteous souls and the foolish, unrighteous souls.

Philo's treatises display the same interchangeability of terms. In certain contexts he distinguishes between the "mind" in the soul, its dominant part, and the soul as a whole. But in *Op.* 135; *Leg.* 3.161; *Som.* 1.34,[9] and other interpretations of Gen 2:7, the basic division lies between body and soul, while the terms "soul" and "mind" (νοῦς or διάνοια) are used virtually interchangeably. In these texts the "divine spirit" (θεῖον πνεῦμα) or the "spirit of life" (πνεῦμα ζωῆς) is the substance (οὐσία) or the means by which this soul or mind is constituted. In *Op.* 135 the terms for the *immortal* part of a person composed of *divine spirit* are both "soul" and "mind" (διάνοια), in *Leg.* 3.161 it is "soul," and in *Som.* 134 it is "mind" (νοῦς). In the latter two passages "soul" and "mind" respectively are identified as "a divine fragment" (ἀπόσπασμα θεῖον). In *Plant.* 18–20 the term for the higher part of a person, the part made according to the Image of God, the Archetype, the Logos of the First Cause, is "soul" or "rational soul." "Spirit" in this passage is not the rational part of the soul, but rather "that Divine and Invisible Spirit."

In several different contexts (e.g., *Det.* 79–95; *Her.* 54–57; *Spec. Leg.* 4.123) Philo draws a distinction between the vital soul that humans share with animals and the rational soul whose essence or source or archetype

---

usage in Jewish exegetical traditions. He closely associates and nearly identifies ψυχή, νοῦς, and πνεῦμα: the spirit in the heart generates thoughts, *Spec. leg.* 1.6; the mind is the πνεῦμα ἔνθερμον, *Fug.* 134; cf. *Som.* 1:30; cf. Diogenes Laertius 7.157; von Arnim, ed., *Stoicorum Veterum Fragmenta*, vol. 2, frg. 96 and frg. 838.

9. Like those from Wisdom cited in the previous paragraph, these are passages that Pearson (*Pneumatikos–Psychikos*, 18–20) uses to explain the origins of the *pneumatikos/psychikos* terminology.

is the Divine Spirit or Logos. His use of this distinction in various contexts indicates that for Philo and the branch of Judaism he represents this is a standard exegetical tradition. It was developed partly (perhaps even primarily) to clarify any seeming discrepancies between Lev 17:11 (blood as the essence of the soul) on the one hand, and Gen 1:26–27 and 2:7 (spirit as the essence of the soul, which is made according to the Divine Image, the Logos) on the other. The higher, dominant (part of the) soul is called variously νοῦς, λόγος, ἄνθρωπος, λογισμός, νοερὰ καὶ λογικὴ ψυχή. *Pneuma* is usually stated as "the essence" of this rational soul.[10] The distinction, however, is not between a *mortal soul* and an *immortal spirit* but between the *soul of blood* (or flesh) and the *soul whose essence is spirit*. In *Det.* 79–90 that which Moses "names" spirit is the *soul*.

Thus the terminological evidence in Philo, like that in Wisdom, will not support the contention that Philo maintains a basic contrast between *mortal soul* and *immortal spirit*.[11] Philo's various interpretations of Gen 2:7 are no different from the rest of his writing in this regard. They provide neither the actual language of the *pneumatikos/psychikos* distinction nor the anthropological division between *pneuma* and *psyche* on which such language might be based. The fundamental anthropological division for Philo lies between *mortal body* and the *immortal soul*. And, in these exegeses of Gen 2:7, following precisely the implication of the text of 2:7b, the (divine) Spirit is the means or the essence by which the soul becomes immortal.

Two Types of Human Beings

Although it may not be possible to determine the precise origins of the *pneumatikos/psychikos* terminology, it may be possible to establish the background and meaning of this highly significant contrast by broadening our approach to include other, parallel language used by the Corinthians. With such a broadened approach we can profitably return to Hellenistic-Jewish interpretation of Gen 2:7. For there are in Philo other standard interpretations of Gen 2:7 besides that contrasting the soul of spirit with

---

10. Philo does use πνεῦμα once for "the dominant part of ourselves," (*Spec. Leg.* 1.171), where the abbreviated form of this traditional exegetical distinction may account for the expression: τὸ ἐν ἡμῖν λογικὸν πνεῦμα ("in your rational spirit"); cf. *Spec. Leg.* 1.277.

11. Pearson, *Pneumatikos–Psychikos*, 18–20.

the soul of blood. And one of these in particular[12] is directly relevant to 1 Cor 15:44–50 and may elucidate the significance of the *pneumatikos/psychikos* contrast in both 1 Cor 2 and 15.

Just as the *pneumatikos/psychikos* contrast in 1 Cor 2:6—3:4 is parallel to that of "the perfect" vs. "children" (τέλειοι vs. νήπιοι) so it is parallel in 1 Cor 15:44–50 to the contrast between "the *anthrōpos* of heaven" and "the *anthrōpos* of earth" or "dust." The Corinthians whom Paul is attempting to "straighten out" in 1 Cor 15[13] are apparently thinking of the *pneumatikos* and the *psychikos* respectively as the person of heaven and the person of earth or as two types of humanity, the heavenly and the earthly. As noted above, an anthropological dualism of immortal spirit and mortal soul expressed in terms of the *pneumatikos/psychikos* contrast as an exegesis of Gen 2:7 is not attested in extant texts of Hellenistic-Jewish theology. Such an exegesis would have to distinguish basically between the two clauses of Gen 2:7b, i.e., between the "breath of life" and the "living soul." But the Philonic interpretations of Gen 2:7 already examined, and the corresponding allusions in Wisdom, divide basically between 2:7a and 2:7b, i.e., between the body of earth or dust and the soul of spirit. The latter distinction, however, points to two things directly relevant to the Corinthian contrast between the two types of human being. (1) The conceptual apparatus for these interpretations of Gen 2:7 is a fundamental duality expressed in terms of earthly/heavenly, mortal/immortal, body/soul, blood/spirit, basically the same contrasts that appear in 1 Cor 15:44–54 in connection with Gen 2:7 (e.g., Philo *Her.* 55–56, *Op.* 135; *Leg.* 3.161; cf. Wis 2:23—3:4; 9:15; 15:11). (2) Moreover, in Philo all of the terms used to express this duality are also used in explanation of a fundamental contrast between two types of humanity, a contrast based on the two creation texts, Gen 1:26–27 and 2:7a. It is this other particular interpretation of Gen 2:7 (and 1:27),[14] this contrast between two types of humankind, which may elucidate the *pneumatikos/psychikos* contrast.

---

12. Apparently rejected as not relevant by Pearson, *Pneumatikos–Psychikos*, 19 n. 26.

13. The other pairs of contrasting terms in 1 Cor 15:44–54—i.e., heavenly/earthly, immortal/mortal, incorruptible/corruptible—represent further the language of the Corinthians whose views Paul is attempting to "correct" by insisting on the historical priority of the psychic or earthly human being to the pneumatic or heavenly human being.

14. It is evident that in Philo's writings we have to contend with a variety of different—and not necessarily related or consistent—interpretations of a given text or scriptural symbol. Philo's treatises display several standard interpretations or uses (a) of Gen

This distinction between the heavenly *anthrōpos* and the earthly *anthrōpos* was probably current prior to Philo.[15] Scholars such as Brandenburger who are influenced by the "history of religions" approach often take the Philonic heavenly *anthrōpos* as a reference to "The Primal Man" (*Urmensch*).[16] As Colpe points out, however, this concept of Primal Man is a synthetic scholarly construct designed to comprehend a variety of material, is historically imprecise, and is inconsistently applied by many scholars.[17] More particularly, the notion of a Gnostic or proto-Gnostic "Primal Man" has little descriptive or interpretative potential for any Philonic material and is hardly appropriate to Philo's texts on the heavenly *anthrōpos*. The latter figure in Philo bears no connotations of a macrocosmic Anthropos or of the *god* Anthropos. The Logos is once called "God's Man" in response to the "one man" in Gen 42:11, and is once called a "second god" (*Conf.* 41; 62; *Q.G.* 2.62). Philo once calls the cosmos "a great and perfect *anthrōpos*" (*Mig.* 220), but he says nothing to suggest that this is in some way identical with the heavenly *anthrōpos*. Of the different characteristics of the composite concept *Urmensch* as delineated by Rudolph,[18] some are applicable to one or another Philonic figure, while others are not applicable to any figure at all. For example, neither the Logos/Sophia nor the heavenly *anthrōpos* seem to qualify as a *redeemer* in any usual sense of the concept. The motif of descent and ascent pertains only to the individual soul (and *not* to the heavenly *anthrōpos*), which comes to sojourn in earthly-bodily reality but then returns to its heavenly home. In terms of *Urmensch*, the best we could salvage—and even this would be almost sheer speculation on our part—would be an androgynous heavenly figure who was the image (vs. "after the Image") of

---

1:26–27 or parts thereof, (b) of Gen 2:7 or parts thereof, and (c) of combinations of parts of Gen 1:26–27 and 2:7. Jacob Jervell, *Imago Dei*, 52–70, has attempted a simplified presentation of this complex Philonic material. Since he is concerned primarily with the *imago dei*, however, he does not distinguish all of the discrete exegetical traditions that Philo uses and combines, although he comments on some of them.

15. Conzelmann, *1 Corinthians*, 286; Brandenburger, *Adam und Christus*, 124–31, and others.

16. Brandenburger, *Adam und Christus*, 117–31.

17. See Colpe, *Die religionsgeschichtliche Schule*, 171–97; Conzelmann, *1 Corinthians*, 284–85, agrees but continues to use the concept anyway.

18. Rudolph, "Urmensch," 1196.

God at the pre-Philonic stage, but certainly *not* the same as the heavenly *anthrōpos* in Philo.[19]

What we do find in Philo repeatedly is a fundamental distinction between two types of human being, the heavenly and the earthly. The distinction between the two types is dominated by the contrast between the *anthrōpos made* after the image and the one *molded* out of earth.[20] The basic terms in this contrast depend on Gen 1:27 ("made" and "after the Image") and 2:7 ("clay," "out of earth," and "molded") respectively. Philo, moreover, uses this distinction primarily to explain a number of enigmas perceived in the text of Genesis 2. It would appear, therefore, that Philo (and his predecessors) found in the Biblical creation account two different types of humankind and that these had become a standard concept in his religious tradition.

> (citation of Gen 2:7) There are two types of human being (ἄνθρωπος): the one heavenly, the other earthly. The heavenly *anthrōpos*, being made after the Image of God, is altogether without part or lot in corruptible and earthly substance; but the earthly one was compacted out of the matter scattered here and there, which Moses calls "clay." For this reason he says that the heavenly *anthrōpos* was not molded, but was stamped with the Image of God; while the earthly is a molded work of the Artificer, but not His offspring. (*Leg.* 1.31.)[21]

In this and related texts (such as *Op.* 134;[22] *Leg.* 1.53, 88, 90–92; 2.4, etc.) we have paralleled all of the basic language of 1 Cor 15:44–54

---

19. That is, this is the most we can conclude once we recognize the Philonic distinctions that Brandenburger (*Adam und Christus,* 118–23) either overlooked or discounted. Brandenburger's claim to find *the* Primal Man in Philonic material will not stand up to a more careful examination of the Philonic passages on which he bases it. The weak link in the argument is on pp. 122–23. Eltester, *Eikon,* on whom Brandenburger relies, is not always accurate in his reading of Philo. See further the warning in Jervell, *Imago Dei,* 65–66.

20. See *Op.* 134; *Leg.* 1.131, 53, 88–95, 2.4; *Plant.* 44; *Q.G.* 1.4, 8; 2.56; *Q.E.* 2.46; *Her.* 57. The "heavenly" vs. "earthly" human beings occur in *Leg.* 1.31 and 90–95, and the "two types of humankind" in *Leg.* 1.31 and 2.4.

21. In this and subsequent quotations from Philo, I have relied upon the translation by Colson and Whitaker (LCL), while adapting toward consistency of English terminology and contextual meaning.

22. *Op.* 134, however, appears to be a special case (so also Jervell, *Imago Dei,* 53) that does little more than make the usual Platonic distinction between the intelligible form or idea of man and sense-perception or empirical man. Focusing on *Op.* 134, a text

except the *pneumatikos/psychikos* terminology. Moreover, this language is all centered around the basic contrast between two types of human: the heavenly *anthrōpos* vs. the earthly *anthrōpos*, who are, respectively, incorruptible vs. corruptible and immortal vs. mortal. There is also here, in an exegesis of Gen 2:7, the language of "after the image" from Gen 1:27, the Image for Philo being the Logos (Sophia) of God, in accordance with which the heavenly *anthrōpos* is created. Philo, furthermore, is concerned with the priority of the heavenly over the earthly. In *Leg.* 2.4 the earthly *anthrōpos* is explicitly called the "second,"[23] although more important is the priority implicit in the comparison whereby the heavenly type is clearly superior in ontological status and value to the earthly. The latter is merely the molded work of the Creator but not the offspring of the divine, and is even said to be mortal by nature (*Op.* 134). It is evident that Paul's polemical argument in 1 Cor 15:44–54, with the pointed transformation of his opponents' view of the priority in 15:46, could be readily understood as directed against such a distinction between two types of humanity.

But Philo's exposition of the two types is much more elaborate and reveals the further significance of the contrast. Philo tends to understand *anthrōpos* allegorically as referring to "mind," or the highest part of the soul. Accordingly he finds that the heavenly *anthrōpos* and the earthly *anthrōpos* refer to two different kinds of mind: the *earth-born and body-loving mind* and the *mind* existing *after the Image*, which has no share in corruptible earthly reality (esp. *Leg.* l.31–33; 2.4–5; cf. *Leg.* l.53–55; 88–89; 90–95; *Plant.* 44–45). The soteriological significance of the symbolism now begins to emerge. In *Leg.* l.53–55 and 88–89 Philo indicates that the mind made after the Image God deems worthy of three gifts of which natural ability consists: facility of apprehension, persistence (practicing noble actions), and memory (retention of holy doctrines).[24] The

---

frequently cited in references to 1 Cor 15:44–54, tends to divert us from Philo's usual understanding of the heavenly *anthrōpos* vs. the earthly *anthropos*, leading us either to false distinctions (such as "the idea man" vs. "the historical Adam"—Conzelmann, *1 Corinthians*, 286) or to dismissing the distinction as merely Philo's Platonic form of thinking.

23. The order in which the two creation accounts of humans are presented in the biblical account just happens to correspond with Philo's more basic pattern of priority.

24. The Greek words are εὐφυΐα, ἐπιμονή, μνήμη. Εὐφυΐα is an Aristotelian term used inclusively of natural and moral goodness. Εὐφυΐα is attested almost exclusively in Philo and in this context. It surely connotes more than "cleverness, tact" (so LSJ)!

molded mind, on the other hand, can only apprehend well. It neither retains nor practices good things, and is soon cast out of the garden. But upon the *anthrōpos* whom God provides with secure knowledge, i.e., the pure mind that has no share in corruptible matter, He also bestows the ability to practice and to remember or guard the virtues and doctrines.²⁵

In these passages the contrast between the two types of human being emerges as a qualitative distinction between people of two different levels of religious-ethical ability and achievement. The heavenly type of humanity or mind, by virtue of the abilities granted by God, or by virtue of its origin after the Image, the Logos/Sophia, has achieved immortality and is secure in its heavenly status. The earthly mind, however, because of its attachment to earthly and bodily realities, is thus

> played upon by forces drawing it in opposite directions and given the high calling to decide between them, that it might be moved to choose and to shun, to win fame and immortality should it welcome the better, and to incur a dishonorable death should it choose the worse. (*Plant.* 44–45)

It is also noteworthy that the distinction between the soul of blood (Lev 17:11) and the soul of Spirit (Gen 2:7b) discussed above is developed by Philo into this same contrast between human types,

> the one that of those who live by reason, the Divine Spirit, the other of those who live by blood and the pleasure of the flesh. This last is a molded clod of earth, the other is the faithful impress of the Divine Image. (*Her.* 54–57)

Two additional passages (*Q.G.* 2.56 and *Q.E.* 2.46) elucidate even more clearly how the two *anthrōpoi* function as paradigms or prototypes for devout Jews of different religious levels. In *Q.G.* 2.56, because the blessing given Noah in Gen 9:1–2 parallels that given to the man made in Gen 1:27–28, Noah is equal in honor, not with the molded and earthly *anthrōpos*, but with the one made in the likeness of God. The heavenly

---

The Neoplatonic metaphorical use of θίξις in the sense of the apprehension of the mind probably leads us in the right direction. Ironically enough, Colson and Whitaker (LCL) do better on εὐθιξία ("facility in apprehending") than on ἐπιμονή and μνήμη in their paraphrase based on contextual usage.

25. Can Wis 4:1–5 be understood as an independent witness to the particular Jewish theological tradition on which Philo is here drawing? There is immortality in the remembrance of virtue (μνήμη ἀρετῆς), but the impious (of the two kinds of *anthrōpoi* here in Wisdom) are unable to persist, even though they may blossom with virtue for a season.

anthrōpos here serves as a paradigm into which a scriptural hero of righteousness is set in the interpretation of his destiny and his significance for the faith. This passage also illustrates a general typological pattern: as the prototype or paradigm, so are those who belong to that type or paradigm. Thus Philo exhorts the souls of intelligent people to follow the paradigm of Noah and the *anthrōpos* made in the Image. The same typological pattern of thought is expressed in other passages as well when the lower prototype, "the earthly mind called Adam," is contrasted with those who belong to the higher type, "the truly alive having Sophia for their Mother" (*Her.* 52–53), or "the people endowed with sight" (*Plant.* 44–46).

When Philo makes a distinction between the contemplative race, or faithful adherents of Jewish religious communities in general, and the prophetic type of people who are "called above" as initiates into the divine mysteries (*Q.E.* 2.46), he is quite clearly speaking to actual communities of devout Jews. That is, he is addressing Jewish communities that (like the community Paul addresses in Corinth) contain an elite of exalted spiritual status, in distinction from the ordinary believers. The "contemplative race," or ordinary faithful Jews, has indeed considerable value to God. Its election is comparable to the ordering of the world and the creation of the earth-born molded human, to all of which is assigned the symbolic number "6." Yet the "calling above" of the prophetic type, symbolized by Moses, is an origin (and destiny) superior to that of the molded humanity's corruptible mixture with the body and earth, and is rather ethereal and incorporeal in accord with the ever-virginal Hebdomad, i.e., Sophia/Logos.[26] From these several Philonic passages it is clear that the heavenly *anthrōpos* and the earthly *anthrōpos*, the two types of humanity, are paradigms, based in creation texts, of different levels of religious endowment or status in the Hellenistic-Jewish tradition represented by Philo.

The argument thus far should perhaps be summarized briefly. We cannot account for the *pneumatikos/psychikos* terminology in 1 Corinthians on the basis of any of the comparative literature previously suggested. Even the Hellenistic-Jewish texts that Pearson adduces do not

---

26. In this passage both *Moses* and the *anthrōpos* after the Image are juxtaposed with the symbolism of the Hebdomad, important in Philo and elsewhere in Hellenistic Judaism (cf. Aristobulus in Eusebius *Praep. Ev.* 9.667a–668b). For Philo the perfect number, Seven, symbolizes Light–Logos–Sophia and thus the human mind insofar as the Holy Logos of the Hebdomad comes upon the soul and replaces the Six and its mortal things (cf., *Leg.* 1.15–18; *Q.G.* 2.41).

show a distinction between mortal soul and immortal spirit from which, supposedly, the terminology was derived. But Dupont and Pearson have pointed in the right direction. The *pneumatikos/psychikos* language is part of or parallel to a fundamental contrast between two types of human being, heavenly and earthly, immortal and mortal, which Paul argues against polemically in 1 Cor 15:44–54. This same fundamental cosmological-soteriological contrast is found in Philo's writings generally, but particularly in the explanations of the two types of humanity based on Gen 1:27 and 2:7a, respectively. Only the specific terminology, *pneumatikos/psychikos*, is missing. It would appear, then, that the Corinthians used *pneumatikos/psychikos* along with the rest of these terms to make the same basic contrast between people of different levels of spiritual ability and attainment, different religious types of people, for whom the heavenly *anthropos* and the earthly *anthropos* were paradigmatic symbols in Philo.

Levels of Spiritual Status

Analysis of the Corinthians' language behind 1 Cor 1–4 leads to the same result. The actual terminology of *pneumatikos/psychikos* is not found in Philo. But the other language of the Corinthians discerned through 1 Cor 1–4, especially the "perfect vs. child" contrast which is parallel to the *pneumatikos/psychikos* distinction (1 Cor 2:6—3:4), is adequately and comprehensively paralleled only in Philo. Thus again, the Hellenistic-Jewish tradition he represents provides the analogy for understanding the Corinthians' religious language.

The distinction between "perfect" and "child," which is adequately paralleled only in Philo,[27] is important and central language in his treatises. Philo makes frequent distinctions between different classes of people or levels of religious status, sometimes distinguishing two, sometimes three classes or levels.

He makes one twofold distinction between the extremes, the wise or perfect or good person as opposed to the foolish or bad or evil person (σοφός, τέλειος, ἀστεῖος, σπουδαῖος vs. ἄφρων, φαῦλος, κακός). He makes another twofold distinction between the wise and perfect as the highest religious status and the child or practicer or one making progress at a lower level of achievement (νήπιος, ἀσκητής, ὁ προκόπτων). The threefold distinction, in effect, juxtaposes these twofold distinctions,

---

27. Pearson, *Pneumatikos–Psychikos*, 27–28.

situating the babes or practicers in between the two extremes with the possibility of moving in either direction.

Thus the τέλειος/νήπιος language is important to Philo's determination of these different levels of soteriological status or achievement. The "solid food" and "milk" refer, as part of this same set of terms, to the different diets appropriate to the respective levels.

> And who also could the *anthrōpos* in each of us be except the mind, who is to reap the benefits from what is sown or planted? But since food for children is milk, and for mature (perfect) people is cake, there must also be as milk-like foods for the soul during its infancy, the elementary education of school studies, and as foods for mature people instruction through wisdom and moderation and all virtue. (*Agr.* 8–9)[28]

Philo's primary concern is with the individual soul or mind and its attainment of perfection. Sometimes he speaks of the process leading toward perfection in terms of a three-stage scheme: beginnings, progress, and perfection (e.g., *Leg.* 3.159; *Agr.* 165). From some passages (e.g., *Agr.* 157–65) it is clear that these terms refer to stages of religious achievement undergone or experienced by pious (Alexandrian) Jews. "Perfection" was a spiritual status that could be reached and established ever more firmly during the soul's sojourn in the body as it attained an ever more intimate relation with Sophia. This language of perfect vs. child is integral to Philo's more extensive exposition of what might be termed patterns of perfection, whose paradigms are the great patriarchs, such as Abraham or Jacob.[29]

A further aspect of this language in Philo, however, is even more particularly pertinent to the Corinthian situation, where Paul found this language of different religious status linked with a divisiveness in the community. Although the *teleios/nēpios* terminology may designate the stages along the process leading to spiritual perfection, the effect of this

---

28. See further, for example, *Quod Omni prob.* 160; *Congr.* 19; *Agr.* 157–62; *Mig.* 28–33; 36–40; *Sob.* 9–10; *Som.* 2.10–11, 234–36; *Leg.* 1.90–94. Compare, in NT writings, Heb 5:12–14.

29. Abraham is a symbol of the nascent σοφός who sojourns with Hagar or school studies as preparation for becoming τέλειος and possessed of Sarah or Sophia (ἀρετή); Jacob symbolizes the practicer who eventually attains the vision of God, symbolized by the name Israel (e.g., *Leg.* 3.244; *Congr.* 154; *Q. G.* 3.20). Erwin Goodenough has laid out these patterns of perfection clearly and sympathetically in *By Light, Light*, chapters 5, 6, and 8, and esp. pp. 136–52 on Abraham.

and related language is to make sharp distinctions between the abilities of the two levels. The wise and perfect are able to transcend the body and psychic passions, while those making progress can only check their effects on the higher self (e.g., *Leg.* 3.131-44). The *teleios* receives perfect goods from God without having to "toil," while the child or "ascetic" acquires virtue only through toil and cannot thus reach perfection (e.g., *Leg.* 3.135). The situation of training, that of the children, is clearly an inferior status. The higher religious ideal is to become perfect or wise. This involves leaving behind the merely infantile and milk-like teachings to feed on Sophia herself. The wise thus come to possess the perfect good and immortality. In fact, the perfect attain such an exalted position as to be changing their ontological status, from corruptible to untreated nature, whereas those making progress lie merely on the border between the living and the dead (*Som.* 2.234-36). The distinction between these two levels of spiritual achievement is often so sharply drawn that the perfect and the children are separated into two distinct groups.

> These are two companies (θίασοι) as leaders of which Moses introduces Isaac and Joseph. The noble company is led by Isaac who learns from no teacher but himself, absolutely disdaining to make use of soft and milky food suited to infants and little children, and using only strong nourishment fit for grown people. . . . The company which yields and is ready to give in is led by Joseph, for he . . . is thoughtful for the wellbeing of the body also . . . and is drawn in different directions . . . and can never attain to fixity. (*Som.* 2.10-11; cf. *Sob.* 9-10)

The Philonic parallels, furthermore, extend beyond the terminology of "perfect vs. babes" to nearly all of the Corinthians' self-designations which can be discerned through 1 Cor 1-4. Judging from Paul's polemical or even sarcastic comments in 1 Cor 1:26 and 4:8-10 the same Corinthians who understood themselves as the wise, perfect, and spiritual, as opposed to the foolish, babes, and psychics, also used terminology such as "nobly born, rich, kings, glorious" (εὐγενής, πλούσιος, βασιλεύς, ἔνδοξος), etc., in reference to their exalted status. As with the *teleios–nēpios* contrast, Philo provides an analogous use of these terms on the basis of which we may better understand the Corinthians.[30] Indeed separately or to-

---

30. Philo, of course, has appropriated this set of terminology from Hellenistic philosophy, where it was standard at least among the Stoics, e.g., *Stoicorum Veterum Fragmenta* (ed. J. von Arnim) 3.85-89, 150-57. Jewish wisdom theology prior to Philo had long

gether, these terms are found throughout some of the same passages in which the *teleios/nēpios* language is used and can hardly be avoided.³¹ True nobility, wealth, honor, kingship, etc., are possessions of the soul (the *teleios* or the *sophos*) secure in its own proper spiritual existence.³² As with *teleios* in the *teleios/nēpios* contrast, the designations of "wise," "nobly born," "king," etc., refer to a spiritual elite. This elite is often quite explicitly contrasted with the foolish and wicked. But in many passages there is also a contrast between the elite who possess wisdom and thereby are rich, well-born, kings, glorious, and those merely of lesser religious achievement. One of these same passages, *Virt.* 174, also indicates that some of those who characterized themselves as rich, nobly-born, strong, and knowledgeable, appeared arrogant even to others (Philo) who valued such characterizations of the *sophos*. It is not only Paul who finds a potential arrogance in those who enjoyed the exalted spiritual status expressed in such terms and the divisive implications are again quite evident.

We have found, therefore, that both of the sets of language to which the *pneumatikos/psychikos* terminology is parallel in 1 Corinthians function prominently in Philo's writings as important expressions of different types of men or of different levels of religious achievement. The Philonic analogy, however, goes one step further. For these two sets of language are fused at points in Philo's writings.

---

since expressed the relation between the wise man and Sophia in the same or similar terms: see, e.g., Prov 8–9; 8:18; Sir 4:11–13; 11:1; 15:5–6; Wis 5:16; 7:7–8; 8:3, 5, 10, 17–18.

31. In fact, Philo devotes the last sub-section of the treatise *De virtutibus* (187–227) to the subject "Concerning Noble Birth," the most striking passage of which (211–19) discusses Abraham, inspired by the divine Spirit, as a paradigm of perfection and kingship (although he was a commoner, ἰδιώτης, cf. Paul's charge against the Corinthians, 1 Cor 1:26–27) as well as of noble birth. Pearson (*Pneumatikos–Psychikos,* 40) notices at least the "noble-birth" in this key passage and devotes an excursus to this spiritual quality.

32. Perhaps it will suffice to quote only one of the many pertinent texts:

> For the wise person is a friend of God rather than a servant... But he who has this allotment has passed beyond the bounds of human happiness. He alone is nobly born (εὐγενής)..., not only rich, but all rich (οὐ πλούσιος, ἀλλὰ πάμπλουτος)..., not merely of high repute, but glorious (οὐκ ἔνδοξος, ἀλλ' εὐκλής)..., sole king (μόνος βασιλεύς).., sole freeman (μόνος ἐλεύθερος) ... (*Sob.* 56)

See further, e.g., *Mig.* 197; *Som.* 2.242–44; *Virt.* 8; *Sac.* 43–44; *Sob.* 55–57.

Indeed, in *Leg.* 1.90–95 Philo expresses the contrast between the heavenly *anthrōpos* and the earthly *anthrōpos* in terms of his general distinctions of two and three levels of religious endowment, more particularly in the language of perfect vs. child. Philo interprets "Adam" in Gen 2:16–17 as the name of the molded *anthrōpos*: "Call him 'earth.'" Thus Adam means the earthly and corruptible mind (γήϊνος καὶ φθαρτὸς νοῦς), for the mind after the Image is not earthly but heavenly. Now it is to this Adam, the earthly mind, and not to the *anthrōpos* after the Image, that God gives the command.

> For the latter, even without urging, possesses virtue instinctively; but the former, independently of instruction, could have no part in wisdom.

The distinction that is implicit here, that between the perfect and the child, Philo proceeds to make quite explicit.

> There is no need, then, to give injunctions or prohibitions or exhortations to the perfect person formed after the Image (τῶ τελείω τῶ κατ' εἰκόνα) for none of these does the perfect person require. The bad person has need of injunction and prohibition, and the child (νήπιος) of exhortation and teaching . . . Quite naturally, then, does (God) command and exhort the earthly mind who is neither bad nor good but midway between these. (*Leg.* 1.90–95)

In this passage Philo fuses or identifies the contrast between the two human types with the standard distinction in levels of religious status. The heavenly *anthrōpos* and the earthly *anthrōpos* are the same, respectively, as the *teleios* and the *nēpios*.

As the Philonic analogy to the language and religious viewpoint of the Corinthians becomes more complete, it is becoming also more coherent and compact. According to the Philonic analogy, Hellenistic Jews, at least in this particular tradition, made distinctions (1) between different levels of spiritual status, expressed in the *teleios/nēpios* contrast and related terminology, and (2) between two types of humanity, heavenly vs. earthly, immortal vs. mortal. Since these distinctions are parallel if not identical, it is not surprising to find that the Corinthians were using another, similar set of terminology, the *pneumatikos/psychikos* distinction, in connection with both.

Possession of Sophia

It is quite clear from what Paul says in 1 Cor 1–2 that the claim to special spiritual status by some Corinthians, and the resultant dissensions in the community, were connected with those Corinthians' obsession with *sophia*.[33] Similarly in Philo, all the language of exalted religious status revolves around *sophia*, the divine agent of salvation as well as of creation. For it is through possession of *sophia* that the soul attains exalted status as perfect, nobly-born, rich, king, immortal, heavenly (e.g., *Mig.* 26–40; *Q.G.* 4.46). The Philonic analogy, however, has not been adequately pursued for the light it may shed on the significance of the *pneumatikos-psychikos* and related language of the Corinthians. Wilckens perceives that for the Corinthian "opponents" Sophia is a personified divine figure. But he obscures the issue by suggesting that they had also identified Sophia with the exalted Christ,[34] and he does not really pursue the Philonic material beyond the only Philonic image for Sophia ("the royal way") that could possibly fit with the "Redeemer-myth" model that he is following.[35] Pearson, perhaps reacting against Wilckens' focus on Sophia as divine person, concentrates on "*sophia* as content" and, similarly, does not pursue the Philonic analogy.[36] A more comprehensive pursuit of this Philonic analogy may further elucidate the significance of the *pneumatikos-psychikos* terminology and other language of differential religious status.

In the earlier development of the Jewish wisdom tradition ḥokmah/ sophia had become the focus of Jewish piety. Wisdom had become identical with the Torah or Law, and was the very content of salvation and true religion. The whole section of Wisdom, chapters 6–10, is a poetic pan-

33. Wilckens (*Weisheit und Torheit*, 5–11) makes this quite clear.

34. Koester's and Colpe's reviews must be used along with Wilckens' exegesis in order to make sense out of the polemical situation in 1 Corinthians. That Sophia, for the Corinthian "opponents," is a personified divine figure is clear, likewise that Sophia is their salvation-content. This does not mean that they also identified Sophia with the exalted Christ (in the sense of the Gnostic redeemer, according to Wilckens), see Koester, 591–92. It is Paul who makes the identification: the true wisdom of God is the historical person, the crucified man, Jesus Christ. Conzelmann (*1 Corinthians*, ad. loc.) does not really clarify the polemical situation with respect to *sophia* in 1 Cor 1–2.

35. Wilckens, *Weisheit und Torheit*, 139–59, following Pascher, Η ΒΑΣΙΛΙΚΗ ΟΔΟΣ; cf. Colpe's review of Wilckens.

36. When he comes to direct discussion of *sophia*, Pearson (*Pneumatikos–Psychikos*, 30–32) moves away from the Philonic material, although he does base his interpretation of *sophia* as *pneuna* on Wis 7:22 and 9:17 and fragments of Aristobulus, as well as one Philonic phrase from *Gig.* 47.

egyric on Sophia as a divine figure, the consort of the *sophos* and agent of his immortality as well as the consort of God. Similarly, in Philo's writings Sophia, or her equivalent, the divine Logos,[37] is the mediator of creation and especially the means and substance of the soul's salvation. Sophia (Logos), perpetually understood as a divine personal figure, is either the wife (spouse) or the mother of the wise. As the divine spring (*Fug.* 177-202; *Post.* 124-319), the spiritual banquet (*Som.* 1.47-51; 198-200; *Fug.* 137-38, 166-67; *Cong.* 172-74), and the "royal way" (*Post.* 101-2; *Quod Deus* 140-80), Sophia is the means or agent of spiritual achievement and security for the wise and perfect. As the divine spring and spiritual banquet, Sophia is also the substance of salvation, the divine nourishment or knowledge. And as the divine land that the *sophoi* or *teleioi* attain (*Mig.* 28-30, 45-46; *Her.* 313-15), Sophia is the soteriological object or goal. It is apparent from such passages that Philo conceives of *sophia* both as the *content* of wisdom possessed by the wise and perfect and as the *means* or agent by which the perfect come to possess the content. This pattern becomes quite explicit at points.[38] Most directly pertinent to our analogy for the Corinthians perhaps are the "by Sophia, Sophia" passages such as *Her.* 98; *Mig.* 39; and *Q.G.* 4.101: thus the wise who desire wisdom "God has entirely approved and has made perfect in the knowledge of Sophia by his Sophia" (cf. 1 Cor 1:21). For Philo, as for Wisdom, the divine figure Sophia (Logos) has rather comprehensive functions. Soteriologically all depends and focuses on Sophia.

Since Hellenistic-Jewish piety of this tradition is thus centered on Sophia, the differences in religious status are due to differences in relationship with Sophia. In fact, the respective relationships are strikingly contrasted in Philo's writings. For the babes, the ascetics who are merely at the elementary stage, Sophia may be the soteriological goal. But they are unprepared for, or incapable of, the intimate relationship with Sophia enjoyed by the wise and perfect. The religious content or teaching appropriate to the ascetics or children is the "school studies" as opposed to

---

37. On the identity of Logos and Sophia generally in Philo, see Wolfson, *Philo*, 1.253-61.

38. The most notorious by now is the "by light, light" paragraph in *Praem.* 43-46, from which, of course, comes the title of Goodenough, *By Light, Light*, which gives an extensive discussion of the function of Sophia as divine light and enlightenment, esp. chapter 6. Compare Wlosok, *Laktanz*, 77-114. Also Klein, *Lichtterminologie*, 11-79. It should he pointed out, however, that "light" is less, rather than more, prominent than some other imagery in Philo's writings.

the true knowledge and wisdom enjoyed by the perfect (e.g., *Agr.* 8–9; *Congr.* 19), that is, the milk-like teachings or mere fragrance as opposed to the solid food of Sophia herself (e.g., *Mig.* 28–33; *Fug.* 202; *Sac.* 43–44). The imperfect who only sojourn with Sophia must practice the mundane duties, whereas the perfect and true-born actually dwell with Sophia and possess the perfect virtues (*Sac.* 43–44). Or, to change the image somewhat, for the babes or practicers, Sophia/Logos is only the teacher, while the perfect possess or dwell in or are married to Sophia/Logos (e.g., *Leg.* 3.1–3; *Som.* 2.234–36).

Sophia also has quite different effects on the different classes of people. Those who dwell in Sophia have passed beyond the toil necessary for the babes. The former are now immune to ensnaring pleasures of the flesh and need not struggle against the corruptible matters of body and the senses (e.g., *Mig.* 26–40). For the perfect, who actually dwell together with Sophia as their life-mate, all the influences that would injure the soul cease, whereas they merely diminish in force for those of lesser status who simply sojourn with Sophia (e.g., *Som.* 2.234–36; *Quod Deus* 1–3; *Leg.* 3.131–44). Those who, drinking and being filled with Sophia, are wise and free and rulers, who thus enjoy the divine wealth (*Post.* 130–39), have completely transcended or rid themselves of the body and earthly influences. Those who have acquired *sophia* are able to pass beyond the earthly values to the spiritual values of wealth, noble-birth, glory, etc.

> Great ventures such as these betoken a celestial and heavenly soul which has left the region of the earth, has been drawn upwards, and dwells with divine natures. For when it takes its fill of the vision of good incorruptible and genuine, it bids farewell to the good which is transient and spurious. (*Quod Deus* 148–51)[39]

It is thus possession of Sophia that renders one perfect, wise, nobly-born, rich, and kingly in status, that makes one a heavenly and immortal and incorruptible soul. Those who have not attained this substantial a relationship with Sophia, however, are still babes living on the milky food of elementary teaching and are mortal insofar as they are still subject to the corruptible bodily and earthly influences. Following our analogy between Philonic writings and the Corinthian "opponents," the *pneumatikos-psychikos* language used by the latter would appear to have similar con-

---

39. See also esp. *Q.G.* 4.46; note the similarity of the language in both texts to that of the Corinthians discerned through 1 Cor 15:44–45.

notations with respect to Sophia as both the content and the agent of salvation.[40]

Conclusion

The *pneumatikos/psychikos* terminology so distinctive in 1 Corinthians appears to be quite important in the religious language of the Corinthians whom Paul is addressing. Yet no adequate comparative material has been found from which to establish the precise origin and significance of this unusual terminology. By broadening our approach, however, to include the language to which the *pneumatikos/psychikos* terminology is parallel in 1 Cor 2:6—3:4 and 15:44–45, there is more than adequate terminological basis for finding in the Hellenistic-Jewish tradition represented by Philo an analogy for how all of this religious language functions. Thus the *teleios/nēpios* contrast, the distinction between the heavenly *anthrōpos* and the earthly *anthrōpos* (related respectively to Gen 1:27 and 2:7a), and the *pneumatikos/psychikos* terminology all can be understood as parallel expressions used by the Corinthians for different levels of spiritual status or different religious types of people.

As we might expect in a religious consciousness focused on Sophia as the content and means of salvation, spiritual status and achievement depend on the soul's relation with Sophia. Possession of Sophia means perfection and immortality for the soul and provides one with all the spiritual benefits and security symbolized by "noble birth," "wealth," "kingship," etc. Those who were still struggling with the milk-like nourishment of elementary doctrines did not share this intimacy with Sophia. For these "children" or "earthly ones" or *psychikoi* were still in need of instruction and exhortation in order to make progress toward perfection. In their lower religious status they were susceptible to corruptible earthly and bodily influences. In contrast stood the "perfect" or *pneumatikoi*, who, by having found their true incorruptible identity in the heavenly *anthrōpos* or by virtue of their possession of Sophia, far transcended the corruptible and threatening conditions of earthly reality.

40. It is difficult, on the basis of Paul's formulations in 1 Cor 2:10–16 and 12:4–11; 14:2, 12, etc., to determine whether the Corinthians were thinking in terms of the *pneuma*. Determination of this may not be very important for the purposes of this essay, however, since in our Hellenistic-Jewish analogy the soteriological functions of the Spirit are always parallel to or identical with those of Sophia/ Logos, as, e.g., in Wis 7:22–30; *Her.* 259–66; *Gig.* 27, 47; *Quod Deus* 1–3.

2

Wisdom of Word
and Words of Wisdom

In recent scholarship on 1 Corinthians the role of *wisdom* (σοφία) has become a focal point. Scholarly investigation has concentrated primarily on *sophia* as the means and content of salvation, searching for its background in Jewish wisdom speculation or a Gnostic Sophia-myth, and arguing whether it is Paul or his opponents who are responsible for the Wisdom-Christology in Corinth.[1] In 1 Cor 1–4, however, Paul reacts against *two* aspects of *sophia*: wisdom in speech as well as wisdom as the means of salvation. He strongly insists that eloquent speech is not an appropriate expression for the gospel (1:17; 2:1–5; 4:20). *Sophia* as persuasive speech is closely related, apparently, to *sophia* as a means of knowing God (1:21), and both of these aspects together must be considered the organizing principles of his polemical argument from 1:17 to 3:4. In his elaborate play on words in 1:18–25 Paul rejects both aspects of wisdom. In 2:1–5 he directly disclaims eloquence. Then in 2:6—3:4 he sarcastically derides the Corinthians' obsession with *sophia* as the means of salvation.

With all the interest in Gnosticism and Wisdom-Christology, however, *sophia* as eloquent speech has been somewhat neglected. With the exception of the older work by Weiss, commentaries have devoted very little attention to the motif of speech in 1:17; 2:1–4, 13; 4:19–20.[2] The one

---

1. The most noteworthy studies are Knox, *St. Paul and the Church of the Gentiles*, chapters 3 and 4; Wilckens, *Weisheit und Torheit*, as corrected by two very important critical reviews by Koester (1961) and Colpe (1963); the recent commentary by Conzelmann, *1 Corinthians*; and Feuillet, *Le Christ*.

2. Weiss, *Korintherbrief*; Lietzmann, *An die Korinther*, provides virtually nothing. Conzelmann does not really comment on the appropriate phrases in 2:4 and 13, or on

major and influential study that has dealt more extensively with wisdom as eloquent speech, that of Johannes Munck, lumps the eloquence together with wisdom as the means (and content) of salvation, and finds "from the conjunction of 'word' and 'wisdom' that we have here Hellenistic features of Greek complexion."[3] Thus when eloquence has been discerned as an important element in the Corinthian situation, it has been understood primarily in terms of the rhetoric of popular Hellenistic philosophy. New Testament scholarship is thus in the anomalous position of finding that the one aspect of *sophia* in Corinth represents Jewish wisdom speculation or a kind of proto-Gnosticism, while the other aspect of *sophia*, persuasive speech, is wisdom like that of Greek philosophy.

Wisdom as Eloquence

The solution to this anomaly requires more serious attention to the Hellenistic-Jewish tradition represented by Philo and the Wisdom of Solomon, for this may be the background to the particular religiosity which Paul is challenging in 1 Corinthians.[4] Not only is eloquence an important religious possession in this tradition, but it is closely connected with *sophia* as the means of salvation as well. The high evaluation of eloquence was of long standing in the Jewish wisdom tradition. In literature such as Proverbs 1–9, Sirach, and Wisdom 6–9—writings that have been important for tracing the development of wisdom speculation and Wisdom-Christology—eloquent speech is a prominent motif. From

---

logos in 4:19; Barrett, *First Epistle to the Corinthians*, sees that speech is being discussed, but goes too far in finding reference to rhetorical art and technique (Weiss, *Korintherbrief*, 23, had warned against that reading!). Wilckens does not investigate the possibility that speech has something to do with the Corinthians' *sophia*, either in *Weisheit und Torheit* (cf. 44ff.) or in "σοφία." 523. Hence back to Weiss—esp. 22–23 and 48ff., including comparative material—and of course Munck's treatment (see next note). On 1 Cor 2:4 see also Bultmann, "πείθω κτλ.," 9.

3. Munck, "Church without Factions," chapter 5, esp. 140ff. and 150ff. Funk, "Word and Word," fuses the Corinthians' wisdom and speech into "word" or "language," and somewhat assimilates Paul's response into the Corinthians' language, but never ventures to indicate precisely what "language" they are speaking.

4. Munck ("Church without Factions," 143–44, 153), still viewing the milieu in which Christianity arose as containing two dominant cultural forces: the essentially secular Greek or Hellenistic, expressed in popular philosophy or rhetoric, and the more religiously oriented Jewish, which has little to do with the Hellenistic, was limited to the alternative Greek or Jewish wisdom. He thus did not seriously consider Hellenistic-Jewish traditions as possible background for the Corinthian situation.

the beginning of Proverbs 1–9 *sophia* as the content of instruction and discipline is closely associated with skill in the use of speech. Proverbs 1:2–7 accumulates a number of associations that are similar to those in 1 Corinthians.

- to know wisdom and discipline (γνῶ ναι σοφίαν καὶ παιδείαν)
- to understand words of wisdom (νοῆσαί τε λόγους φρονήσεως)
- to receive subtle turns of arguments (δέξασθαί τε στροφὰς λόγων)
- to conduct judgments (καὶ κρίμα κατευθύνειν, cf. 1 Cor 4:3–5)

Sirach makes the same close association of *Sophia* with eloquent speech (cf. 6:5; 18:28–29; 38:33; 39:1–6). In Wisdom turns of speech and skill in public discourse are important benefits of the relationship with Sophia (esp. 8:8, 12, 18).

This same high evaluation of speech becomes quite elaborate and explicit in the treatises of Philo. Despite Munck's impression, Philo displays a consistent evaluation of eloquence. He criticizes its abuse and distortion[5] but highly values its proper use. Occasionally Philo criticizes sophistry in order to make various polemical points. The clever arguments of the sophists and rhetors contrast with the composed, reasoned discourse that penetrates to the soul of the listeners (*Vita Cont.* 31; *Det.* 69–78; *Leg.* 1.74–78). The most basic charge against the sophists, that of the discrepancy between argument and action, or word and will, was a common argument in Philo's and other philosophers' rhetorical repertoire. Such harangues or snide passing comments should also be viewed as an integral part of the intergroup rivalry and polemics that were a standard feature of Hellenistic culture. Nearly every philosophical group and individual attacked its competitors as being charlatans, magicians, empty sophists, and the like.[6] Thus also for Philo and other Jews who

---

5. In two passages, *Conf.* 129 and *Sac.* 13, Philo seems to express a strictly negative attitude toward eloquence. But these comments must be evaluated in their contexts and in accordance with Philo's method of dialectical contrast whereby a valuation will depend on what is being contrasted. *Conf.* 129 is followed by further explication that clarifies that this is not a condemnation of persuasive arguments in general, but only of "every argument which would persuade the mind to turn away from holiness." In *Sac.* 12–13, Philo, in good Platonic tradition, continues Plato's own negative judgment of the myth-makers, but not of eloquence itself.

6. Paul felt compelled to disclaim such an identity, cf. 1 Thess 2:1–8 and 2 Cor 2:17.

saw themselves as several cuts above the ordinary traffic in religion and philosophies, just as the sorcerers could not stand before Moses, so mere sophistry could not be confused with true (Jewish) wisdom (e.g., *Her.* 302-3 and *Mig.* 85).

His rejection of empty sophistry, however, does not mean that Philo has no use for speech or eloquence.[7] Philo is fond of contrasting sophistry with true wisdom or philosophy (e.g., *Mig.* 171; *Post.* 101), the sophists with the true σοφός (e.g., *Q.G.* 3.33). But *sophia* for Philo includes speech in its proper function, and in non-polemical contexts even sophistry has its value. In *Sob.* 9 (cf. *Fug.* 208-9) Isaac inherits wisdom (σοφία) and Ishmael sophistry (σοφιστεία). For, as this is explained briefly,

> the mere babe (νήπιον παιδίον) has the same relation to the mature man (ἄνδρα τέλειον) as the sophist to the sage (σοφός) and the school studies to the sciences concerned with virtues.

These Philonic texts indicate that Philo rejected what he considered the misuse of eloquence partly because he values its proper use in conjunction with true wisdom (e.g., *Her.* 302-3).

Philo illustrates more extensively his high evaluation of eloquent speech and its role in the religious life of the wise in *Mig.* 70-85. In discussing Gen 12:1-3, Philo elaborates on three gifts that God bestows on the soul. After it has relinquished mortal things God grants the soul the viewing and contemplation of immortal things (*Mig.* 2-52). Secondly, he gives the soul progress in abundance of virtue and goodness (*Mig.* 53-69). The third gift (*Mig.* 70-85), without which the others are not secure, is εὐλογία which by wordplay on καὶ εὐλογήσω σέ means a combination of virtue, mind, and speech. The wordplay is of the essence here, however, and one should keep in mind that εὐλογία connotes primarily fine language, eloquence, and plausibility, as well as praise or blessing.

That eloquence is the primary significance of this third gift in Philo's mind is confirmed by the ensuing interpretation, which explains the proper function of speech, including its integral relation with mind. God

---

For such a charge against opponents used simultaneously as an exhortation to the faithful to avoid such things as empty disputes about words, cf. 1 Tim 6:3-5; 2 Tim 2:14-17.

7. Philo begins with the usual word-deeds discrepancy charged against the sophists, but insists that mind and speech are absolutely necessary. Only by bringing his speech, mind and action into harmony could one be considered perfect (τέλειος). Cf. the same point more briefly put, *Mos.* 2.212, more discursively, *Mut.* 236-48.

grants the gift of εὐλογία in both divisions of λόγος, i.e., mind and speech, because the recipient should both conceive the noblest thoughts and express the ideas masterfully (cf. *Som.* 1.102–14). For perfection (τέλειώτης) depends on both. The relation of Aaron to Moses in Exod 4:10ff. is used to illustrate the function of speech in its relation to mind.[8] Moses, the all wise, who symbolizes mind, from the time that God began to flash to him the light of truth by means of the immortal words of knowledge and wisdom itself (διὰ τῶν ἐπιστήμης καὶ σοφίας αὐτῆς ἀθανάτων λόγων), begins to take eloquence and persuasion (speech symbolized by Aaron) more seriously. Even though the mind can move among intellectually apprehensible objects unaided, yet when it is dealing with matters affected by sense and the body (symbolized by Egypt) it will need the skill and the power of speech (καὶ τῆς περὶ λόγους τέχνης ὁμοῦ καὶ δυνάμεως, *Mig.* 77, cf. 82). So he calls Aaron to his aid. Speech, the mind, and God are seen to have a close relation. "Thoughts" are the words or *logoi* of God. As mind is the prompter or interpreter of speech, so God is of mind (78–81). Philo cannot resist stating this yet another way, in reference to Exod 7:1 (84). Aaron, or *logos*, is also called "prophet," when mind (Moses) is inspired and entitled "God." For it is the prophetic race (γένος) that interprets the thoughts of God when possessed by a divine inspiration and ecstasy. Philo concludes with the victory of *sophia* over sophistry, Moses over the sorcerers. The obvious implication is that true *sophia* includes speech properly functioning as the complement of mind, or, as he had stated in *Mig.* 73, speech as well as mind is necessary for perfection.[9]

It is worth noting, finally, with respect to the positive evaluation of eloquence by Philo, that the boldness of speech (παρρησία) that Munck stressed as a prominent mark of the Greek sophist also figures importantly in Philo's comments regarding the speech of the *sophos*, e.g., *Her.* 14–21.

> Keeping quiet is advisable for the ignorant, but for those who desire knowledge and also love their master, bold speech (παρρησία) is most necessary ... those who have put their faith in the divine

---

8. Parallel to their relationship in the other major interpretation, i.e., Moses symbolizing the Λόγος proper and Aaron the Λόγος as immanent structure of the world, Moses is here interpreted as "mind" and Aaron as "speech." See also the further explanation in *Det.* 38 and *Her.* 16–19; and cf. also *Mos.* 2.112–15; 127–30; *Q.E.* 2.110–11.

9. Cf. *Mig.* 168–70, where speech accompanies the σοφός, *i.e.*, the mind worthy of sovereignty, or the "king."

love of wisdom should speak . . . with a great cry (14). Moses reaches such a courage even to reproach God. He reaches such a limit "because all σοφόι are friends of God. . . And παρρησία akin to friendship." (20-21)

Not only do Wisdom and Philo have a keen appreciation for fine speech, however, but they both connect speech integrally with *sophia* as the means and content of salvation as well. In the Hellenistic-Jewish tradition represented by Wisdom and Philo, Sophia (or in Philo the equivalent Logos) has become the central content and agent of religion. Accordingly, impressive speech is one of the key gifts of Sophia (Wis 8:8, 12). Sharing words (λόγοι) of Sophia is the mode of intimacy with her and skillful communication of these words the expression of this intimate soteriological relationship (see Wis 8:12-18). Similarly in Philo, it is the revelation to the all-wise Moses of the "immortal words of Knowledge and Wisdom herself" that brings him to appreciate and employ eloquence of speech (*Mig.* 76). It is those who have come to trust in the divine love of *sophia* who should employ bold speech (παρρησία, *Her.* 14). Considered in the context of the whole Philonic corpus, eloquence may not compare with immortality and perfection as one of the primary or most central soteriological benefits of Sophia (= Logos). And eloquent speech would not appear to be a natural counterpart of the primary imagery used for Sophia—the divine dwelling place of the wise, the divine Spring (Rock), the spiritual banquet, the divine Light, or the royal way.[10] But eloquence is clearly an effect and an important expression of the soul's intimate relationship with Sophia, which is both the means and the content (or goal) of salvation.[11]

We find, then, in at least one branch of Hellenistic-Jewish theology a high evaluation of eloquent and persuasive speech. Like other Hellenistic philosophers and religious propagandists Philo makes a standard critique of those who abuse eloquence, the "sophists," "charlatans" and "quacks."

10. The latter, "the royal way," is perhaps the least prominent of these, occurring prominently only in *Post.* 101-2; *Quod Deus* 140-80. More important in the Philonic corpus as a whole are: Sophia as the divine dwelling place of the wise, e.g., in *Mig.* 28-30, 45-46; *Her.* 313-15; Sophia as the divine Spring or Rock or the spiritual banquet, *Sac.* 86; *Her.* 191, 79; *Fug.* 137-39, 177-202; *Leg.* 3.162-73; *Leg.* 2.86; *Det.* 115-17; *Som.* 2.221-22; and Sophia as the divine Light, e.g., *Mig.* 39-40; *Spec. Leg.* 1.285-88. On the latter see Goodenough, *By Light, Light*.

11. Besides the "by light, light" passage made famous by Goodenough, there are a few passages, quite explicitly stated, on "by Sophia, Sophia": *Her.* 98; *Mig.* 39; *Q.G.* 4.101.

But eloquence used properly as the integral mode of communicating σοφία is the expression appropriate to the mind that possesses knowledge of the divine. Thus coupled with its "brother," mind, speech is one of the endowments necessary for becoming perfect (τέλειος) and wise (σοφός). The orientation throughout is clearly toward the possession and expression of the immortal, divine thoughts viewed as God's gifts provided by Sophia.

This Hellenistic-Jewish tradition expressed in Wisdom and Philo elucidates the two aspects of *sophia* to which Paul reacts in 1 Corinthians, the "wisdom of word" as well as the more soteriologically substantive *sophia*. Now Conzelmann has offered a simple and direct explanation for the resemblances that a few passages in Paul's letters bear to certain texts from Jewish wisdom literature: Paul was a wisdom-teacher who founded a Christian wisdom-school.[12] This novel hypothesis, however, works with categories that are too general and vague, makes subordinate or unusual themes in Paul's letters into dominant ones, and rests largely on passages such as 1 Cor 1:18ff. and Rom 1:18ff., where Paul is actually rejecting or strongly qualifying views represented by certain wisdom-literature (e.g., Wis 13–14).[13] Bringing sapiential material directly to bear on Paul's letters in this way, moreover, does not allow for the polemical situation behind 1 Corinthians. With regard to *sophia*, it is quite clear, as noted at the outset, that Paul is *rejecting* wisdom of word as well as wisdom as the means of salvation. We should thus investigate the use of eloquence among the Corinthians.

Eloquence has not usually been discerned as one of the factors in the Corinthians' religiosity probably because it is not a theme distinctive to 1 Corinthians. Similar to his comments in 1 Cor 2:1, 4, Paul had written earlier in a non-polemical context, 1 Thess 1:5: "For our gospel came to you not in word λόγος) only, but also in power (δύναμις) and in the Holy Spirit, with full conviction." It was just standard technique for a popular philosopher or religious propagandist to deprecate his own ability in eloquence and reasoning power (cf. Dio Chrysostom, *Or.* 12.15ff.; 31; and 32). There thus may be an element of this in Paul's denial of persuasive wisdom in 1 Cor 1:17—2:5, as in 1 Thess 1:5.[14] But is there in fact

12. Conzelmann, "Paulus and die Weisheit," 234ff.

13. Conzelmann apparently has carried this picture of Paul's relation to Wisdom-speculation and sapiential traditions over into his commentary.

14. In this sense Paul can be said to be practicing what he is preaching against.

something distinctive in 1 Cor 1–4 over and above Paul's subordination of means of communication to effective conviction in the delivery of his gospel?

An affirmative answer is required by the distinctive formulations in 1 Cor 1:10—4:21 and by the specific reference these formulations appear to have to the Corinthian situation. Paul rejects *logos* in connection with *sophia* in the following formulations:

1:17 "to preach the gospel, not in wisdom of speech" (οὐκ ἐν σοφίᾳ λόγου); Paul's message (λόγος) is that of the cross, 1:18.

2:1 "proclaiming to you the mystery (witness) of God not with superiority of speech or wisdom" (οοὐ καθ᾿ ὑπεροχὴν λόγου ἤ σοφίας).

2:4 "My message and my preaching were not in persuasive words of wisdom" (ὁ λόγος μου καὶ τὸ κήρυγμά μου οὐκ ἐν πειθοῖς σοφίας λόγοις).[15]

2:13 "we speak (about the things granted to us by God) not in words taught by human wisdom, but in those taught by the Spirit . . ." (οὐκ ἐν διδακτοῖς ἀνθρωπίνης σοφίας λόγοις).

4:19–20 "I will find out not the speech of these arrogant people, but their power. For the Kingdom of God (consists) not in speech but in power." (οὐ τὸν λόγον . . . ἀλλὰ τὴν δύναμιν).

The only one of these passages that could be even partially explained from 1 Thess 1:15[16] is 1 Cor 2:4. But in 1 Thessalonians "speech" and "Spirit and power" are complementary (indicating the attitude with which Paul comes to the Corinthian situation), whereas in 1 Cor 2:4 the demonstrations of Spirit and power stand in opposition to persuasive (speech of) wisdom. Moreover, over and above 1 Thess 1:5, 1 Cor 2:4 mentions explicitly the element of persuasiveness and connects this persuasive

---

15. See the treatment of the textual variants in Conzelmann, *1 Corinthians*, 55.

16. Cf. 1 Thess 2:13; 1 Thess 2:1–8; and Phil 1:15–18 are not directly pertinent here, since they are rather apologies for the sincerity of his ministry, denying flattery, 1 Thess 2:5, but not mentioning eloquence.

speech directly with σοφία. Furthermore, the importance of "speech" in connection with "wisdom" in the Corinthian situation is indicated by the frequency with which Paul mentions it in the course of 1 Cor 1:10—4:21 (cf. also the mention of speech alongside *gnosis* in the introductory *captatio benevolentiae* 1:5).

It appears, then, that some of the Corinthians included eloquence as an element in their spiritual achievement. It is difficult to determine what forms it had taken at Corinth, e.g., whether Paul was being criticized for lacking, or praised for possessing eloquence. In any case, there were some in Corinth who were boasting (4:19) of their wisdom including their wisdom in speech (1:19). This can best be understood by analogy with the expressions in Wisdom and Philo. These Corinthians had come into an intimate relationship with *sophia* as the means and probably also the content or object of their salvation. Possession of Sophia meant immortality and perfection. Similarly this intimacy with Sophia endowed them with eloquent expression of her revelations (2:4).[17] They could thus enjoy and impart "words" (λόγοι) of *sophia* disclosed to them by Sophia.

In the person of Apollos there is even a possible historical link between the Hellenistic-Jewish tradition represented by Philo and the Corinthian situation, although such a direct link is hardly necessary for the analogy to be valid and helpful, given the general mobility of people, ideas, and religious cults in the Hellenistic-Roman world. Munck discounted the significance of his Alexandrian origins.[18] But perhaps we should take more seriously the tradition about Apollos in Acts 18:24, 26, that he, an Alexandrian Jew, was an *eloquent man . . .* and well versed in the scriptures, and that he was noted for *speaking boldly* (παρρησιάζεσθαι) in his evangelizing. Paul insists that there is no conflict between himself and Apollos (1 Cor 3:5-9). But he insists too much! Paul is apparently presenting a common front with Apollos in order to counter the Corinthian divisiveness that is clearly linked with Apollos (1:10-17; 3:5-15, with the warning in 3:10-15; 4:6). Indeed his reputation for eloquence is not the only element of the tradition that links Apollos with the conflicts behind

---

17. Λόγος and λόγοι, in 1 Cor 1:5,17; 2:1, 4; 4:19-20, probably refer to speech and not to transmitted Jesus-sayings. Only λόγοι in 2:13 could possibly be an allusion to Jesus-sayings. But eloquence could easily have been attributed to Jesus Christ as the great mouthpiece of Wisdom and to certain apostles as the bearers of sayings of wisdom. But cf. James M. Robinson, "LOGOI SOPHON," 87 n. 39.

18. Munck, "Church without Factions," 143-44.

1 Corinthians. Although he "spoke and taught" *accurately* the things concerning Jesus, it was necessary for Priscilla and Aquila, two close associates of Paul from his Corinthian mission, to take him aside and expound to him the way of God *more accurately* (Acts 18:25–26). Moreover, his major deficiency, according to the tradition in Acts 18:25, was his misunderstanding of *baptism,* which was one of the basic sources of the conflict in Corinth (1 Cor 1:12–17). If anyone had cultivated a wisdom-school, in Corinth at least, it was not Paul but Apollos. Through the latter's ministry some of the Corinthians apparently had come to regard the (Christian) gospel as wisdom, the leaders as teachers of wisdom, and themselves as wise. This wisdom was, to be sure, "like that of the Greeks," a mixture of philosophy, religion, and rhetoric.[19] But this was understood by Apollos and others as Sophia, the Divine Teaching to be contemplated in Scriptures. Indeed Sophia had been understood for generations as the real focus and substance of Jewish religion by Hellenistic Jews such as Philo, and this *sophia* included eloquent speech as an important facet.

Wisdom, Eloquence, and Spiritual Status

The analogy between the Corinthians and the Hellenistic-Jewish tradition represented in Wisdom and Philo is not confined, however, to their common understanding and use of eloquence and wisdom. The similarity extends to much of the Corinthians' religious language in 1 Cor 1–4 insofar as it can be discerned through what Paul says in response.[20] A brief survey of some of these other aspects will show that the Corinthians' eloquence is an integral part of a whole pattern of religious expression and will help clarify, indirectly, what Paul writes in 1 Corinthians.

The Corinthians, for example, judging from Paul's almost sarcastic polemic in 2:6—3:4, were apparently making distinctions in religious status or achievement expressed in terms such as τέλειος vs. νήπιος, the mature or perfect who enjoy the solid food (of *sophia*) vs. the babes who could handle only milk-like nourishment. These Corinthians also referred to the exalted status of perfection as being "powerful," of "noble birth," "wealthy," and "reigning like kings," according to Paul's rejection of such language in 1 Cor 1:26 and 4:8. This is all standard language for

---

19. Ibid., 152–54.

20. For detailed analysis that sorts through Paul's argument for the language and principles of the Corinthians, see Hurd (*Origins*) and the recent commentaries by Conzelmann and Barrett.

Philo who used it to make the same distinctions in religious status: the perfect or wise as the highest status, vs. the babes or ascetics or those making progress as the intermediate state, and the bad or worthless persons who are obviously lost.[21]

For example:

> Since food for babes is milk, and for mature (perfect) men is cake, there must also be as milk-like foods for the soul during its infancy the elementary education of school studies, and as foods for mature (perfect) men instruction through wisdom and moderation and all virtue. (*Agr.* 8-9)

At points this distinction in status also parallels Philo's contrast between the *heavenly man,* created according to the Divine Image, and the *earthly man,* who, like the *nepios* or ascetic, is caught between immortality and the detrimental bodily-earthly forces and requires instruction (διδασκαλία; e.g., *Leg.* 1.90-94). The situation of the babe or practicer is clearly an inferior status. The higher religious goal is to become perfect and wise. This involves leaving behind the merely infantile teachings to feed on Sophia herself. Or, following Philo's mixed metaphors, the wise and perfect dwell in Sophia, or contemplate wisdom by means of Sophia, who is God's archetypal Light (*Mig.* 28-40). The wise thus possess perfect good and immortality.[22]

---

21. In interpreting 1 Cor 2:6ff., Wilckens, *Weisheit und Torheit,* 53ff., and Lührmann, *Offenbarungsverständnis,* 113-14, both follow Reitzenstein's derivation and interpretation from Hellenistic mysteries, *Mysterienreligionen,* 338-39. Actually, τέλειος and this whole set of terms, τέλειος, νήπιος, etc., were common usage in many philosophical, ethical and religious contexts, see belling, *MDT* 8 (1972) 68-69, including those of Greek-speaking Hellenistic Judaism. Delling provides a reasonably comprehensive listing of the uses of *teleios* in various connections by Philo, 71-72. Neither Delling nor Bertram, in the article on *nepios, TDNT* 4 (1967) 912-13, however, really cover the *teleios/nepios* terminology and the distinction of religious status or achievement it expresses in Philo.

22. All of this language of the different levels of spiritual attainment forms part of Philo's more extensive exposition of what might be termed patterns of perfection whose types or paradigms are the great patriarchs. Goodenough has delineated these patterns of perfection clearly and sympathetically in *By Light, Light,* chapters 5, 6, and 8, in particular. On Philo's use of Hellenistic ideas of education, e.g., interpreting Abraham, Isaac, and Jacob as paradigms of education, through teaching, nature, and practice, respectively, see Colson, "Philo on Education," 153-62. The extent and manner in which Philo has appropriated the language and ideas of Hellenistic *paideia* is a subject that still awaits a more thorough investigation.

As with τέλειος (and "the heavenly man") the designations εὐγενής, βασιλεύς, πλούσιος, etc., in Philo also refer to a spiritual elite (*Sob.* 55–57; *Sac.* 43–44).²³ The wise, nobly born, rich, kings are contrasted either with the foolish and wicked or with those merely of lesser religious achievement. *Virt.* 174 shows that one who claimed the highest status could use the antitheses to rich, honored, wise—i.e., poor, dishonored, ignorant—in reference, not to the wicked, but merely to those whom he considers to be of ordinary religious status. *De virtutibus* 174 also indicates that some of those who characterized themselves as rich, nobly-born, strong, and knowledgeable, appeared arrogant even to others (Philo) who valued such characterizations of the σόφοι. This latter is important for attempting to discern the nuances of this language as Paul directs it back at the Corinthians. As is the case with one's status as τέλειος, the σοφός is constituted rich, nobly-born, king, glorious, etc., by virtue of intimacy with Sophia (e.g., *Her.* 313–15).

Philo's discussion of speech in *Det.* 32–49, 65–68, 132–33, not only displays a high estimation of eloquence, including the necessity of possessing it in order to reach perfection, but it connects the highly valued eloquence with these distinctions of religious status. Those of the middle or practicing status lack even the dream of subtlety with words, while those who truly pursue the Divine have their speech fortified by the arts of eloquence. Only the latter, the *perfect*, who possess the proper eloquence along with the dominant mind, maybe recipients and "interpreters" of divine thoughts and teachings.²⁴ Those in the intermediate status, the ascetics, who are seeking education, are not perfect precisely because they do not possess eloquent speech. Instead they must be instructed in wisdom by the speech of the perfect as one of its proper functions (*Det.* 66; cf. *Her.* 19).

---

23. See further, e.g., *Abr.* 272–74; *Virt.* 8, 187–90; 212–19; *Mig.* 197; *Som.* 2.242–44; Q.G. 4.76. Such terms were likely Stoic and Cynic in origin: von Arnim, ed. *Stoicorum vererum fragmenta*, esp. 3.150, 5–10, frg. 567; 3.155, 20–23, frg. 594; 3.365, 10–14, and further, 3.85–89, 150–57. By the time of Philo, however, such language was common in popular philosophy. Labels and provenance are less important here than the recognition that Philo and the Jewish tradition he represents had appropriated such language and arguments as standard elements in their modes of expression. Philo uses such language both in its literal, social sense and, more prominently, in a spiritual sense in characterization of the faithful Jew of highest religious status.

24. See also Q.G. 4.8, where speech forms a triad with the most pure mind and perfect virtue.

Thus, just as it is a quality necessary for achieving perfection, so eloquence belongs with noble birth, kingship, wealth, etc., as one of the distinctive and enduring qualities of those who have achieved such exalted status. The wise look to the Divine as their country, "their bold speech (παρρησιά), and their great and glorious and inalienable wealth" (*Her.* 27). Perhaps especially noteworthy for the Corinthian situation, where gentiles were converting to the new Jewish religious movement (not yet known, of course, as "Christianity"), is what Philo says of Abraham as the paradigm of *nobility* (εὐγένεια) for all proselytes.[25]

> Abraham, having gained faith, and with it all the other virtues, was regarded as a *king*, since although he was a commoner he possessed a kingly spirit . . . and a more than human perfection. He sought a more holy converse, since he was divinely inspired . . . . For the Divine Spirit, which was breathed upon him from above, dwelt in his soul, investing . . . his speech with persuasiveness (τοῖς λόγοις πειθώ; cf. 1 Cor 2:4) and his listeners with understanding . . . . He is of the highest nobility, . . . the standard of nobility for all proselytes who . . . have come to settle in a better land, whose overseer is Truth. (ἀλήθεια = σοφία; *Virt.* 216–19)

By divine inspiration, Abraham, the paradigmatic pilgrim to the land of Sophia, enjoys persuasive words along with the other qualities of perfection. Similarly in the Wisdom of Solomon, "words of wisdom" and verbal finesse go along with these other exalted qualities of noble-birth, wealth, glory, and immortality, which Sophia possesses and provides to those who have gained intimacy with her (see esp. Wis 8:3, 5, 8, 10–13, 17–18).

Applying this Hellenistic-Jewish analogy to the situation in Corinth, it is clear that some Corinthians had come into an intimate relation with divine Sophia. By this possession of Wisdom they had achieved the highest spiritual status, expressed in terms of being wise and perfect, versus the inferior status of mere "babes." These Corinthians, who, like Abraham, had been "commoners" and mere nothings in the world, felt exalted in their attainment of true wealth, kingship, noble birth, etc., and eloquent

---

25. The whole section of this treatise, *De virtutibus*, is entitled *peri eugeneias*. This is perhaps a good illustration of how Hellenistic Jews have thoroughly assimilated elements of Hellenistic culture.

and persuasive speech was an integral manifestation of the spiritual perfection in which they now possessed the divine teachings of *sophia*.²⁶

Another aspect of Philo's discussions of eloquence that is of particular importance for comparison with the Corinthians is the absence of concern with the social dimension. Moses' conflict with the sophists in Egypt is read to mean the conflict of the mind with the elements of body and sense perception that might subvert it from its proper devotion to wisdom. The problem Philo finds with the sophists is the strife *within* their own souls (cf. *Det.* 72–74, etc.). He even criticizes them, among many other things, for their speeches on the social aspect of justice. He asks rhetorically, "What benefit do these speeches on virtue have *for your own soul?*"²⁷ Philo's whole discussion of speech is rather single-mindedly oriented toward the relation of the individual soul and the divine wisdom. Closely related to this individualistic spiritual orientation in its lack of concern with the social dimension is the conception frequently expressed in Philo that those who occupy different levels of religious status belong to distinct *types* of spiritual existence, or to distinct companies (θίασοι). The noble company or type of the τέλειος disdain milk-like infantile food in their use of strong food fit for the mature (*Som.* 2.10–11; 234–36; *Mig.* 28; *Leg.* 3.140; cf. *Sob.* 9–10 cited above).

If the Corinthians were thinking in similar terms, then it is evident how their eloquence is directly related to what Paul viewed as a spiritual arrogance on their part and to the divisiveness in the newly formed Corinthian community. As the perfect, wise, nobly-born, etc., they

---

26. The fact that the Pneuma is virtually identical with Sophia/Logos in the Hellenistic-Jewish tradition represented by Philo and Wisdom indicates that the λογος σοφίας, etc., Paul discusses in 1 Cor 12 and 14 and the λόγοι σοφίας he rejects in 1 Cor 1–2 may be closely related. Paul provides a suggestive link in the πνευματικος/ πνευματικα terminology. There is, furthermore, in Philo's discussions of persuasive speech cited above, a close connection between eloquent expression of words of *sophia* and the experience of prophetic ecstasy or inspiration by the Divine Spirit. For example, in the close relation between the mind, speech, and God (*Mig.* 78 ff.), when the *logos* as mind becomes inspired then the *logos* as speech becomes "prophet." For it is the *prophetic genus* that interprets the thoughts (*logoi*) of God when possessed by divine inspiration and ecstasy. The discussion of παρρησία in *Her.* 4, 14–15, described as eloquence of the soul heard by God and not by any mortal, is also strikingly similar to Philo's portrayal of prophetic inspiration, and cannot help but remind one of Paul's cautionary discussion of glossolalia in 1 Cor 14:2–5.

27. See Jonas, *Gnostic Religion*, 278–81, on Philo's mystified understanding of ἀρετή, compared with the classical Greek view.

viewed themselves as occupying a spiritual status distinctly superior to the rest of the community, who still required instruction in order to make further progress in wisdom. As the perfect who possessed *sophia* and the eloquent means of communicating the divine teachings perhaps they even saw it as their proper role to instruct those of lesser achievement. That such a distinction between members of the community would be divisive would not even occur to them. For such a possession of Sophia and her spiritual benefits was oriented almost exclusively toward the achievement of spiritual security by the individual soul (vs. the body). To achieve immortality the soul had to detach itself from the influence of corruptible earthly and bodily elements that were seen as diversions from its own proper devotion. "For a perishable body weighs down the soul" (Wis 9:15). Eloquence in communication, ironically, as an integral aspect of the individual soul's achievement of perfection and immortality, was part of a religiosity that had no concern for the vitality of the community. Lacking Paul's Christocentrism and oriented toward individual possession of *sophia* and perfection, the Corinthian τέλειοι apparently did hold strong attachments to their particular apostle but this had a divisive effect on the community as a whole (1:10–11; 3:4).

Paul's Rejection of *Sophia*

If Paul is being viewed by the Corinthians as a wisdom teacher and evaluated negatively and/or positively on such a model—or more likely, being compared with the eloquent Apollos (4:3; cf. 2 Cor 10:10)—then the sharpness of his insistence that he had not preached and taught with wise speech and persuasive wisdom in Corinth becomes directly intelligible. His rejection of *sophia* indicates that he well understands the language of Apollos and his Corinthian followers. In good rhetorical fashion he pointedly derogates his "opponents'" wisdom as merely "wisdom of the world" or "the wisdom of men."[28] That is, these phrases are hardly to be taken at face value as references to (secular) Greek philosophy but are rather polemical references to the heavenly Sophia, the divine agent of creation and salvation, the very soteriological content with which Paul sees the Corinthians as being overly possessed.

---

28. Ἀποδείχις in 2:4 is also rhetorical terminology—see e.g. Diogenes Laertius 7.45; Epictetus 1.24.8; 2.25.1–2; further Weiss, *Korintherbrief.* 50.

Paul, however, counters primarily not with the rhetorical language of persuasive speech, but with the crucified Christ. Although, in terms of the hermeneutics of language, there is a formal parallelism between "wisdom of word" and "word of the cross," the fundamental contrast for Paul is certainly not "thus a contrast between two words."[29] There is no parallelism of substance. Paul rejects *sophia* as the means of salvation (1:21–24) by replacing it with the crucified Christ as the true "power" and "wisdom" of God. He rejects *sophia* as persuasive speech (2:1–5) by replacing it with demonstrations of spirit and power. And, whether it is intentional or not, his constructions in 1:17b and 2:1–3 are juxtapositions of thoughts that stand in utter contradiction. In his play on words (esp. σοφία, σοφός), Paul may begin with the Corinthians' language of *word* in the anomalous phrase "the word, the one of the cross"—which he knows very well will sound like just plain foolishness to the wise Corinthians. But by 2:5 he has made quite clear what the real contrast is for him: he is concerned that the Corinthians' faith rest in the *power* of God rather than in the *wisdom* of men.

Besides rejecting *word* as the object of faith in favor of the *power* of God, i.e., the crucified Christ, Paul also rejects both the presuppositions and the implications of the Corinthians' "words of wisdom" (λόγοι σοφίας). The Corinthian τέλειοι understood themselves, apparently, as the recipients and interpreters of the mind of God, or Wisdom. Their claim to possession of wisdom and to unassailable spiritual discernment, however, appeared to Paul as utter arrogance. As he moves toward his abrupt castigation of the τέλειοι / πνευματικοί in 3:1–4, Paul cites what must be one of their spiritual principles: "The πνευματικός judges (discerns = ἀνακρίνει) all things, but is himself to be judged by no one."[30] For Paul this principle enunciated in 2:15 would be unthinkable. It sets the πνευματικοί in the place of God Himself (which, of course, may be precisely where they thought they were). Paul, therefore, in transition to

---

29. Pace, Funk, *Language*, 275–83.

30. Apparently the Corinthians' spiritual judgment included in its jurisdiction the authority and ministry of apostles. Surely Paul's comments in 4:1–5 are not just hypothetical. He is too much on the defensive. Some in Corinth must have been criticizing him heavily. In the divisive situation in Corinth, criticism of an apostle by some was apparently the counterpart of others' boasting in that apostle. Paul's comments in 9:3ff. are also defensive in tone and may allude to the same problem. But "those who would examine me" in 9:3 could refer as easily to accusers outside the Corinthian community (see Conzelmann).

the abrupt reversal of 3:1, asks rhetorically and polemically, quoting Isa 40:13: "For who has known the mind of the Lord as to instruct him?"[31] In fact, Isa 40:13 here in 2:16, and all of the other scriptural passages (λόγοι σοφίας) that Paul adduces to support his case (e.g., those in 1:19; 2:9; 3:19, 20),[32] state either that no one yet has really known the mind of God, or that God destroys the "wisdom" of the "wise." Paul thus clearly and sharply rejects the presuppositions of the Corinthians' eloquent articulation of λόγοι σοφίας, i.e., rejects as arrogant their claim to know the mind of God.

Paul also vigorously rejects the implications of the Corinthians' enjoyment of eloquent speech and other manifestations of their exalted spiritual status. In 3:1–4 he challenges the Corinthian τέλειοι with the divisive effects of their excited involvement in the speech of wisdom and other πνευματικα. Paul's response here and in chapters 12–14 to the arrogant, individualistic, other-worldly spirituality is to call for egalitarian, communally edifying use of spiritual gifts.

Funk suggests that Paul enters into the Corinthians' language context.[33] Now Paul is indeed quite aware of the particular language (of Hellenistic-Jewish wisdom) that these Corinthians are speaking. He trades them quote for quote from the scriptural λόγοι σοφίας, and even is able quite skillfully to turn their own language against them (including ανθρώπινη σοφία, τέλειος, etc.) in an almost sarcastic rhetorical tour de force. Paul indeed uses their words and phrases—in the process of strongly qualifying if not diametrically opposing their meaning. But he certainly does not enter into their language in the deeper sense of language implied by Funk. Paul is concerned about historical-eschatological events, such as the crucifixion of Christ and the parousia, and about the eschatological community in its social-historical extension. The *language* of the Corinthian τέλειοι, utterly lacking Paul's Christocentrism and his eager eschatological orientation, was focused on heavenly Sophia and

---

31. And Paul adds: "But we have here the *mind* of Christ"—Christ of course having been clearly identified previously in the argument as that crucified one, 1:23 and 2:2; cf. 2:8.

32. Munck argues ("Church without Factions," 144–46) that Paul is not working from a Jewish florilegium of scriptural quotations, as Cerfaux had contended, but quoting from memory.

33. Funk, *Language*, 284–87.

her spiritual benefits, with no appreciation for anything other than the immortality of the individual soul. The Corinthians devalued the very concrete manifestations of God's *power* that Paul so highly valued. Even if he had attempted to enter into the Corinthians' language, it would have provided him no medium for expression of his basic concerns. Paul, however, remains throughout within his own language of eschatological events and manifestation of God's power. He insists to the Corinthians that for them to live in their language of σοφία and σοφία λόγου is divisive and inappropriate, "For the kingdom of God does not consist in *logos* but in *power*."

3

Spiritual Marriage with Sophia

Seele: Mein Freund ist mein!
Jesus: Und ich bin dein!
Beide: Die Liebe soll nichts scheiden!
(Bach, Cantate No. 140)

'Let Him kiss me with the kisses of his mouth.'
Who is it speaks these words? It is the Bride.
Who is the Bride? It is the soul thirsting for God.
(St. Bernard, Sermon VII on the Song of Songs)

I loved Her and sought Her from my youth
and I desired to take Her for my bride,
and I became enamored of her beauty.
(Wis 8:2)

E. R. Dodds is not pleased with the asceticism he finds rampant in late antiquity.

> Contempt for the human condition and hatred of the body was a disease endemic in the entire culture of the period; while its more extreme manifestations are mainly Christian or Gnostic, its symptoms show themselves in a milder form in pagans of purely Hellenic education.[1]

---

1. Dodds, *Pagan and Christian*, 35–36.

Among Christians one of the primary forms and theological understandings of this asceticism was a spiritual marriage with the Divine Savior. This sacred or mystical marriage of the soul with the Logos/Christ emerged clearly in the writings of Origen.[2] It spread widely in the East, especially in connection with monasticism, while Ambrose regularized this mode of religiosity in the West. The ascetic spiritual marriage of the soul with Christ the Bridegroom reached its most explicit and elaborate expression among later mystics such as Mechthild of Magdeburg, Teresa of Avila, and St. John of the Cross.

Regarding the background of Christian spiritual marriage there is some dispute. Underhill, followed by Chavasse, finds its roots in Neoplatonism.[3] Harnack, on the other hand, looks to Gnosticism.[4] As Dodds suggests regarding asceticism generally, however, the roots of this spiritual marriage lie further back. Recent Christian theological scholarship, in fact, looks further back, deriving the spiritual marriage of the soul with Christ from the earlier tradition of the spiritual marriage between Christ and his Church (e.g., Eph 5:23–32). The latter, the primary tradition, is seen as clearly rooted in primitive Christianity and its scriptural tradition, from Hosea's metaphor of Israel as the wife of God through the Song of Songs understood allegorically as the relationship between God and his people.[5] From this primary tradition of Christ and his Bride the Church developed an "individual bridal mysticism, based on the principle that what is true of the ecclesiastical collectivity is true of each individual."[6]

All of these derivations of the individual Christian spiritual marriage with Christ/Logos, however, overlook the fact that spiritual marriage was already a prominent motif in Hellenistic Judaism. Dodds' suggestion that the Jews are among those to blame for the ascetic "disease" smacks a bit of "blaming the victims." But the symbolism of spiritual marriage with the divine Savior and the ascetic impulse that accompanies it are strikingly manifest in literature such as the Wisdom of Solomon and Philo's trea-

---

2. Especially in the *Commentary on the Song of Songs*, but elsewhere as well. See Dölger, "Christus als himmlischer Eros"; and Quasten, *Patrology*, 2:98–100.

3. Underhill, *Mysticism*, 426; Chavasse, *Bride of Christ*, 173.

4. Harnack, *History of Dogma*, 2:295n.; 3:129.

5. Gross and Mussner, "Brautmystik, biblische," 660–62; Schmid, "Brautschaft, heilige"; Schlier, "*Hieros Gamos*," 265–76; Sampley, *One Flesh*.

6. Rush, "Death," 81–82.

tises. The spiritual marriage with Sophia expressed in an ascetic life even found concrete expression in the Jewish group called the "Therapeutae."

An important predecessor of the Christian "individual bridal mysticism," therefore, was the spiritual marriage with Sophia in Hellenistic Judaism. The individual marriage with the divine Savior is surely a religious tradition or pattern separate from the idea of the Church as the Bride of Christ. And the roots of Origen's and others' nuptial religiosity can be elucidated by a survey of the rich material in Philo and Wisdom.

The importance of Hellenistic-Jewish spiritual marriage, moreover, is not restricted to intellectual history in Alexandria from Philo to Origen. For the occurrence in certain Hellenistic-Jewish circles of asceticism linked with devotion to Sophia also elucidates some of the earliest "Christian" asceticism, in particular that in the community addressed by Paul in 1 Corinthians.[7]

Spiritual Marriage with Sophia in Wisdom and Philo

One of the most important motifs in Philo's and Wisdom's exposition of the relationship between God, the divine Sophia, and the individual soul is that of a spiritual marriage.[8] Whatever the origin of the motif of συνουσία with Sophia, Philo surely presupposes this manner of expressing the soul's relationship to the Divine as indigenous to Jewish piety and

---

7. Nearly all interpreters agree that asceticism was being practiced by at least some of the Corinthians in the newly formed community. In the most extensive recent treatment of early Christian sexual morality, Niederwimmer, *Askese und Mysterium*, 80–82, disagreeing somewhat with the scholarly consensus, finds in Corinth only ascetic tendencies rooted in baptismal teachings. Niederwimmer does not notice any motif of individual spiritual marriage in early Christianity, and considers only eschatologically-oriented Palestinian Judaism (including the teaching of Jesus) and Jewish Christianity as the background of early Christian asceticism. He mentions Wisdom and Philo only cursorily in connection with the background of the *hieros gamos* of Christ and the Church in Eph 5:22–33.

8. Philo (and/or the Jewish tradition on which he draws) uses several basic images to express the central importance of Sophia and her salvific relation to the soul of the σοφός. Sophia is the divine spring (*Fug.*177–202; *Post.*124–39); and a spiritual banquet (*Som.* 1.47–51, 198–200; *Fug.* 137–38, 166, 167; *Cong.* 172–74) from which the σοφοί or τέλειοι obtain divine nourishment or teaching. Sophia is also portrayed as divine light (*Mig.* 39–40; *Spec. Leg.* 1.285–88), as the proper spiritual dwelling place of the wise (*Mig.* 28–30, 45–46; *Her.* 313–15; *Q.G.* 4.46–47; *Q.E.* 2.39), and as the "royal way" (*Post.*101–2; *Quod Deus* 140–80). Recent discussion of some of these images in Mack, *Logos und Sophia*, 133–78.

theology.⁹ Indeed, at least since the time of Ben Sira it had been a standard mode of expression for Jewish sapiential piety (see, e.g., Prov 9:1–6; 4:6–9; Sir 4:11ff.; 14:22–27; 15:3–8).

Wisdom presents a contemplative speculation and panegyric on the personified divine Sophia, influenced by Hellenistic philosophy and mystery religions.¹⁰ Wisdom also manifests a close and intense personal relationship between the sage and his divine lover. As "Solomon" testifies:

> I loved her and sought her from my youth
> and I desired to take her for my bride,
> and I became enamored of her beauty.
> ...
> Therefore I determined to take her to live with me,
> knowing that she would give me good counsel
> and encouragement in cares and grief.
> ...
> When I enter my house, I shall find rest with her,
> for companionship with her has no bitterness,
> and life with her has no pain, but gladness and joy.
> When I considered these things inwardly,
> and thought upon them in my mind,
> that in kinship with Sophia there is immortality,
> and in friendship with her, pure delight,
> I went about seeking how to get her for myself. (8:2, 9, 16–18)

In this spiritual intercourse, Sophia is the agent or means as well as the object or substance of salvation. She imparts knowledge and revelation. But she also is the understanding and illumination she imparts. Therefore intercourse with her means possession of the spiritual substance and status that she mediates.

> If riches are a desirable possession in life,
> what is richer than Sophia who effects all things?
> And if understanding is effective,

---

9. Wilckens concentrates on this motif in his treatment of σοφία in Jewish wisdom literature, "σοφία," 499ff. See also Goodenough's exposition of Philo's interpretation of Abraham, Isaac, and Jacob in *By Light, Light*, chapters 5–6.

10. On the relations of Wisdom with Hellenistic philosophy, Larcher *Études*, esp. 201–23, 237–44, 254–62; and Reese, *Hellenistic Influence*, esp. 6–17, 36–50.

> who more than she is fashioner of what exists?
> Because of her I shall have glory ... and honor ...
> ... in kinship with Sophia there is immortality,
> and in friendship with her, pure delight,
> and in the labors of her hands, unfailing wealth,
> and in the experience of her company, understanding,
> and renown in sharing her words. (8:5–6, 10, 17–18)

Marriage with Sophia is also the means of the soul's relation to God. Sophia is, before anything else, God's consort:

> She glorifies her noble birth by living with God,
> and the Lord of all loves her.
> With Thee is Sophia, who knows thy works.... (8:3; 9:9; cf. 9:4)

By imparting knowledge, or herself, Sophia also brings the soul into her own intimacy with God: the soul thus stands immortal and incorruptible before the Divine presence (8:13, 17; 6:19), and enjoys the divine love and even the very divine essence (7:25–29). Intercourse with Sophia thus imitates God's union with her, and is the sage's personal *experience* of the Divine—revelation, salvation, and divinization.

In Philo's writings the spiritual marriage has become elaborate and sometimes complex.[11] The central image, however, is the marriage of the soul/mind with Sophia (or her equivalents, Arete, Episteme, Logos).

> The fitting lot of those who have been held worthy of a self-taught and self-learned *Sophia* is, apart from any agency of their own, to accept from God's hands the Logos as their plighted spouse and to receive Episteme, the wife of wise men (σοφῶν σύμβιον). (*Post.* 78)

In its origin, this imagery of spiritual marriage is related to the respective *genders* of the words that have become central symbols of the self

---

11. The soul can be related to the Divine through a variety of interchangeable relationships between two or three figures. The soul/mind can be mated with God or Sophia (Ἀρετή) or the Logos. Correspondingly, in the three-figure relationships both and the σοφός can be mated with Sophia (as in Wisdom) alternately or simultaneously. Many of the pertinent Philonic passages represent standard traditional interpretations of the Genesis patriarchal narratives in allegories of divine triads: for example, God–Sarah (Sophia/Aretē)–Abraham; God–Rebecca (Constancy)–Isaac. See esp. Goodenough, *By Light, Light*, chapters 5–6.

and the divine agent of salvation. Once this soteriological symbolism was established in Jewish piety, the gender of the terms apparently became problematic for a reflective theologian such as Philo. On the one hand, he works from traditional patriarchal assumptions about sex roles in the family and society. On the other hand, he is anxious to preserve the sense of divine initiative, the prevenience of divine grace. Hence, on the spiritual level, Sophia takes on the masculine roles of husband and father as well as the feminine roles:

> Let us then pay no heed to the discrepancy in the gender of the words, and say that the daughter of God, even Sophia, is not only masculine but father, sowing and betting in souls aptness to learn, education, knowledge, wisdom, good and laudable actions. (*Fug.* 52; see context, and *Abr.* 99–102)

From some of these Philonic passages one might conclude that such symbolism is merely a complex of standard traditional metaphors used in passing by Philo to describe the soul's intellectual relation to the divine ideas and that there is no real personal religious relationship implied. There are, however, at least three important interrelated reasons for drawing the opposite conclusion, i.e., that Philo uses this symbolism to express an intimate relationship with a divine figure. The same material makes it clear moreover, that this religiosity, focused on the relationship with Sophia, was tending toward a general asceticism.

First, as in Wisdom, Sophia is both object and means of salvation. Indeed, as Pascher demonstrated and Wilckens emphasizes, in a whole series of passages Philo portrays a "Wisdom mystery" with certain resemblances to the mystery of Isis, as described by Apuleius and Plutarch.[12] Or, to state the case more cautiously with Goodenough, spiritual marriage with Sophia, the Mother of the Universe and the divine person represented by scriptural symbols such as Sarah or Leah, was the central symbolism in the "Great Mystery" described by Philo.

> For this is a divine mystery and its lesson is for the initiated who are worthy to receive the holiest secret, even those who in simplicity of heart practice the piety which is true and genuine, free from all tawdry ornament... Moses, the holiest of men... shows us Sarah conceiving at the time when God visited her in solitude (Gen 21:1), but when she brings forth it is not to the author of her

---

12. Pascher, Η ΒΑΣΙΛΙΚΗ ΟΔΟΣ, 9–10, 262–64; Wilckens, "σοφία κτλ.," 501.

visitation, but to him who seeks to win wisdom (σοφία), whose name is Abraham ... God is the Father of all things, for He begat them, and the Husband of Sophia, dropping the seed of happiness for the race of mortals into good and virgin soil .... (*Cher.* 42–49)

In this and many other Philonic discussions of the sacred triads (Abraham-Sarah-God, etc.) we have the same pattern as in Wisdom. Sophia is the means of the souls' ultimate salvation, she is the mediator of the divine essence. This happens in the mind's spiritual intercourse with Sophia because she is also in mystical union with God. It should be added that in Philo the wise man possesses Sophia in his soul, which is similar to, if not as dramatic as, Lucius' preservation of Isis in his innermost heart.[13]

Second, Philo lives in a metaphysical and anthropological dualism by which he views the body and sense perception as the problem soteriologically. In good Platonic fashion, the true self is really the rational soul or the mind. The body not only fails to cooperate with reason in the pursuit of virtue and salvation, but it is an actual hindrance. "The task of wisdom," therefore, "is to become estranged from the body and its cravings" (*Leg.* 1.103; cf. Wis 9:15). Philo reads the "wife" in Gen 2:24 as "sense-perception" and "the father" and "mother" as God and Sophia. Hence when a man becomes "one flesh" with sense-perception, it means abandoning God, the Father, and Sophia, the Mother of all things. The two sides of this dualism are irreconcilable, although the body and the senses can be controlled, especially if the mind is divinely aided. This dualistic view of reality and the self have certain clear implications for behavior for one truly intent on partaking in the higher, divine essence.

> For Leah estrangement on the human side brings about fellowship with God, and from Him she receives the seed of wisdom, and is in birth-throes, and brings forth beautiful ideas worthy of the Father who begat them. (*Post.* 135)

> [Interpreting Deut. 23:12] Why go forth? Because the soul cannot have dealings with any of the body's friends while it abides with good sense and spends its days in the house of *Sophia*. For then it is nourished by food more divine, which it finds in all knowl-

---

13. Apuleius, *The Golden Ass*, book 11, discussed below.

> edge, and for the sake of this it actually disregards the flesh. (*Leg.* 3.152)

Philo, in fact, draws ascetic conclusions on this basis (*Leg.* 3.153–59), specifically with reference to eating, drinking, and the lower appetites. He even draws the implications for marriage quite explicitly. There are two kinds or two levels of marriage: that made by pleasure, which is a union of bodies, and that made by Sophia, which is of souls seeking purification and perfect virtues (*Abr.* 99–102).[14] In the latter the devout mind is either virgin or wife in its relation with Sophia/Logos.

> As a virgin, the mind keeps itself pure and uncorrupted from the malignant passions and pleasures. . . . As a wife she dwells with the good Logos . . . who impregnates her with excellent thoughts. (*Spec. Leg.* 2.30)

Third, this higher, spiritual kind of intercourse (that with Sophia or her equivalent, or with God) involves a change in one's marital status and sexual behavior. This new status forms a striking contrast to the former this-worldly marital status.

> Those (souls) who are free of self-love and hasten to God obtain . . . as from a husband the sowing of good thoughts and intentions. . . . Among men the opposite thing comes about, for when a man comes in contact with a woman, he marks the virgin as a woman. But when the souls become divinely inspired, from (being) woman they become virgins, throwing off the womanly corruptions which are (found) in sense-perception and passion. Moreover, they follow after and pursue the genuine and unmated virgin, the veritable Sophia of God. And so, rightly do such minds become widows and are orphaned of mortal things and acquire for themselves and have as husbands the Orthos Logos of Nature, with whom they live. (*Q.E.* 2.3)

Somewhat the same contrast is made in *Cher.* 50. Depending on how the symbolism was understood, this could almost be taken as prescribing recovery of virginity as a necessity for spiritual marriage with the Divine.

> For the union of human beings . . . turns virgins into women. But when God begins to consort with the soul, He makes what before was a woman into a virgin again, for he takes away the degenerate and emasculate passions . . . and plants . . . unpolluted virtues.

---

14. Note that this is standard teaching, not just Philo's; cf. *Cher.* 43–44 in context.

> Thus He will not talk with Sarah till she has ceased from all that is after the manner of women, and is ranked once more as a pure virgin (cf. Gen 18:11). (*Cher.* 50)

In fact, this passage is followed by an exhortation to the soul to live the virgin life in the house of God, clinging to *Episteme,* and to abandon outward matters that are defiling (*Cher.* 52).

The Ascetic Inclination in Wisdom and Philo

It is not difficult to imagine how ideas or beliefs such as these about spiritual marriage with Sophia could involve, or be developed in the direction of, an asceticism in this-worldly affairs. Both Philo's and Wisdom's language would seem to favor such an asceticism. The question can be sharpened, perhaps, by asking to what extent Philo and Wisdom are advocating a sexual asceticism in such passages.

In the first main section of Wisdom (1:1—6:11) both theme and structure are a running contrast between two groups of people: the righteous, saved through wisdom, whose "souls are in hands of God," on the one hand, and the impious, unrighteous sinners who have given themselves over to lawlessness and death, on the other.[15] The passage 3:13—4:6, taken by itself, seems very asymmetrical, even inconsistent. Viewing this sub-section, however, in the larger context of chapters 1–6 we realize that, instead of a polemic against Jewish marriage with pagans,[16] it forms an integral part of the continuing contrast between the righteous and the impious. This sub-section carries on this contrast in the imagery of sexual union and its fruits, a standard topic in traditional wisdom literature.

But something has changed from earlier Jewish or Israelite attitudes toward marriage, child-bearing and sexual virility. The sapiential spiritual-

---

15. This tradition contrasting the righteous and the impious sinners in Jewish wisdom literature is originally a development from Deutero-Isaiah; see Isa 57:1–13.

16. Commentaries that find here a polemic against Jewish marriage with pagans also reveal an implicit contradiction in their interpretation. Geyer, *Wisdom of Solomon,* for example, finds in 3:13 a reference to Jewish women in Alexandria marrying Gentiles, but he also emphasizes how revolutionary the thoughts of both 3:13 and 14 are. Now what is the real thrust of this passage in Wisdom? Fichtner, *Weisheit Salomos,* 21, bases the interpretation "Jews who marry Gentiles" on the "bastard slips" in 4:3 and the clear allusion there to Isa 57:3ff. But Wis 3–4, like Isa 57, is much more likely the characterization of religious *apostasy* or unfaithfulness in sexual terms than a specific reference to marriage with pagans. And the whole is quite clearly spiritualized in Wisdom.

ization process has relativized the older, this-worldly values whereby the bearing of many children and physical wholeness were signs of divine blessing and religious qualification.[17] True fruitfulness and virility are now sought in the spiritual virtue of the soul by which it achieves immortality. Most important, soteriologically, is the relation of the soul with ἀρετή—which in Wisdom, as in Philo, is similar to, if not the same as, σοφία. It is blessed to be *barren* (στεῖρα) and *undefiled* (ἀμίαντος); and *childlessness* (ἀτεκνία) with *virtue* brings immortality. It is blessed to be a eunuch and to enjoy a special gift of faith.[18] Wisdom 3:13—4:6, to be sure, does not explicitly enjoin sexual asceticism. But it is clearly a step in that direction.

From his writings in general it is quite clear that Philo is not making any absolute demand for sexual continence. Although he emphasizes the deeper, spiritual meaning of scripture discerned through allegorical interpretation, he still retains a sense of the validity and importance of the Jewish Law as it bears on social life.[19] Thus, he sees the human practice of sexual intercourse as Nature's mode of reproduction—according to natural, hence divine law. On the other hand, there are two sets of material in Philo's writings that point to an ascetic inclination in his religiosity and even, apparently, to an ascetic ideal.[20]

In all of his three great series of writings, the *Allegorical Interpretation*, the *Special Laws*, and the *Questions*, Philo speaks very sharply about sex and the sex drives. Sexual intercourse is strictly proscribed; it is allowed

---

17. See, e.g., Pss 127 and 128. Already in Sir 16:1–4 the old values are strongly qualified with the emphasis now being on the sapiential quality of one's children, rather than on quantity.

18. A development from Isa 56:2–3.

19. Goodenough, *Jurisprudence*, argues that in the *Special Laws* Philo actually reflects legal practices in Alexandria.

20. I mean asceticism in a more specific and sexual sense than portrayed in Philo's exposition of "Jacob" as a type of "ascetic," i.e., a disciplined "practicer" of virtue. However, for Philo the importance of Jacob as a *type* of religious figure who eventually experiences the vision of God (becomes "Israel"—seer of God) also points in the direction of this ascetic ideal. See, for example, passages interpreting Jacob's wrestling, etc., in the obvious treatises: *On the Change of Names* (*De mutatione nominum*), esp. 14; 44–45; 81–82, 87; and *On Dreams* (*De somniis*), esp. 1.129ff; 238ff.

only for reproductive purposes.²¹ The sex drives he sees as threateningly strong. He exhorts his readers to "cut off" these excessive drives.²²

Philo also appears to be presenting us with an ascetic ideal. He does this not only in passages such as those on spiritual marriage (e.g., *Cher.* 42–52), but in his portrayal of the great Jewish mystagogue, Moses, as well. The most striking expression of this ascetic ideal is significantly placed just at the beginning of the description of Moses in his role as priest, his central religious function (*Mos.* 2.66ff.). As the paradigmatic wise man and priest Moses enjoys divine inspiration and a reciprocal love with God.

> But first he had to be clean, as in soul so also in body, to have no dealings with any passion, purifying himself from all the calls of mortal nature, food, drink, and intercourse with women. (*Mos.* 2.68)

Philo mentions Moses' lengthy but temporary abstinence from food and drink, following Exod. 34:28. He specially emphasizes, however, that the sexual abstinence was long-standing and perpetual.

> This last he had disdained for many a day, almost from the time when, possessed by the Spirit, he entered on his work as a prophet, since he held it fitting to hold himself always in readiness to receive the oracular messages. As for eating and drinking, he had no thought of them for forty successive days, doubtless because he had the better food of contemplation, through whose inspiration, sent from heaven above, he grew in grace.... (*Mos.* 2.69)

It is worth noting also that Philo connects this sexual abstinence specifically with the ecstatic experience of the Divine and with Moses' role as a prophet receiving oracles. The ability to experience or be possessed by the Divine presupposes a purity from the defilement of mortal nature (cf. *Q.E.* 2.3; *Cher.* 52). Philo does not elsewhere describe Moses or any of the other great paradigmatic Jewish figures as sexual ascetics in such explicit terms. But *Mos.* 2.66 ff is a strikingly blunt description of the great mystagogue Moses at a key point in his *Life*. Taken along with other passages already cited this apparently represents an ascetic ideal. And

---

21. E.g., *Spec. Leg.* 3.133; 34–36; *Abr.* 248; *Praem.* 108.
22. E.g., *Leg.* 2.74; *Spec. Leg.* 1.9; *Q.G.* 3.48; 4.86.

Moses here sounds strikingly similar to the Therapeutae whose contemplative and ascetic life Philo described very admiringly.

Asceticism and Spiritual Marriage with Sophia among the Therapeutae

That the particular spiritual orientation expressed in Philo and Wisdom not only *could* but *did* go with a rigorous asceticism is exemplified by the Therapeutae. It is interesting that Philo, in *On the Contemplative Life*, does not treat the Therapeutae as an aberration but rather as almost typical of the devout Jews who "pursue wisdom" (φιλοσοφεῖν). He cannot resist the temptation of generalizing from the particular group of Therapeutae, whose realization of the contemplative life he so admires, to the Jewish religion generally, which he calls "the Therapeutic genus" (*Vita Cont.* 2–20).[23] But it is clear from Philo's language in *Vita Cont.* 21–22— where he gradually narrows his focus from the οἰκουμένη, to Egypt, to the particular settlement of Therapeutae near Lake Mareotis—that he is discussing an actual mystical ascetic group of Jews. Here, living in simple houses with special cells for meditation, live a number of Jews totally devoted to private contemplation of the Divine (24–29) combined with group observance of the Sabbath and ecstatic special celebrations in a community sanctuary (30–32). In striking contrast to the usual situation among Jewish groups and to Philo's general attitude toward women,[24] this group includes women on an equal or near equal basis. For example, the women shared fully in the ecstatic celebrations.

The primary purpose of the Therapeutae, according to Philo, was contemplation of the divine essence. They did this primarily by meditation on the Scripture, seeking through allegorical interpretation to find the deeper meaning that is hidden beneath the symbols of the literal text (28). The aim of this continuous meditation was apparently to live in the soul alone—i.e., in contrast with bodily, societal, worldly concerns—to realize a kind of spiritual strength or virtue (and thus be citizens of heaven and cosmos). Their longing for, or anticipatory realization of, "the immortal and blessed life," moreover, seems to have involved a close relationship with σοφία / ἀρετή, who according to Philo, was their guide,

---

23. See also, for example, *Q.E.* 2.42–43, 46, where "the contemplative race" or *genus* refers to the Jews generally.

24. See Meeks, "Image," 174–79.

source, sponsor and companion. The phrase τις ἅπαξ ὑπὸ σοφίας ἀχθείς denotes a distinctive and particular relationship. Once someone (of the Therapeutae) has come under the guidance of Sophia, he or she would no longer tolerate the turmoils of life in cities and the distractions of social intercourse, and would seek a life of solitude (ἐρημία). The substance of the contemplation to which they devote themselves is understood as a banquet of doctrines lavished by Sophia (35). It is, moreover, Arete (= Sophia) who commends them to the Father-Creator and secures for them his love (90). As in Philo and Wisdom, Sophia appears to be the agent and the substance of their religious life. Their ecstatic experiences appear to be specially important as a means toward attainment of the highest spiritual status, the vision of the Divine (12, and 83–88). These ecstatic experiences arise out of celebration of the Exodus spiritually or allegorically understood. In fact, it is the seeing and experiencing of this deeper meaning of the Exodus, a divine work that transcends reason, thought, and hope, that so fills both men and women with the Divine that they all join in ecstatic song, celebrating their salvation as if led by Moses and Miriam (87).[25]

Of particular interest is the rigorous asceticism practiced by the Therapeutae. These people have left the turmoil of city life and the distractions of social intercourse for the lonely solitude of private meditation (19–20; 25–28). Life for them was extremely private and simple. The diet was sparse in the extreme—even the "Banquets" consisted on only water and bread seasoned with salt and hyssop (37; 73). Apparently, according to Philo, the concentration on (the truths of) wisdom was so intense for some that they went three or even six days without food (34–37). The foundation of their souls, on which they build the other virtues of the souls' life was ἐγκράτεια (34).[26] Their asceticism was understood and expressed according to a dualistic pattern. None of them would partake of food or drink before sunset "since they hold that (on the one hand) the pursuit of wisdom is appropriate to the light, whereas (on the other hand) the needs of the body are appropriate to the darkness, so they assign the day to the one and a small part of the night to the other" (34).

---

25. There is hardly "something like a ritual unification of the sexes" here, contra Meeks, "Image," 179.

26. On the ascetic implication of ἐγκράτεια, esp. in Philo, see Grundmann, "ἐγκράτεια κτλ.," 340–42.

Sexual asceticism is quite clearly central to their rigorous devotion. Most of the women in the community were elderly virgins (68). Some members of the community had entered the practice in their prime and remained virgins, others had left not just property and friends but family, children and/or spouse as well for the rigors of divine contemplation (13; 18; 68). Most striking of all is the direct connection between the virginity of the women and their intimate relation with Sophia. Just as their enjoyment of the nourishment provided by Sophia meant abstention from ordinary food (35), so their intimate relation or sacred intercourse with Sophia meant abstention from ordinary sexual life in favor of more spiritual benefits:

> Women also share in the festival, the majority of whom are elderly virgins, who have kept their chastity not under compulsion, like some of the Greek priestesses, but of their own free will, because of their zeal and love for Sophia. Desiring to have her as their life-mate (desiring to cohabit with her as their spouse) they have spurned the pleasures of the body; they desire no mortal offspring, but immortal children which only the soul dear to God can bring to the birth unaided, because the Father has sown in her spiritual rays, by which she is able to behold the truths of Sophia. (*Vita Cont.* 68)

The metaphors are mixed, or rather the "persons" in the spiritual intercourse are mixed—Sophia being the life mate while the Father sows the spiritual seeds of σοφία. But more is involved than mere metaphor. The abstention from normal sexual relations, including separation from one's wife or husband, is connected with and occurs because of a higher, spiritual marriage with Sophia. The intense and exclusive contemplation of the divine mate leaves no time, energy, or interest for any of the normal social or marital relations. Six days of the week from dawn to sunset are devoted to meditation on the Divine and the deeper meaning of the scriptures, the latter being the substance of the *sophia* with whom one is so intimately and intensely mated. The dualistic pattern of asceticism, noted in 34–35, is focused most intensely and personally in the *hieros gamos* in 68. The Therapeutae give up normal conjugal relations (their "mortal life" having ended) in favor of spiritual intercourse with divine Sophia, the substance, agent, and sponsor of their salvation, their "immortal and blessed life."

Contemporary Devotion to Isis

This pattern of spiritual marriage with a divine Savior was not confined to Hellenistic Jews and, later, Christians. The same or similar pattern occurs in contemporary devotion to Isis. Recent scholarship has drawn attention to the similarity between portrayals of Sophia and the traits of the goddess Isis, and suggests that the widespread cult of Isis must have influenced Hellenistic-Jewish sapiential piety.[27] More particularly, for our present purposes, devotion to Isis provides a pagan example, parallel to the Hellenistic-Jewish material, of the intense and intimate personal relationship with a divine figure which includes sexual asceticism. Some of our best evidence indicates that in some cases initiation into Isis was not merely "rebirth" but was in effect a spiritual marriage with the corresponding abandonment of marital and/or other sexual relations. Many were those individuals who felt themselves fortunate enough to be chosen by "the Queen of heaven" for initiation into her mysteries. Public cults of Isis were well-known and widely established from early Hellenistic times.[28] But our attention here must focus on one of the most remarkable personal religious phenomena of antiquity, the dedicated personal devotion to Isis portrayed by Apuleius in the autobiographical book 11 of *The Golden Ass*.[29]

Not only is Isis the agent of Lucius' salvation, but he feels himself personally cared for and loved by the goddess as well. He has been buffeted about in the form of a lowly and despised ass by the fickle and inexorable Fate. But Isis, Queen of heaven, natural mother of all life, supreme divinity, comes with solace, relief, and transforming salvation (11:1–16). Through her providence "the sun of his salvation" rises; she prolongs his life, makes it blessed and glorious (11:5–6). She is not just his Savior, rescuing him from the grip of Fate (11:15, 25). She also regenerates him,

---

27. See, for example, Conzelmann, "Mutter," 225; Reese, *Hellenistic Influence*, 6–12, 36–49.

28. On the Isis cult in the Hellenistic and Roman world, Nilsson, *Geschichte*, 2:120–31, 624–39; Merkelbach, *Isisfeste*; Vidman, *Isis und Sarapis*, esp. chapters 2–4, 7; Nock, *Conversion*, chapter 9 and passim; and the review article by Jonathan Z. Smith.

29. Festugière, *Personal Religion*, chapter 5, is a most sensitive and insightful treatment of "Lucius and Isis." For the reliability of Apuleius' descriptions of Isis and her cult, see Nock, *Conversion*, 149ff. The translations that follow draw on Festugière; Lindsay, *Golden Ass*; as well as Adlington in the Loeb edition.

giving him *new* life (11:21, 24). Her attention, moreover, is constant and regular; she visits him each night in visions (11:19).

Lucius responds with an intense emotional attachment to Isis. Festugière says there is no analogy to be found among the Greek mysteries, such as the Eleusinian. "Lucius feels that he is loved. He believes in the love of Isis. This faith of his is absolute. How could he *not* be loved by Isis, when she herself sought him out in his misery."[30] After his initial "salvation" he cannot bear to leave the temple when the other devotees return home: "But I could not bring myself to move one inch from where I was; looking intently at the image of the goddess I bethought myself of all of the adventures I had had" (11:17). He remains for steadfast contemplation of the Goddess, seeking and enjoying visions and communications from her. "As soon as I could, I went again before the face of the Goddess, I made my lodgings within the temple precinct, and entirely shared the life of her priests and was an inseparable worshipper of her great godhead" (11:19).

He is eventually initiated into her mysteries, in which he passes through a cosmologically symbolic death to be reborn and dramatically revealed as the sun, i.e., the consort of Isis.[31] Even then, it is only with great difficulty that he can tear himself away from her presence in the temple:

> But I could hardly bear to break the ties of intense affection that bound me to the place. Prostrating myself before the Goddess and watering her feet with my tears, I addressed her, gulping back the sobs that disturbed my articulation (11:24, Lindsay).

Lucius does manage to depart the temple, and eventually re-enters more ordinary social and professional life. But he does two things that indicate his continuing spiritual love for Isis. He becomes a daily worshipper at her temple in Rome, nothing mattering to him so much as this daily supplication to the goddess. Most importantly, since Isis had com-

---

30. Festugière, *Personal Religion*, 182. K. H. E. de Jong, *Mysterienwesen* 56–57, also emphasizes the close, exclusive personal relationships in the Isis religion. There is also evidence from the Isis inscriptions in Thessalonika (in *Inscriptionae Graecae* 10.2.1) that show a real warmth of personal piety (mostly 1st–2d AD).

31. This pattern of death and spiritual marriage in the initiation into Isis is strikingly parallel to the individual bridal mysticism of "death as spiritual marriage" which Rush, "Death," finds focused in the Christian initiation rite of baptism.

manded him to keep her remembrance "fast as in his heart's deep core," he now nurtures an inner devotion to his Savior and true love.

> So I shall try the only thing which a devotee, though poor in all else, can: I shall always keep Thy divine appearance and Thy most holy godhead locked in the privacy of my heart and shall conjure them up in my imagination (11:25).

Lucius' intimate relation with Isis is ascetic. The continuing favor of Isis, in fact, is contingent on this ascetic aspect of his dedication.

> More, if you are found to merit my love by your dedicated obedience, religious devotion, and *constant chastity*, you will discover that it is within my power to prolong your life beyond the limits set to it by Fate (11:6).[32]

The rigor of the discipline required by Isis even makes Lucius hesitate before initiation (11:19). In the most recent general survey of asceticism in antiquity and the early church, Lohse concludes that sexual asceticism must have been widespread in the Isis cult, it being witnessed by both pagan and Christian writers. Lohse thinks that sexual asceticism may have been a religious duty for the priests and priestesses of Isis.[33] Most interesting with regard to the practices among the Corinthians of separating from wives or husbands is the report by Tertullian that priestesses of the African Ceres (Isis) freely give up their marriage, and thenceforth deny any contact with males, including kissing their own sons.[34] The case of Lucius, which is surely an autobiographical expression of Apuleius himself, is even more striking. Here an ordinary initiate and devotee feels a deep emotional attachment to Isis. He has been given new life through her, has been dramatically initiated and portrayed as her consort. He cherishes her divine image in his innermost heart[35] and continues his

32. *Tenacibus castimoniis* in 11.6; cf. *castimoniorum abstinentiam* in 11.19. Festugière, *Personal Religion*, 162–63 n. 32, demonstrates that "*castimonia* in the plural without any associated determinative, seems at least to include also abstinence from sexual intercourse, and this is, after all, the primary sense of *castimonia* (cf. Livy 39.9.4)." He also argues, on the basis of the context of Lucius' life devoted to Isis in her temple and the contrast with the profligacy of his earlier life, that Lucius' dedication and discipline included sexual abstinence. See further, on the chastity of the priests of Isis, de Jong, *Mysterienwesen*, 56–57, 69ff.

33. Lohse, *Askese and Mönchtum*, 38.

34. Tertullian, *De exhortatione castitatis* 13.2.

35. A motif of spiritual marriage picked up both by Christian mysticism and by romantic love.

daily contact with her long after his extremely intense initial devotion and habitation in her temple. In complete contrast to the wantonness of his earlier life, he now leads a life of exclusive devotion to his goddess.

Sophia and Asceticism in Earliest Corinthian Christianity

Spiritual marriage with Sophia seems to underlie one of the earliest cases of asceticism in a "Christian" community, that addressed by Paul in 1 Corinthians. It is sometimes suggested that the asceticism Paul deals with in 1 Cor 7 is rooted in a realized eschatology.[36] This interpretation of the Corinthian situation finds in the Corinthians' language behind 1 Cor 15:12 and 4:8 an expression of a spiritually realized resurrection such as that expressed in 2 Tim 2:18.[37] But Paul says explicitly in 1 Cor 15:12 that some of the Corinthians were denying the resurrection of the dead, and in 4:8 the "already" is Paul's own formulation. In his discussions of the ethical problems that have emerged in the Corinthian community (1 Cor 6–10) Paul significantly gives no indication whatever that any are related to a "realized eschatology." Indeed in 1 Cor 7:23ff. it is Paul who argues for a qualified asceticism on the basis of the imminent eschatological crisis, an odd tactic if he were concerned about an overly zealous eschatological enthusiasm.

The hypothesized realized resurrection in Corinth is usually seen as based in a baptismal experience of dying and rising with Christ, as in Col 2:12–13 and Eph 2:5–6. But the Corinthians hardly understood their baptism so Christocentrically. As Meeks points out, theirs was a baptism of *sophia*, and as Koester makes clear, they did not identify Sophia and the exalted Christ.[38] The Corinthians, rather, according to 1 Cor 1:13 (and 10:2) are thinking of a baptism of *sophia* by or into the name of their particular apostle or wisdom teacher. Moreover, it is quite clear that the divisiveness in the community and what Paul sees as the arrogance of

---

36. Recently, for example, Cartlidge, "1 Corinthians 7," 227ff.; Wayne Meeks, "Image," 199, 202. Niederwimmer, *Askese und Mysterium*, 75, sees less the Corinthian asceticism than the (supposed) Corinthian libertinism as an expression of a radical "enthusiasm"; but he neither demonstrates the presence of this enthusiasm in Corinth nor explains what the enthusiasm is, other than "gnosticizing."

37. Käsemann, "Primitive Christian Apocalyptic," 119–20; Robinson, "Kerygma and History," 32–33; Schniewind, "Die Leugner," 273.

38. Meeks, "Image," 202; Koester, review of Wilckens.

some are connected with their devotion to Sophia,[39] which Paul rejects in 1 Cor 1–4. It would appear than that the focus of the Corinthians' faith is the divine Sophia, and that the ascetic separation of husbands and wives advised against in 1 Cor 7 should be viewed in this connection.

It has also become increasingly clear that the background of the Corinthians' devotion to Sophia is the particular tradition of Hellenistic Judaism represented by Philo and Wisdom.[40] Considerable agreement has developed concerning the particular language and principles in 1 Corinthians that represent the Corinthians' religious point of view. Nearly all of these terms, principles and ideas of the Corinthians are extensively paralleled in Philo's writings and in Wisdom.[41] Perhaps the most striking passages where most of these terms and ideas come together are Wis 7–10; *Mig.* 28–40; *Her.* 247–83; *Post.* 1.24–129; *Abr.* 255–76; *Virt.* 179–80; 212–19; *Q.E.* 2:39–40. Because these language parallels are so extensive and comprehensive it is possible to use Wisdom and Philo as an analogy from which to understand the Corinthians whom Paul is admonishing. For, although we have somewhat fragmentary evidence in 1 Corinthians, in Wisdom and Philo all of these terms and ideas can be seen to be expressions of the same consistent religious viewpoint. Although a concrete link is hardly necessary, there happens to be one in the person of Apollos. From what Paul says, in however conciliatory a tone (1 Cor 3:5–15; 4:6), Apollos' ministry in Corinth has clearly generated the excitement about Sophia and exalted spiritual status—and he is known from early

---

39. Clearly argued by Wilckens, *Weisheit und Torheit*, although the Corinthian situation must be understood more in terms of Koester's incisive critique (see his review).

40. Helmut Koester, "GNOMAI DIAPHOROI," 149–50; Dupont, *Gnosis*, 172–80; Pearson, *Pneumatikos–Psychikos*, chapters 3–5; Hamerton-Kelly, *Pre-Existence*, esp. 138–42.

41. Many of these terminological parallels have been noted by the commentaries, but none of the studies of 1 Corinthians have pursued a systematic analysis of the possible interconnections of these terms and traditions. This is ironic, since the *same* passages in Wisdom or Philo can be cited as "parallels" for different terminology from *different* points in 1 Corinthians. Thus it is clear from *Leg.* 1.88–95, for example, that the contrast between two types of men, heavenly and earthly (1 Cor 15:45ff.) is equivalent to the distinction between two levels of religious status, the "perfect" vs. the "babes," etc. (1 Cor 2:6—3:4). Or, in *Plant.* 62–72, the wise man who, by possession of Sophia, possesses all things including true wealth and kingship (1 Cor 1:26; 4:8; 3:21), whose lot is heavenly as opposed to earthly (15:46–47), also possesses knowledge that "God is One alone" (8:4); see chap. 1 above.

Christian tradition as a Jew from Alexandria, eloquent and well-versed in the scriptures (Acts 18:24).

The vortex of this whole Corinthian pattern of religious thinking is the divine figure Sophia. She, as spiritual food and drink and the spiritual rock (1 Cor 10:3–4),[42] as *gnosis* of theological truth (1 Cor 8:1, 4),[43] is the very content of salvation. As the guide through the spiritual exodus (1 Cor 10:1–2)[44] and as the Spirit who inspires prophetic ecstasy (1 Cor 12:7–10; 14:1–14),[45] Sophia is also the means or agent of salvation. Sophia provides those who know or possess her with an exalted, secure and indelible spiritual status. They become wise, perfect, immortal, kingly, wealthy, powerful, nobly born, etc., as opposed to the inferior status of the babes or earthly men (1 Cor 1:26; 2:6–3, 4; 4:8–10; 15:46–50).[46] Not mentioned by Paul in 1 Corinthians but integral to this same religiosity focused on Sophia in Wisdom and Philo, are the images of Sophia as the divine place where the wise dwell, as divine light, and as the divine lover or spouse of the wise.[47] Is it conceivable that the Corinthian πνευματικοί ("spiritual ones") also thought in terms of a spiritual marriage with Sophia and that this is related to their asceticism?

Even more striking than the similarities in religious language between the Corinthian spirituals and Wisdom and Philo are the extensive parallels between the Corinthians and the Therapeutae. These parallels, moreover, are the more important since we have here not merely linguistic similarities but an actual Hellenistic-Jewish group devoted to Sophia and individually practicing an asceticism related to spiritual marriage with

---

42. Paul, borrowing the Corinthians' symbols here, in order to qualify them sharply in 10:5–13, has surely just substituted Christ for Sophia in 10:4. On Sophia as spiritual food and drink, see *Sac.* 86; *Her.* 191, 79; *Fug.* 137–39, 177–202; *Leg.* 3.162–73. For Sophia as the rock, see esp. *Leg.* 2.86; *Det.* 115–17; *Som.* 2.221–22.

43. Cf. generally: Wis 7:17; 10:10; 15:2–3; *Leg.* 3.46–48, 126; *Quod Deus* 143; knowledge that "God is One," etc., *Spec. Leg.* 1.30; *Opif.* 70–172; knowledge about non-existence of other gods and idols: Wis 13:1; 14:22; 15:2–3; *Dec.*7–8; *Spec. Leg.* 1.15–30.

44. Sirach 24:4; Wis 10:15–21; *Mos.* 1.166; Philo interprets the central symbols of the exodus story as referring to Sophia/Logos. Cf. the "royal way," *Post.* 101–3; *Quod Deus* 140–80. On the latter, Joseph Pascher, Η ΒΑΣΙΛΙΚΗ ΟΔΟΣ, and Ulrich Wilckens's "σοφία κτλ.," 500ff.

45. Cf., Wis 7:27; 8:8; 9:17; *Pier.* 249–66; *Spec. Leg.* 4.49; *Gig.* 47; *Quod Deus* 1–3; *Fug.*166.

46. Cf. Wis 7:8, 11; 8:3, 5, 10, 17–18; *Mig.* 28–40; *Som.* 2.215, 242–54; *Sob.* 55–57; *Her.* 313–15; *Leg.* 1.90–95.

47. *Mig.* 28–30, 39–40; on the spiritual marriage with Sophia, see pp. 41–47 above.

Sophia. The Corinthians apparently drew spiritual edification and even a kind of spiritual security from the higher meaning of sacred scripture, and concentrated in some way on celebrating or learning from the Exodus symbols spiritually understood (1 Cor 10:1–4 and the implications of Paul's warning in 10:5–13; cf., *Vita Cont.* 25–31; 78; 85–88). Although their "spiritual gifts" were a divisive rather than a cohesive force for the community as a whole, some of the Corinthians, like the Therapeutae, were enjoying ecstatic experiences and revelation of wisdom or interpretation (1 Cor 12:8–10; 14:2–4, 26–27; cf., *Vita Cont.* 12, 25–31, 83–88). The Corinthians also display a dualistic division between body and soul whereby the soul as the true self has transcended mortal and earthly matters such as the body and enjoys the immortality and perfection appropriate to its heavenly status (1 Cor 15:12, 45ff.; 4:8–10; 2:6—3:4; cf. *Vita Cont.* 13, 34). This is all related to a sexual asceticism being practiced by at least some, who have left their spouses or are remaining unattached, believing that "it is well for a man not to touch a woman" (1 Cor 7; cf. *Vita Cont.* 13, 18, 68). As with the Therapeutae, and in contrast to the usual situation in Jewish groups, women play a prominent part, sharing in the ecstatic experiences and spiritual gifts as well as in the practice of asceticism (1 Cor 11:5; 14:34–35; 7:2–3, 8, 10).[48] It would appear, finally, that the focus of these Corinthians' religiosity is the divine Sophia; that is, all of these other features of their spiritual substance and religious practices are aspects of or benefits of their relation with Sophia.

From the analogies in Philo and Wisdom, and especially that of the Therapeutae, the relation between the Corinthians' devotion to Sophia and their sexual asceticism emerges quite clearly. The spiritual marriage with Sophia, so prominent in the analogous cases, provides the connecting link.[49] Some of the Corinthian *pneumatikoi* had come to believe

48. The community of Therapeutae—in which women (1) have equal participation with men, including ecstatic expression, (2) are ascetically separated from husbands and/or are ascetic virgins, and (3) are devoted to Sophia as divine agent and content of their salvation—thus provides a far better and more complete parallel to the Corinthians' religiosity (discerned through 1 Cor 1–4; 7; 12–14) than the "realized resurrection" explanation derived from comparison with the "heretics" opposed in 2 Timothy. Niederwimmer, *Askese und Mysterium*, 220, curiously ignores this ascetic Jewish group.

49. It is quite striking in comparison with the Corinthian situation that Wisdom describes the intercourse with Sophia in language virtually identical to that used by the Corinthian spirituals to describe Sophia and the special status she imparts. Especially in Wis 8:2–18 it is evident that much of the other key soteriological terminology coheres around the marriage with Sophia as the central image.

that "it is better not to touch a woman" since the true intercourse was a spiritual one with Sophia. Some of these persons were apparently shifting their marital relationships from an earthly plane, which included sexual activity, to an exclusively spiritual plane, with sexual asceticism (implied in 1 Cor 7:5–6, as well a 7:1). Some were even, like the Therapeutae, separating from wife or husband—becoming widows or widowers to mortal matters in order to achieve a heavenly marriage of immortality with Sophia (1 Cor 7:10–11, 27a).[50] The Philo passages cited above (e.g., *Spec. Leg.* 2.30; *Q.E.* 2.3; *Cher.* 42–52) illumine how these Corinthians probably understood their relationship with Sophia:

> the soul cannot have dealings with any of the body's friends while it spends its days in the house of Sophia. For then it is nourished by food more divine, which it finds in all knowledge, and for the sake of this it actually disregards the flesh. (*Leg.* 3.152)

The Background of Individual Spiritual Marriage with Christ

The Corinthian asceticism would appear, therefore, to be rooted in the same pattern of spiritual marriage as that in Wisdom, Philo's writings, *The Golden Ass*, and among the Therapeutae. Although modern scholars apply the concept of "sacred marriage" somewhat broadly, to cosmic forces and divinities as well as to human relationships,[51] the pattern delineated above involved the particular relationship of a human soul with its divine Savior. It was celebrated in a special rite of initiation, as in the ease of Lucius with Isis, but the relationship was one of the perpetual mystical intercourse. This pattern involved not the spiritualization of sex, in which ordinary sexual relations are understood as symbolic of higher religious realities,[52] but the sublimation of sex, including abstinence from ordinary

---

50. By discerning more precisely the particular religious orientation and motivation of the Corinthians' asceticism perhaps ground work can be laid for more precise discussion of the asceticism that Paul favors in a qualified way and on the basis of a very different orientation and motivation.

51. See standard literature such as Eliade, *Sacred and Profane*, 146, 170–71; and van der Leeuw, *Religion*, 1:199–201, 369–70. The Greek term *hieros gamos*, of course, refers to a ritual action as used in the "history of religions." In biblical scholarship the term is applied, for example, to the interpretation of the Song of Songs with reference to God and Israel and to Eph 5:22–33. See Schlier, "Excursus," 265–76; and Niederwimmer *Askese und Mysterium* 134–37, and the literature cited there.

52. As among the Lurianic Kabbalists at Safed, Israel, in the sixteenth and seventeenth centuries; see Scholem, *Kabbalah*, 139–45.

sexual relations. For Philo, the Therapeutae, and the Corinthians this sublimated intercourse with the divine Sophia elevated the human self into an immortal ethereal existence. For the Therapeutae, Lucius, and apparently for some of the Corinthians, such a spiritual marriage was total and exclusive, hence required a sexual asceticism on the worldly level, even to the point of leaving one's spouse or, for Lucius, totally abandoning his earlier promiscuous activities. Indeed, given the marked cosmological and anthropological dualism in Wisdom and Philo—whereby the true self is the soul or mind and the body is other[53]—it is not surprising that the intimate bond between the soul and Sophia would lead to asceticism.

Despite Paul's opposition to spiritual marriage with Sophia—or perhaps partly because of his attempt to replace Sophia with Christ (1 Cor 1:24; 8:6; 10:4)—it became a prominent Christian soteriological and mystical symbol. In a paradigmatic incident in the *Acts of Thomas* (1:10–15), a writing probably independent of Pauline influence, where the young couple do not consummate their marriage in "filthy intercourse," but give themselves entirely to Christ, the bride says: "I have had no intercourse with a short-lived husband . . . because I am yoked with the true man."[54] Among the Church Fathers Origen provides the first well-developed expression of individual Christian spiritual marriage, including an appeal to Pauline texts such as 2 Cor 11:2, now individualistically interpreted. As Rush points out, he applies the Song of Songs not just to Christ and his Church but to the individual marriage of the soul with Christ the Logos as well. Standing near the beginning of the same tradition that Bernard would draw on nine centuries later, Origen writes:

> Let us bring in the soul whose every desire is to be joined in fellowship with the Word of God and to enter into the mysteries of His wisdom and knowledge, as into the chamber of a heavenly bridegroom. The soul . . . prays that her clear and virgin mind

---

53. For a general discussion of this legacy of classical Greece to Western culture, see Ricoeur, *Symbolism of Evil*, Part II, chapter 4; and Dodds, *Pagan and Christian*, esp. 29ff.

54. The *Acts of Thomas*, in Hennecke and Schneemelcher, *New Testament Apocrypha*, 447–50. Although it is extremely difficult to reach a precise interpretation of the references and allusions to "the mystery of the bridal chamber" in the *Gospel of Philip*, it would appear to belong to this same pattern of spiritual marriage with the divine mate. Spiritual impregnation of the τέλειος is by a sacred kiss (*Gospel of Philip*, logion 31; cf. 55) and actual cohabitation is rejected (73; 126). See Meeks, "Image," 189–91.

may have the light of the illumination and the intercourse of the very Word of God . . . (The soul says) in prayer to God, 'Let Him kiss me with the kisses of His mouth.' (*Commentary on Song of Songs* 1)[55]

It may be stretching things, however, to claim that "he is the father and creator of bridal mysticism."[56] Following Origen, individual mystical marriage with Christ accompanied by asceticism became a dominant pattern of Christian spirituality, especially in monasticism. The ground had been well-prepared, however, by the long-standing practice of spiritual marriage with Sophia-Logos among Hellenistic Jews and even in earlier Christian communities that, like Origen later, were strongly influenced by Hellenistic-Jewish traditions. Moreover, in this devotion to a Savior as one's divine spouse we see one significant theological self-understanding of the asceticism that, as Dodds suggests, begins "further back," before the third century.

Such asceticism may well be a "neurosis," as Dodds charges. But their "neurosis" surely had a very positive, even therapeutic significance for the ascetics themselves. As we know from literature of the Hellenistic-Roman period such as *The Golden Ass* or Gnostic treatises, external reality, the world of society, politics, and even the cosmos, was experienced as hostile and threatening.[57] What is more, with weakened support from tribe, community or other social group to help hold them together personally, individuals found it difficult to understand and control various "internal" forces, such as bodily passions and "appetites." As Jonas points out with regard to Gnosticism, these internal forces really correspond to the unreliable chaos of forces invading from the outside.[58] To maintain some form of conscious individuality or identity over against powers threatening from within and without it was necessary for the self to generate power of its own and to find security in a transcendent source.

Paradoxical as it may seem, both libertinism and asceticism work toward the same end, generation, and concentration of one's spiritual power

---

55. Origen, *In Canticum* 1.1 (*GCS* 8); translation following Tollinton, *Selections*.

56. Cf. Rush, "Death," 82.

57. On such characteristics and effects of Hellenistic-Roman civilization, see Dodds, *Pagan and Christian*, chapters 1–2; and idem, *Greeks*, chapter 8; Nock, *Conversion*, chapters 7–9; and Jonas, *Gnostic Religion*, chapter l.

58. That is, what Jonas, *Gnostic Religion*, 281–82, says of the later, more extreme case of Gnosticism holds for the earlier situation as well.

over against a hostile environment.[59] Libertines demonstrate that they are so strong as to be unaffected by ordinary requirements, thus manifesting that they have overcome the oppressive order. Ascetics seemingly take the route of self-deprivation, a renunciation of power. But this self-deprivation in sexual relations, eating habits, etc., makes possible an intensification of the ascetic's spiritual forces. Deprivation on the worldly level is experienced as personal transcendence on the spiritual level. Asceticism, moreover, is closely connected with other means of achieving transcendent power such as ecstasy,[60] as appears in the cases of the Corinthian *pneumatikoi* and the Therapeutae. Philo's comments about the change of marital status (*Q.E.* 2.3; *Cher.* 50), the practices of the Therapeutae, and Lucius' emotional outpouring of devotion all express how such an asceticism can generate the power necessary for spiritual transcendence and security. Similarly, by virtue of their intimacy with Sophia the Corinthian spirituals are "powerful," "of noble birth," and "reigning like kings," in utter contrast to their previous status (1 Cor 1:26–27; 4:8–10). For a transcendent security is found in the form of a caring divine figure who loves the soul and to whom the soul responds with love and devotion.

The individual who entered spiritual marriage with Sophia, Isis, or Christ thus gained a transcendent inner strength, a secure basis from which to fight against threats from both within and without. Lucius was able to overcome his own lust and the fickle fortunes of Fate. The σοφός in Wisdom or Philo was able to resist the debilitating weight of the body and to escape the corruptible contingencies of the material historical world in general. Some, such as Lucius (Apuleius?) and Philo, were then able to function adequately *in* the world (e.g., Lucius as a lawyer in Rome, Philo as a leader and emissary of Alexandrian Jews) even if they were not *of* the world. They could function in the world of affairs even though they could not really share in shaping their own destiny. Others, such as the Therapeutae and the later Christian monks, simply removed themselves from interaction in ordinary social affairs.

Paul objected to the Corinthians' devotion to Sophia because it seemed individualistic, arrogant, and divisive (1 Cor 1–4). He insisted that the primary purpose of spirituality was to edify the community and that the primary spiritual gift was a socially oriented *agape* with com-

---

59. Van der Leeuw, *Religion*, 456–57.
60. Ibid., 487.

munal extension. Dodds, indeed, suggests that it was this cultivation of community among otherwise isolated and threatened people that accounted for the growth and success of the Christian movement.[61] Paul's successors such as Origen, far from following the apostle in rejecting devotion to Sophia (Logos) and the corresponding asceticism, actually embraced individual mystical marriage with the Logos. But they did, in effect, come to a compromise or synthesis by understanding the individual bridal mysticism within the larger context of the mystical union of Christ and his bride the Church.

---

61. Dodds, *Pagan and Christian*, 136–38.

4

Gnosis in Corinth

Scholars are gradually relinquishing the belief that the Corinthians were Gnostics. As a noted student of Gnosticism concludes, we find in Corinth "at most only the first tentative beginnings of what was later to develop into full-scale Gnosticism."[1] In fact, a kind of agnosticism has emerged with regard to the early Christian community in Corinth. "The position in Corinth cannot be reconstructed on the basis of the possibilities of the general history of religion."[2] I suggest, however, that it is possible to determine with some degree of precision the nature and background of the proto-Gnosticism in Corinth: Hellenistic-Jewish religiosity focused on σοφία (*sophia*) and γνῶσις (*gnosis*).

The use of one's *gnosis* was one of the principal points of contention between Paul and those in the Corinthian church who considered themselves strong and wise. The statements in 1 Cor 8:1 and 4: "we all have knowledge," "no idol exists in the world," and "there is no god but One," are now generally recognized as Corinthian slogans quoted by Paul.[3] First Corinthians 8:6 as well is thought by some scholars to reflect the viewpoint of the strong Corinthians;[4] but this is somewhat less obvious, and analysis of this issue must await clarification of the principles that are most certainly from the Corinthians. The two quotations in 8:4 are, in effect, particular principles of the Corinthians' *gnosis*. In the most substantive recent commentary on 1 Corinthians, Conzelmann suggests

---

1. Wilson, "How Gnostic," 65–74.
2. Conzelmann, *1 Corinthians*, 15.
3. Hurd has tabulated scholarly opinions (*Origin*, 67–68); more briefly, Conzelmann, *1 Corinthians*, 7 n. 54; see especially Jeremias, "Gedankenführung," 273–74.
4. Conzelmann, *1 Corinthians*, 7.

three possibilities for the nature of the Corinthians' *gnosis:* it can be understood as popular philosophical enlightenment on the nature of the gods, or as illumination of the pneumatic, or as a specifically Gnostic insight (into the depths of being).[5]

There is, however, a fourth possibility that fits far better with other aspects of the particular situation of conflict in the nascent Corinthian community that Paul had "planted" and Apollos "watered" (1 Cor 3:5). It is becoming increasingly clear that Hellenistic-Jewish speculation about and devotion to Wisdom forms the background of the Corinthians' obsession with *sophia* which Paul addresses in 1 Cor 1–4.[6] Perhaps an investigation of the Hellenistic-Jewish background of the Corinthians' principles cited in 1 Corinthians 8 can illuminate both the specific nature of the Corinthians' *gnosis* and its relationship to other aspects of the Corinthians' religiosity.

A philologically-centered approach that searches primarily for comparable words and phrases and then brings these directly to bear on particular words and phrases in the biblical text sometimes fails to consider broader patterns of thought. Conzelmann, for example, in dealing with 1 Cor 8:4 and other passages, lists an abundance of comparative phrases and formulas.[7] But he apparently does not consider it important to investigate the possible interconnections, for example, between the various Stoic passages he lists or between the many Philo passages he cites. He thus does not discern that Philo in particular displays a whole pattern of language and thought that is relevant to the polemical situation in Corinth.[8] It is important to take such patterns and interconnections into consideration. In particular it would be well to keep in mind how Paul's argument in 1 Cor 8 may be related to what he said in 1 Cor 1–4, how the Corinthians' principles of *gnosis* in 1 Cor 8 may be related to their obsession with *sophia* as discerned through 1 Cor 1–4, and whether the same comparative material elucidates different aspects of the Corinthians' viewpoint and thus (indirectly) Paul's argument as well.

---

5. Ibid., 140.

6. Koester, "GNOMAI DIAPHOROI," 310–11; Pearson, *Pneumatikos-Psychikos*, chap. 2; Hamerton-Kelly, *Pre-existence*, 112–23; Horsley, "Wisdom of Word," chap. 2 above; and idem, "Spiritual Status," chap. 1 above.

7. Conzelmann, *1 Corinthians*, 140–45.

8. Pearson, *Pneumatikos-Psychikos*; Hamerton-Kelly, *Pre-existence*, 121–22; Horsley, "Wisdom of Word," chap. 2 above; and idem, "Spiritual Status," chap. 1 above.

With this perspective in mind I will attempt to demonstrate that the principles of gnosis and general religious viewpoint of the "strong" Corinthians can be found in that Hellenistic-Jewish theology represented by Philo and the Wisdom of Solomon. This particular tradition of Hellenistic-Jewish religion should thus illuminate Paul's conflict with the "strong" and "wise" Corinthians.

The Hellenistic-Jewish *Gnosis* behind the Principles in 1 Cor 8:1, 4

"We All Possess 'Gnosis'"

The insights of Bultmann's investigation of the term *gnosis* are still valid even though his organization of the material may no longer be entirely satisfactory. Relying primarily on Reitzenstein and Hermetic literature, and partly on Neoplatonic philosophy and Christian Gnostic literature, Bultmann constructed a synthetic picture of "the Gnostic usage," which he then used to interpret the Corinthian *gnosis*.[9] Nearly all of the principal generalizations that Bultmann makes regarding "the Gnostic usage," however, also fit the understanding of *gnosis* found in the Septuagintal wisdom literature, especially Wisdom, and in the treatises of Philo. Bultmann himself noted in this Hellenistic-Jewish literature "a plain subjective element of profound religious knowledge in the mystical and Gnostic sense."[10]

More particularly, already in this Hellenistic-Jewish literature, *gnosis* (or its equivalents, such as ἐπιστήμη) connotes a content possessed as well as the act of knowing. It is used in the absolute sense (e.g., *Fug.* 164; *Mos.* 2. 98; *Decal.* 1) or with a genitive of an object known. The latter is most frequently "knowledge of God" (e.g., Wis 15:2–3; *Fug.* 165; *Quod Deus* 143), but can also be "knowledge of truth" (*Prob.* 74), or "knowledge of holy things" (Wis 10:10), or even the commonplace "Stoic" definition of σοφία.[11] If not explicitly described as a *charisma*, knowledge is clearly

9. Bultmann, "γινώσκω κτλ.," 692–96, 709.

10. Ibid., 701; and similarly in Bultmann's review of Dupont, *Gnosis*, 22–23; see also the more extensive analysis of *gnosis* in Philo by Jonas, *Gnosis und spätantiker Geist*, 99–121.

11. γνῶσις θείων καὶ ἀνθρωπίνων πραγμάτων καὶ τῶν αἰτίων, "Knowledge of divine and human matters and the causes"; 4 Macc 1:16; Philo, *Congr.* 79; Aristobulus, in Eusebius, *Praep. Ev.* 667c; cf. Cicero, *Off.* 2.2.5; Seneca, *Ep.* 89; Plutarch, *Placit. philos.* 1.2.

divine and is given by God or by his consort Sophia (Wis 7:17; 10:10; *Quod Deus* 92; *Op.* 70–71). The recipients thereby have a special religious status, as "wise" or "righteous" or "perfect."

Whatever cosmic or divine content is imparted serves the salvation of the individual soul. Knowledge is a soteriological goal or content that brings divine power or even immortality to the soul (Wis 15:2–3).[12] Although Philo, like Plotinus after him, avoids the term *gnosis* in reference to the ultimate vision of God,[13] he does refer to the goal of the perfect way leading to God, i.e. *sophia*, as γνῶσις καὶ ἐπιστήμη Θεοῦ ("knowledge and understanding of God"; *Quod Deus* 143), or as ἐπίγνωσις τοῦ ἑνός ("knowledge of the One") and γνῶσις καὶ ἐπιστήμη καὶ τιμὴ τοῦ ἑνός ("knowledge and understanding and honor of the One"; *Leg.* 3.46–48, 126). Knowledge is thus an integral aspect of the personal mystical piety in both Wisdom and Philo. Goodenough, through his sensitive and penetrating interpretation of Philo's religious mentality, has provided us with a vivid sense of the "subjective element of profound religious knowledge" in Philo's writings.[14] Similarly, in the book of Wisdom, the *hieros gamos* (sacred marriage) described in chapter 8 expresses a profound personal intimacy with the heavenly Sophia, one manifestation of which is *gnosis*. The Hellenistic-Jewish religion represented in Wisdom and Philo had long since appropriated the language of the mysteries.[15] Thus, well before the genuine Christian Gnostics and mystical Neoplatonists, Hellenistic Jews such as Philo were enjoying a mystical *gnosis* with a clearly other-worldly orientation.

If we attempt to determine more precisely what "knowledge" is for Philo and Wisdom, three significant aspects in particular emerge. First, knowledge is almost always directly or indirectly knowledge of God (e.g., Wis 15:2–3; *Virt.* 178–79, 213–16; *Leg.* 3.46–48, 100, 126–27). This is the case even when "knowledge" appears in the absolute sense (*Fug.* 164; *Mos.* 2.98). Second, knowledge is parallel or similar to *sophia* (Wis 9:10–11; 10:10; *Leg.* 95; *Quod Deus* 143; *Fug.* 76; *Mos.* 2.98). Third and

---

12. Aristobulus, in Eusebius, *Praep. Ev.* 688a, says that after the soul's forgetfulness and vice have been abandoned on the true sabbath, i.e. reason, we receive γνῶσις ἀληθείας (*gnōsis alētheias*).

13. Bultmann, "γινώσκω κτλ.," 702 n. 60.

14. Goodenough, *By Light, Light*.

15. Goodenough, *By Light, Light*, chapters 1, 9–10; Wolfson, *Philo*, 1.36–54; Larcher, *Etudes*, 255–59; Reese, *Hellenistic Influence*, 33–50.

more precisely, knowledge is the particular religious and theological content of *sophia*, i.e. the ontological and especially soteriological knowledge of divine teaching supposedly derived from the Scripture (Wis 10:10; 4 Macc 1:16–17; *Quod Deus* 92; *Cong.* 7:9; *Spec. Leg.* 1.30, 50, 269).

These three aspects of Hellenistic-Jewish "knowledge" are all directly relevant to the Corinthian situation and may help us discern more precisely how the "strong" Corinthians understood their *gnosis*. Judging from the other Corinthian principles cited by Paul in the immediate context, 1 Cor 8:4, their *gnosis* was theological, i.e. knowledge of God. Moreover, the close relation between *gnosis* and *sophia* in Philo and Wisdom enables us to determine, by analogy, how the Corinthians' *gnosis* may have been related to the *sophia* rejected by Paul in 1 Cor 1–4. Although this relation must be further elaborated below, it may suffice at this point to suggest that *gnosis* was not identical with *sophia* for the Corinthians. But it apparently was an expression of the *sophia* they possessed. "Knowledge" probably referred to the particular religious content of *sophia*, including such fundamental theological principles as "there are no idols in the world" and "there is no god but One."

"There Is No God but One"

Henology was a problem with which the philosophers of antiquity were preoccupied since the pre-Socratics.[16] The word θεός (*theos*), and eventually the name Zeus had come to mean "divinity," the divine principle in which all gods found unity. In religious philosophy there developed, as it were, a kind of henological confessional form of two or more declarations of unity: for example, Marcus Aurelius 7.9, an affirmation of the interconnectedness of all things in terms of one cosmos, one God, one essence, one law, one truth, and even one perfection. The principle repeated by Josephus in *Ant.* 4.201 (and not derived from Exod 20:25–26 or Deut 12:5), "for God is one and the Hebrew race is one," is probably a similar declaration.[17] Even more clearly Eph 4:4–6 should be compared

---

16. On Parmenides and Heraclitus see Jaeger, *Theology*, chapters 7, and p. 174; on Hellenistic "monotheism" see Martin P. Nilsson, *Geschichte*, 427–29, 569–78; for Hellenistic Judaism, see Nock, Roberts, and Skeat, "The Guild," 59; and Marcus, "Divine Names"; on the formula "One God," its background, and uses, see Peterson, *EIS THEOS*; and Neufeld, *The Earliest Christian Confessions*, 34ff.

17. Cf. Josephus, *Apion* 2.193; Philo, *Spec. Leg.* 67; *2 Bar.* 49:24.

with this henological confessional form traditional in Hellenistic religious philosophy.

The Corinthians' slogan quoted in 1 Cor 8:4, however, is the basic Jewish confession that "God is one."[18] Its credal character appears in a variety of Hellenistic-Jewish literature, such as Pseudo-Sophocles.[19] For Josephus, that "God is One" is the teaching of the first principle of the Decalogue in his summary, *Ant.* 3.91 (cf. 8.343). For Philo, that "God is One" is the lesson Moses continually teaches in the Laws (e.g., *Spec. Leg.* 1.30) and is the second major principle in a five-part summary of essential Jewish doctrine (*Op.* 170–72; cf. *Conf.* 170–71).

This does not exhaust the central significance of this principle of knowledge for Philo's religion, however. For the knowledge or vision *of God*, as reached via the perfect way, i.e. *sophia*, is the goal of his mystical contemplation, as in the γνῶσις καὶ ἐπιστήμη Θεοῦ ("knowledge and understanding of God") of *Quod Deus* 143. Moreover God, for Philo, is essentially "the One," "the truly Existing One." Thus the knowledge of God is repeatedly expressed as the vision or recognition of *the One*, as in *Leg.* 3.48, 126, cited above.

Moving back, by analogy, to the Corinthians' *gnosis*, it becomes clear that it is inadequate to say with Conzelmann that the confession that there is "one God" is "the self-evident presupposition of their faith."[20] This principle is rather the central and essential content of their faith. This would be true even if all of those who had joined the Christian community in Corinth were already (Hellenistic) Jews, whose conversion to the new religious movement was a repentance or return to the proper knowledge of the One (see *Virt.* 178–79). But especially in the mission context of early Christianity, in which Gentiles were being converted, i.e. becoming proselytes to this new movement (which must have appeared basically as a branch of Judaism), the confession that there is no god but the One would have been central. For the essence of one's conversion to the true faith would be the realization that God is one—and that other gods are non-existent (see *Virt.* 212–19, to be discussed below).

---

18. General discussion by Cohen, "Unity of God," 425–79.

19. As quoted in Hecataeus, "Histories," in Eusebius, *Praep. Ev.* 690d: εἷς ταῖς ἀληθείαισιν εἷς ἐστιν θεός.

20. Conzelmann, *1 Corinthians*, 142.

"An Idol Is Nothing in the World"

Conzelmann may be right that "the Corinthians argue after the fashion of Greek enlightenment philosophy."[21] It would be historically more adequate and precise, however, to view these Corinthian principles as arising out of a Hellenistic-*Jewish religion* of enlightenment. For, as he himself points out, Hellenistic Judaism had long since incorporated certain Hellenistic philosophical arguments concerning the nature of the gods' into its own polemic against polytheism.[22] In fact, not only did writers such as Philo, Aristobulus, and the authors of Wisdom and the *Epistle of Aristeas* feel at home in much of the language of Hellenistic philosophy, they even assumed that the Greek enlightenment had learned all its wisdom from Moses and the Jews.[23] Moreover, if the term εἴδωλον was included in the Corinthians' principle (and is not Paul's rewording) then it is not a question of Greek enlightenment philosophy at all, but a matter of basic Hellenistic-Jewish theology. For εἴδωλον as used here in the sense of a false god was the product of Hellenistic-Jewish translation and development of the Jewish (biblical) critique of heathen gods, and has no meaning like this in pagan Greek.[24]

That the Corinthian *gnosis* of the One God and the nothingness of idols arises from a Hellenistic-Jewish religion of enlightenment can be made clearer by contrasting the critique of false gods in Wisdom and Philo (1) with the attitude toward images in contemporary philosophy, on the one side, and (2) with another and very different Jewish critique of false gods, on the other side.

(1) Wisdom and especially Philo had, to be sure, assimilated some of their arguments against false gods from Hellenistic philosophy. It is not surprising that a reflective Hellenistic-Jewish mentality that emphasized the transcendence of God found affinities with a revived, though thoroughly eclectic, Platonic philosophy and absorbed its ontology. Philo

---

21. Ibid.

22. On Hellenistic-Jewish critique of false gods and idols, see Eising, "Weisheitslehrer"; Delling, "Josephus"; Wendland, "Therapeuten"; and idem, *Die hellenistische-römische Kultur*, 106ff., 140ff.; Wolfson, *Philo*, 8–17, 27–34.

23. This was a standard contention of "Jewish apologetics"; see generally Friedlander, *Geschichte*, 77ff.; Geffcken, *Zwei griechische Apologeten*, esp. the introduction; Dalbert, *Theologie*; more imaginative recent treatment by Georgi, *Gegner*, 95ff.; and see the sensible comments by Tcherikover, "Jewish Apologetic."

24. Büchsel, "εἴδωλον κτλ.," *TWNT* 2:377 = *TDNT* 2:377–78.

heavily criticized the Stoic ("Chaldean") theology and ontology for its deification of the cosmos itself (e.g., *Mig.* 176–83; cf. *Cong.* 49; *Mut.* 16; *Abr.* 68–71). It is indicative of these affinities between Hellenistic-Jewish theology, such as that in Wisdom and Philo, and a reviving Platonism that we find so many similarities to "Jewish" polemics against false gods in the Academic "critique of Stoic" theology in Cicero, *Nat. Deor.* 3.[25]

This same eclectic Platonic philosophy, however, takes a very positive stance toward *images* as an aid for people who otherwise would not be able to conceive of the divine. The later middle-platonist rhetor, Maximus of Tyre 2.3, 9–10 gives full expression to this positive evaluation of images, finding some beneficial function even in Egyptian honor of animals. This view of statues and pictures can be documented, however, at least as early as Varro (Augustine *Civ.* 8.5). Although it is no longer fashionable to push ideas such as this back to Posidonius,[26] this attitude probably gained currency during the eclectic revival of Platonism following Posidonius and Antiochus of Ascalon,[27] i.e. at least by the time of Cicero and Philo. The positive view of images and statues must be fairly standard and widespread by the time of Dio Chrysostom's strong defense of the renowned sculptor Pheidias (*Or.* 12, esp. 12.57–59) and Plutarch's justification of the symbolism of Egyptian animal worship *(Is. et Os.* 74–76). Thus, not only does Greek enlightenment philosophy of the period not use the terminology of "idols" but, more importantly, the very philosophical tradition from which Hellenistic Judaism and early Christianity were most likely to borrow (eclectic Middle-Platonism) took a very positive view of images.

(2) Within Judaism itself there were two distinctive traditions of polemic against idols or false gods. Bousset pointed out some time ago that at least since the exilic times there had been two lines of judgment of paganism.[28] The one line, expressed prominently in Deutero-Isaiah, derided the heathen gods as nothings and their worship as foolishness, since the idol-gods are merely the lifeless products of human craftsmanship—in contrast to the one, true, living God, usually described in terms of his creative activity. This is the most frequently encountered tradi-

---

25. Esp. 3.20–64; for example, neither the world nor heavenly bodies are gods, 3.23, 40, 51; deification of animals and of men is mere superstition, 3.39–41, 47, 49–50.

26. As in Geffcken, "Bilderstreit," 296–97.

27. Luck, *Akademiker*, 32ff.

28. Bousset, *Religion*, 304–5.

tion of idol-critique, and at least traces of it appear in nearly all types of Jewish literature of the Hellenistic-Roman period. It should be pointed out, however, that this tradition is far less prominent in apocalyptic literature such as *1 Enoch* and *Jubilees* than in the wisdom tradition and Hellenistic-Jewish literature, in contrast to the impression given by Bousset. The other attitude toward paganism, exemplified in passages such as Deut 4:19; 29:25; Jer 16:19; or Mal 1:11, held that whereas God had chosen Israel for his own people, He had subjected the other peoples to the subordinate cosmic powers—hence heathen polytheism was more or less God-ordained.

Since Bousset wrote, especially since the discovery of the Dead Sea Scrolls, we have a far better appreciation of the distinctiveness and importance of apocalypticism in Palestinian Judaism. It is necessary now to sharpen the picture of the two distinct traditions of polemic against pagan deities as they appear in the Hellenistic-Roman period—somewhat changed from the exilic period.

The tradition that contrasts lifeless idols (along with the "ignorance" in which idolatry is based) with the one, true, creating and redeeming God (along with "knowledge" of Him) is continued especially in Hellenistic-Jewish literature, such as Bel and the Dragon, as well as Wisdom and Philo. This tradition has been supplemented with other distinct arguments against false gods, such as a commonplace condemnation of Egyptian animal worship. Some of these additional arguments have been appropriated from Hellenistic philosophy, such as the already Judaized Euhemeristic argument[29] in the *Epistle of Aristeas* 135–37, 139 (and Wis 15–21; *Spec. Leg.* 1.28) and the critique of the deification of cosmic elements and heavenly bodies in Wisdom and Philo. The most elaborate development and sophisticated combination of these arguments against pagan idolatry and theology (as Bousset realized) is the same schematized three-part polemic appearing both in Wis 13–15 and in Philo, *Decal.* 52–82; and *Vita Cont.* 3–9. This schematic polemic argues successively against worship of (a) cosmic elements and heavenly bodies (Wis 13:1–9; *Decal.* 53–65; *Vita Cont.* 3–5); (b) impotent, manufactured idol-gods (Wis 13:10—15:13; *Decal.* 66, 76; *Vita Cont.* 7); and

---

29. On Euhemerism, see Nilsson, *Geschichte*, 11, 286–89; Taeger, *Charisma* 1:375–76, 295–96; Dörrie, *Königskult*, 218–24.

(c) Egyptian animal deities (Wis 15:14-19; *Decal.* 76-80; *Vita Cont.* 8-9), as increasing stages of ignorance, foolishness, and offensiveness.[30]

The other distinct traditional Jewish polemic against idol-gods appears prominently in apocalyptic literature such as *Jubilees* and *1 Enoch*. This other tradition, although it agreed that idols are "nothings" and lifeless human products, saw in idolatry the service or the influence of demons (*Jub.* 11:4-6; 22:16-22; *1 Enoch* 19; 99:6-10; *T. Naph.* 3:3-4). Most interesting for the conflict between Paul and the Corinthian dissidents is the connection of this other polemical tradition with the motif of divine judgment. Biblical texts on which this tradition draws connect the critique of idolatry as the service of demons with a recitation of Israel's historical disobedience in, and punishment for, its sacrificing to idols (Deut 32:17-21; Ps 106:28-40 [LXX Ps 105]). Paul himself draws on this tradition in formulating his argument against the implications of the Corinthians' *gnosis* in 1 Cor 10:20-22 as well as in 10:1-13.[31]

Wisdom and Philo, on the other hand, focus their critique of false gods and idols around an absolute antithesis between *ignorance of God* and *knowledge of God*. Ignorance of God is synonymous with supposing that idols or heavenly bodies are gods. Knowledge of God means knowing that other gods do not exist, that idols are mere foolishness. Knowing God/the One, moreover, means righteousness and immortality (Wis 13:1; 14:22; 15:2-3; Philo, *Decal.* 7-8, etc.). It is this Hellenistic-Jewish tradition expressed in Philo and Wisdom that most precisely parallels and most helpfully illuminates the Corinthians' *gnosis* that God is One and that idols are nothing.

It may be useful to make more explicit what is already implicit, that this Hellenistic-Jewish tradition also elucidates the significance of the phrase "in the world" (ἐν κόσμῳ) in the Corinthians' slogan. According to this Hellenistic-Jewish critique, the mistake that polytheists and idol-worshippers have made is to believe that certain things in the world such as heavenly bodies or forces of nature are divine (Wis 13:2-3; *Vita Cont.*

---

30. Philo uses parts of this scheme also in *Spec. Leg.* 1.15-30; 2.255-56; *Ebr.* 107-10. He has in addition several arguments against false theology that do not seem to be developments of any of these other traditional critiques, but which differently develop the contrast of knowledge of the One true God with ignorance, false opinions, and false doctrines, as in *Ebr.* 43-45; *Virt.* 178-80, 212-19; cf. Josephus, *Ant.* 8. 343, 10.50; *Apion*, 252-54.

31. For a "Jewish" attitude toward idols and other gods that is midway between Paul's and that of these Corinthians, see Trypho's comments in Justin Martyr, *Dialogue* 55.2.

3–5; *Decal.* 53, 58–59), whereas true piety, the Jewish faith, recognizes that all these things are merely part of the *creation,* and that the true, Existent One is the *Creator* of the whole cosmos. This is the significance of the frequency with which God is described as "Begetter," "Father," "Maker," or "Cause" in the several Philonic and Wisdom passages in which knowledge is discussed (Wis 13:1, 4–5; *Vita Cont.* 5; *Decal.* 53, 61, 64; *Spec. Leg.* 1.14, 20, 22, 30; *Ebr.* 107; *Virt.* 213–16). Indeed the purpose of Hellenistic-Jewish polemics and proselytizing was to convert and convince Gentiles as well as Jews that there were no divine entities (gods or idols) in the world, which itself was the handiwork of the true God, its Creator.

A number of the Philo passages most pertinent to the Corinthians' slogans have brought us into the context of proselytism. Perhaps the significance of their *gnosis* for the "strong" Corinthians may become clearer through closer attention to the mission situation of the early church.

The Mission Context: Hellenistic Judaism and Early Christianity

In their application of the law of Moses Paul's Jewish contemporaries were scarcely all the "strict constructionists" that modern biblical theology has sometimes made them out to be—striving to reach righteousness by scrupulous observance of the precepts of the Law. "Judaism" in various forms and localities was an expanding "world religion" in the first century CE.[32] There is reason to believe that in this period proselytes were not generally required to undergo particular rites of purification. Baptism for proselytes is mentioned neither in the apocryphal literature nor in Josephus when he refers to converts to Judaism. Zeitlin argues that prior to 65 CE Gentiles were not deemed susceptible to the laws of purity and impurity and were not subject to these laws.[33] Many statements to this effect are found in the Tannaitic literature. Principles such as 'one who denies idol worship recognizes the entire Torah' are preserved even in Rabbinic traditions—although not meant literally, at least by the rabbis.

While one should beware of making statements that by implication include all groups of Jews in this period of diversity, there is substantial

---

32. On Jewish missionary activity, see Nock, *Conversion,* 77–79; and Georgi, *Gegner,* 83–107, and the earlier literature cited there.

33. Zeitlin, "Proselytes," esp. 875–77.

evidence that many Jews and Jewish groups in the first century CE had simplified and rationalized their religion to the point of accepting proselytes merely on the basis of rejection of false gods and worship of the One true God.[34] Philo writes, in *Virt.* 102:

> He (Moses) holds that the incomers (ἐπηλύτας) too should be accorded every favour and consideration as their due, because abandoning their kinsfolk by blood, their country, their customs and the temples and images of their gods . . . they have taken the journey . . . to the clear vision of truth and the worship of the One and truly existing God.

In another example, the Jewish merchant Ananias, who apparently also proselytized, insisted to Izates, King of Adiabene, that the king could worship God without being circumcised, since worship and devotion to God are superior to circumcision. Such a liberal or "liberated" attitude appears all the more sharply by contrast with the more scrupulous stance. A much stricter Jew from Galilee named Eleazar persuaded Izates to undergo the operation (Josephus, *Ant.* 20.34–48).

Certainly the Pharisees, Essenes and others in Palestinian Judaism were strict in observance of the Law, including its application to proselytes. Paul's report in Gal 2 of his conflict with Peter, James, and other leaders of the church in Jerusalem points to the continuation of this stricter attitude into the early church. But Hellenistic Jews such as Philo and Ananias took a very different view. Philo may have felt compelled to defend circumcision to both Jews and Gentiles (*Mig.* 89–92; *Spec. Leg.* 1.2–10). But he refers to it very few times elsewhere in his extensive writings, and then he spiritualizes its meaning (*Som.* 2.25; *Spec. Leg.* 1.305, note the context of 304–9!)—whereas the knowledge of the One God is a central idea throughout Philo's writings. With regard to proselytes in particular Philo writes in *Q.E.* 2.2:

> (Scripture) makes it clearly apparent that in reality the sojourner is one who circumcises not his uncircumcision but his desires and sensual pleasures and the other passions of the soul . . . What is the mind of the sojourner if not alienation from belief in many gods and familiarity with honoring the One God and Father of all?

---

34. For Philo's attitude, expressed in an already standardized form, see *Spec. Leg.* 1.55–54, 308–9; 4.578; *Virt.* 102; *Q.E.* 2.2.

This mission situation in the Corinthian community to which both Paul and Apollos had been apostles would have involved basically two types of people: (1) Hellenistic Jews who had joined the movement, which was in effect a splinter group of the Jewish synagogue;[35] and (2) Gentiles, including *sebomenoi* such as Titius Justus, who had converted to this movement that apparently understood itself as the renewal or fulfillment of the Jewish religious tradition. Philo's use of the knowledge of the One God vs. the nonexistence of false gods is directly relevant to such a mission-situation. For in several key passages (in addition to *Q.E.* 2 cited above) transposition from ignorance to knowledge—either as *repentance* by Jews or as *conversion* by Gentiles—consists precisely in the move from service of false gods to knowledge of the One God.

Whether his apologia is addressed to Hellenistic Jews or Gentiles or both, the purpose of Philo's introduction to the Therapeutae in *De vita Contemplativa* (3–5) is to present this model mystical group as an exemplary worship of the one true God, in sharp contrast to worshippers of false gods. This is the first main point made and probably the principal point of the whole treatise. In other passages, such as *Spec. Leg.* 1.15–30, the transition from ignorance to knowledge takes place by learning doctrines about the One God vs. false gods.[36] Philo would appear to have forgetful or lapsed Jews in mind in his exhortation concerning repentance in *Virt.* 175–86 (but note the ἐπηλύται "incomers," in 182) where he describes the transformation from ignorance to knowledge as simultaneously a change from unrighteousness to righteousness and timidity to self-confidence (179–80). In the next section of the same treatise *(Virt.* 212–19) Philo is apparently thinking of proselytes as he describes the transition of Abraham from his "Chaldaean" knowledge of the many (i.e. ignorance and total lack of "nobility") to knowledge of the One, the Existent, the Maker of all.

If, thus, the notion that rejection of idols and worship of the One God as the essence of repentance or conversion to (true) Judaism was current among Hellenistic Jews, it is easy to understand how the prin-

---

35. On the Hellenistic-Jewish community and synagogue in Corinth, see Stern, "Jewish Diaspora," 159; *CII* no. 718; on the reliability of the traditions in Acts 18:2–3, 7–8 regarding Aquila and Priscilla, the conversion of the "ruler of the synagogue" Crispus and his household, and the split in the Corinthian synagogue, see Haenchen, *Acts*, 537–39.

36. Might the λόγος σοφίας ("word of wisdom" and the λόγος γνώσεως ("word of knowledge") in 1 Cor 12:8 be reference to revelations of just such doctrines?

ciples "an idol is nothing in the world" and "there is no god but One" could be so centrally significant for some of the Corinthian converts to the new movement (the early church). For it was precisely by learning such doctrines that they would have attained knowledge of God and, simultaneously, the enlightened self-confidence of having transcended such mundane issues as eating idol-meat.

Far from being an isolated tradition in certain Hellenistic-Jewish texts, however, *gnosis* as conversion to belief in the One God was an integral and central aspect of a whole distinctive pattern of religion. In Philo's interpretations of Abraham as the "standard of nobility" for all proselytes (*Virt.* 212–19) we find striking parallels to other aspects of the Corinthians' religious viewpoint. For "nobility" is one of the terms the Corinthians used to express their new-found exalted spiritual status gained by virtue of their possession of *sophia*.

The Broader Pattern of the Corinthians' Religious Viewpoint

Not just in 1 Cor 8 but throughout the letter Paul is repeatedly taking up language of the Corinthians in his arguments against their principles and self-understanding.[37] Although not as obvious as in chapter 8, it is nevertheless sufficiently clear that in 1 Cor 1–4 Paul is taking issue with:

(1) the Corinthians' focus on *sophia* both as the means of salvation and as eloquent speech (1:17—2:5), and

(2) their claim of exalted spiritual status expressed in terms of being "wise," "strong," "nobly born," "rich," "kings," (esp. 1:26 and 4:8–10) and as "perfect" and "spiritual" over against those who were merely "children" and "psychical" (2:6—3:4).

Then, in subsequent sections of the letter, he qualifies or even rejects:

(3) the feeling of ethical security expressed in the claim that "all things are possible/permissible for me" (6:12 and 10:23; cf. 10–12);

(4) a sexual asceticism whereby husbands and wives are separating for religious reasons (7:1, 5, 10–11);

(5) a spiritualizing interpretation of the exodus, the cloud, the rock, and the heaven-sent food and drink (10:1–4, 5–13);

---

37. Hurd, *Origin*, chapters 3–5; Conzelmann, *1 Corinthians*, 6–7, 14–16, etc.

(6) enjoyment of individual ecstatic experiences (12–14); and

(7) a denial of the resurrection of the dead (15. 12), apparently on dualistic grounds of soul vs. body, heavenly vs. earthly.[38]

Since numerous passages in Philo's writings provide an analogy for nearly every aspect of the Corinthians' religious language and viewpoint, it is possible to discern, on the basis of Philo's expressions, how the various aspects of this religious mentality may have fitted together. I have attempted to demonstrate elsewhere how, by analogy with extensive Philonic material and a few key passages in Wisdom such as chapter 8, the Corinthians' possession of spiritual status as "wise," "perfect," "nobly born," "rich," etc., is in contrast with those who were still mere babes in the faith and still being nourished on more elementary, milk-like teachings.[39] "Knowledge" is integral to this same pattern of religious expression.

The focus usually lies on *sophia* (or the equivalent in Philo's writings, the Logos). But *knowledge* is closely related and occasionally almost takes the central role. Writes Philo in *Plant.* 62–72, "only the mind which is enraptured by the beauty of Sophia is perfectly purified and able to renounce all created things and *to know the One alone*, the Uncreated One (ἓν μόνον οιδε καὶ γνωρίζει τὸ ἀγένητον)," which means *true wealth and kingship* for the *wise person* (cf. *Mig.* 197; Wis 6:15–21; 7:7). Similarly, in *Som.* 1.50–51 those who enjoy the love-charms of Sophia and banquet on her teachings and yet still have an unquenchable craving for knowledge are contrasted with those who are able only to inhale the aroma, that is, those of lesser spiritual status who have not achieved intimacy with Sophia. Throughout such passages, knowledge is closely associated with Sophia, basically as the substance or specification of *sophia*, and sometimes even interchangeable with *sophia*. Thus, in one of the most important "*sophia* by *sophia*" passages, *Mig.* 39–40, the seeing of the divine Light, i.e. Sophia, is said to be identical with knowledge (ἐπιστήμη; cf. further *Mig.* 41 and Wis 6:22), and in *Post.* 78, *Episteme* is substituted for Sophia (Logos) as the life-mate of the wise person.[40] In a passage di-

---

38. That is, *not* on the basis of an already realized spiritual resurrection, as I have attempted to explain in chap. 8, "No Resurrection."

39. Ibid.; and "Spiritual Status," chap. 1 above.

40. One of the most prominent ways of conceiving of Sophia in Wisdom and Philo is as the spouse or life-mate of the *sophos*, as in Wis 8; Philo, *Fug.* 52; *Spec. Leg.* 2.29–31; Q.E. 2.3; *Cher.* 52; *Vita Cont.* 64ff. The separation of certain Corinthians from their spouses may well have arisen out of just such an understanding of their relation with Sophia.

rectly relevant to the way in which the "wise" and "perfect" Corinthians (behind 1 Cor 2:10-15) must have understood the Spirit (= Sophia? cf. Wis 9:17) and its revelations, the Spirit of God is interpreted as "the pure knowledge (ἐπιστήμη) in which every wise person naturally shares" (*Mig.* 23-27). These few passages should suffice to demonstrate how integral "knowledge" is to this Hellenistic-Jewish religiosity focused on Sophia, who provides her devotees with exalted spiritual status, a religiosity to which that of the Corinthian *teleioi* must have been very similar.

All the more striking are the parallels to nearly every discernible aspect of the Corinthians' religious language and viewpoint in a few Philonic passages from which we have already illustrated the understanding of "knowledge." These should make clear how the *gnosis* of the "strong" Corinthians fits into a distinctive pattern of religiosity similar to that expressed in Philo. In Philo's portrayal of the standard of nobility for all proselytes, *Virt.* 212-19, Abraham's transposition from "knowledge of the many" "to know the Existent . . . the One Cause," etc. (γνῶναι τὸ ὄν . . . ἓν αἴτιον, 215-16), made him a "king," even though he was only a commoner (ἰδιώτης), brought him "perfection" and "nobility," and brought him to dwell in a better land in which the overseer is Truth.[41] Moreover, he was divinely possessed, for the divine Spirit lodged in his soul, thus investing his words with persuasiveness (τοῖς λόγοις πειθώ, 217; cf. 1 Cor 2:4; 1:17; 2:1) and making him a "prophet" (cf. 1 Cor 14:37). The only principal aspect of the Corinthian pneumatics' mentality missing here is the opposition between the soul as the true self and the burdensome bodily and earthly matters (cf. Wis 9:13-18), a dualism to which the idea of the resurrection of the dead (body) seemed completely unthinkable. This body/soul, earthly/heavenly dualism is prominent, however, in two of the other Philonic passages dealing with knowledge. Thus, in *Leg.* 3.46-48:

> The actions of the wise person are upheld by Word and Truth . . . When he had received from God the Tent, namely, Sophia, in which the wise person dwells, he fixed and made it fast . . . not in the body, but outside it . . . (thus he) returns to the knowledge of the One.

---

41. Ἀλήθεια is here substituted for σοφία, which is usually the land in which the σοφός comes to dwell, as in *Mig.* 28-30, 45-46; *Her.* 313-15; *Q.G.* 4.46-47; *Q.E.* 2.39.

Similarly, in *Quod Deus* 120-61, the passage in which the goal of the perfect way leading to God, i.e. Sophia, is said to be γνῶσις καὶ ἐπιστήμη Θεοῦ ("knowledge and understanding of God") knowledge is diametrically opposed to earthly matters, such that those who have learned *sophia* will abandon earthly wealth, noble birth, and glory for the heavenly (οὐράνιος) and incorruptible (ἄφθαρτος) benefits (144, 148-51; cf. some of the language in 1 Cor 15:47-50).[42] This religious viewpoint easily becomes an ideology of sexual asceticism (136-37; cf. 1 Cor 7:1, 3, 5).[43] This same extended passage, moreover, also includes the closely interrelated motifs of divine possession and heaven-sent blessings of spiritual drink and nourishment (138-39, 155-58; cf. 1 Cor 14; 10:3-4). The same passage, finally, contains an extensive discussion of "consciousness" (125-35; ἔλεγχος, σύνειδος, συνείδησις), which is closely related to the possession of knowledge both for Philo and for the strong Corinthians. Thus, coming to knowledge of the One, which is simultaneously the possession of wisdom and the attainment of exalted spiritual status, entails the prophetic ecstasy of divine possession and the enjoyment of spiritual food and drink as well. It means also a certain alienation from the body and other earthly matters such as ordinary marital relations, as the soul or true self finds its immortality in intimacy with God and/or Sophia.

This sense of how *knowledge* thus fits together with other terms and concepts in the same distinctive Hellenistic-Jewish religiosity also leads to a more precise understanding of two further aspects of the strong Corinthians' *gnosis* portrayed in 1 Cor 8. It may be possible to determine behind 1 Cor 8:6 a confessional formula used by the Corinthians (see chap. 5 below). And the close relation of "consciousness" to knowledge points us to the specific way in which the ethical stance of the strong Corinthians may be grounded in their *gnosis*.

---

42. For the way in which this whole set of contrasts (earthly/heavenly, mortal/immortal, corruptible/incorruptible) functioned in Philo and, probably, for the Corinthian *pneumatikoi* as well, see my chap. 1 above: "Spiritual Status."

43. There is little evidence that Philo practiced or encouraged others to practice sexual asceticism, but his ideological expressions certainly tend in that direction, as in *Cher.* 42-52 and *Q.E.* 2.3.

Two Further Aspects of the Corinthians' Gnosis

The Corinthian Confession of Faith in God and Sophia in 1 Cor 8:6

First Corinthians 8:6 reads almost like a further explication of the statement "there is no God but One." Indeed, Conzelmann suggests that 8:6 "is eminently suited to the Corinthian Christology."[44] This interpretation rests on the assumption that it was the Corinthians who had identified Christ with heavenly Sophia, and views the formula in 8:6 as the type of λόγος/εἰκών/σοφία Christology.[45] In his important critical review of Wilckens' interpretation of 1 Cor 1–2, Koester has argued decisively that it was not the Corinthians but Paul who identified Christ with Sophia.[46] The "wise" and "perfect" Corinthians who were obsessed with Sophia held not so much to an exaltation *Christology* as an exaltation *Sophialogy*. It was Paul himself, in attempting to counteract their non-Christological enthusiasm with Sophia, who claimed that the true *sophia* of God was the crucified Christ (1 Cor 1:24), thus first making the identification.

I have attempted to demonstrate elsewhere that 1 Cor 8:6 is an adaptation of a traditional Hellenistic-Jewish form of predication regarding the respective creative and soteriological roles of God and Sophia/Logos, which Philo or his predecessors had adapted from a Platonic philosophical formula concerning the primal principles of the universe.[47] What was already a fundamental tenet of the Hellenistic-Jewish religion expressed in the book of Wisdom appears in more philosophical formulation in Philo: that God is the ultimate Creator and final Cause of the universe, and that Sophia/Logos is agent (and paradigm) of creation or the instrumental (and formal) cause. Thus in *Quod Det.* 54 (cf. *Fug.* 190) faithful Jews are exhorted to

> Accord a father's honour to Him who created the world, and a mother's honour to Sophia, through whom (δι' ἧς) the universe was brought to completion.

The confession of the One God is thus held together with that of his consort and first-born Sophia/Logos, who is the agent of creation

---

44. Conzelmann, *1 Corinthians*, 144.

45. Ibid., 49, for extensive literature on the background of this type of Christology in Jewish speculation on Sophia/Logos.

46. Koester's review of Wilckens, *Weisheit und Torheit*.

47. See chap. 5: "Confessional Formula."

as well as salvation. The dual creative and soteriological role of Sophia/Logos appears in *Sac.* 8 in language very similar to what we encounter in Corinth.

> But he (Moses) is translated 'through the Word' of the Cause, *through which* also the *whole world* was formed. This is in order that you may learn that God values the wise person as the world, for by the same Logos he makes the universe and leads the perfect person from earthly matters to himself.

What we find in 1 Cor 8:6 is Paul's christological transformation of this Hellenistic-Jewish formula concerning God and Sophia/Logos. As in 1 Cor 1:24 Paul has replaced the Corinthians' Sophia with Christ. We can thus discern directly behind Paul's formulation in 1 Cor 8:6 another of the "strong" Corinthians' principles of *gnosis*, another very fundamental theological statement concerning the One God as Creator and final Cause and his consort Sophia as the agent (efficient cause) of creation and salvation.

Sophia, Gnosis, and the Security and Freedom of the Wise and Perfect

The close connection of "consciousness" with "knowledge" in Philo suggests the way in which the Corinthians' *gnosis* informs their liberated ethical stance. Not only, in their enlightened spiritual state, do the strong know that "an idol is nothing in the world"; they also believe themselves, as it would appear, to be morally incorruptible. From some further passages in Philo and Wisdom it may be possible to discern more clearly how such a sense of one's inability to sin can be rooted in the possession of *sophia* and *gnosis*.

Philo claims in passages such as *Quod Deus* 3-4, *Fug.* 117-18 and *Leg.* 3.126-27 that as long as Sophia (or her equivalent, the Logos, or γνῶσις τοῦ ἑνός!) is present in the soul, an unintentional offence is impossible and none of the messengers of falsehood can gain access to the reason. Sophia, symbolized by the cloud of the Exodus story *(Her.* 203-5; cf. *Mos.* 1. 116; Wis 10:17-18; cf. 1 Cor 10:1-2), similarly provides an absolute security for souls who possess wisdom/knowledge, while it brings vengeance and misery to those barren of knowledge. Or, in another image, for the perfect who have Sophia as their life-mate, the influences that harm the soul totally cease, whereas for those of lesser religious stature they merely diminish. Those who possess *gnosis* have thereby complete righteousness and immortality, as explained in the midst of the long critique of idols in Wis 15:2–3:

> For even if we sin we are thine, knowing (εἰδότες) thy power; but we will not sin, because we know that we are accounted thine. For to know thee (ἐπίστασθαί σε) is complete righteousness, and to know (εἰδέναι) thy power is the root of immortality.

Thus secure in their new *gnosis* of the One God, the Corinthians perhaps also believe, again with Wisdom (14:27) that the worship of the nameless idols (εἴδωλοι) is the beginning and cause and end of every evil.

Neither Philo nor Wisdom addresses the specific issue of idol-meat, which had clearly become a point of conflict in the Christian community in Corinth. We have no way of knowing precisely how the eating of idol-meat by the "strong" had provoked such a conflict—whether, for example, the "strong" were attempting self-consciously to demonstrate their spiritual security and liberty by deliberately eating meat that had been offered to idols or just happened to eat idol-meat along with other actions which, in their enlightened consciousness, they considered a matter of complete indifference. In any case, it is clear that a religious viewpoint, such as that expressed in Philo and Wisdom, with a firm sense of purity and security gained through intimacy with Sophia and the possession of *gnosis*, could result ethically in a sense of liberation from, or indifference toward, traditional purity regulations. Since von Soden's influential article on "sacrament and ethics," it has become a standard observation that the strong Corinthians were super-sacramentalists.[48] But there is no evidence in 1 Corinthians itself that the Corinthians found their security through the "Christ-sacraments." It was Paul, not the Corinthians, who introduced the notion of an almost magical influence of a cultic meal (1 Cor 10:16–21). If the Corinthians are practicing some sort of "sacrament" at all, it is a highly spiritualized one, in which the "spiritual food" and the "spiritual drink" are understood as a Wisdom-banquet, as in our Philonic analogy (e.g. *Som.* 1.47–51, 189–200; *Fug.* 137–38, 166–67; *Cong.* 172–74). In any case, whether or not it was sacramentally expressed, the Corinthians' sense of ethical purity and security was rooted in their possession of *gnosis* and *sophia*.

---

48. Von Soden, "Sakrament."

The Corinthians' *Gnosis* and Paul's Response

Because Conzelmann believes that "the position in Corinth cannot be reconstructed on the basis of the possibilities of the general history of religion,"[49] he leaves the nature of the liberating *gnosis* an open question: popular philosophical enlightenment, or pneumatic illumination, or Gnostic insight. His skepticism is unwarranted, however, for a systematic survey of pertinent Hellenistic texts reveals a fourth alternative for the nature of the Corinthians' *gnosis:* Hellenistic-Jewish religion of enlightenment. On the basis of the analogous use of language and ideas in Wisdom and Philo it is clear that the Corinthian *gnosis* is part of a whole pattern of religious self-understanding. This pattern, moreover, includes nearly all of the other Corinthian concepts or principles to which Paul objects in the different sections of 1 Corinthians. It is also clear that the enlightened ethical stance encountered by Paul in 1 Cor 8–10 is grounded in just this pattern of religiosity in which *sophia* and *gnosis* are means and content of salvation. This Hellenistic-Jewish religiosity, moreover, *includes* two of the three general possibilities that Conzelmann suggested: popular philosophical enlightenment and pneumatic illumination.

What Paul responds to, therefore, is not a Gnostic libertinism, as derived from Reitzenstein, elaborated on by Schmithals, and still presupposed by commentators such as Barrett,[50] but a Hellenistic-Jewish *gnosis* at home precisely in the mission context. Whereas Gnosticism of almost any form was hostile to the creation and the Creator-God, this Hellenistic-Jewish *gnosis*, despite its apparent alienation from the body and "earthly" matters, focused precisely on the knowledge of the One true God as the Creator, in contrast with cosmic forces or idols that are in fact non-existent.

Paul's theological argument in response to the *gnosis* of the strong Corinthians is indeed "dialectical."[51] His dialectical style and procedure here, however, are mostly a function of the polemical situation. Conzelmann suggests that for Paul the content of the Corinthians' *gnosis* "is in itself correct."[52] But this would not appear to be the case. Not only

---

49. Conzelmann, *1 Corinthians*, 15.

50. Reitzenstein, *Mysterienreligionen*, 75–79, 333–96; Schmithals, *Gnosis*; Barrett, *First Epistle to the Corinthians*.

51. Conzelmann, *1 Corinthians*, 138.

52. Ibid., 138.

does Paul challenge the effects and effectiveness of the *gnosis* (8:1b and 2; cf. 3:18), but he takes issue with the content as well.

The thrust of Paul's response to the *gnosis* of "the strong" is not completely clear from the immediate context of 1 Cor 8. For example, we may reasonably surmise that Paul has relations with other members of the community in mind when he speaks of love in 8:3 and declares that "love builds up" in his discreet "put-down" of the Corinthians' *gnosis* in 8:1b. Yet this is not at all clear from the context, where he speaks only of the love of God. Paul's seemingly narrow focus here, however, can be explained from his method of dealing with the Corinthians. He starts purposely from their presuppositions. Just as he quotes their principles in 8:1 and 4, so he purposely begins his response by focusing where "the strong" focus: on the individual's relation with God and the content of their knowledge. He then gradually moves his discussion into the broader context of the community and the history of salvation, beginning with 8:7: "But not all possess gnosis." To deal adequately with Paul's comments on the social-ethical implications of the Corinthians' *gnosis* would require exegesis of the whole section of the letter, 1 Cor 8–10. But it is possible from the perspective of this section (and the letter as a whole), to discern how Paul challenges and changes the *content* of the Corinthian gnosis in 1 Cor 8:3, 5, 6.

In 8:3 Paul shifts the Corinthians' viewpoint around in two decisive ways: from a static cognitive and epistemological stance to a dynamic affectional relationship, and from knowledge of God to being known by God. As has been pointed out in previous treatment, in the latter shift Paul is referring to God's initiative in the sense of God's gracious election or redemption (cf. Gal 4:9).[53]

In 8:5 Paul in effect contradicts one of the Corinthian principles of *gnosis*, that "an idol is nothing in the world," by asserting parenthetically the actual existence of "many so-called gods and lords in heaven or on earth." The key to Paul's own point of view here lies in 1 Cor 10:19–22, where he asserts that in sacrificing to idols pagans are really worshipping demons. As noted above, besides the extensive and systematic critique of false gods found prominently in Hellenistic-Jewish literature such as Wisdom and Philo, there was another, different critique of idolatry and

---

53. Bultmann, "γνώσκω κτλ.," *TWNT* 1:709–10 = *TDNT* 1:708–11; Niederwimmer, "Erkennen und Lieben," 93–94.

paganism distinctive to apocalyptic literature. This other critique, which saw in paganism the work or the service of demons, is precisely what Paul presupposes in his response to the Corinthians' *gnosis*. In response to the Hellenistic-Jewish enlightened wisdom-theology, Paul asserts his own apocalyptic perspective on the demonic powers that rule the world. It does not become clear, however, until 1 Cor 10:14–21 (and perhaps 10:5–13) how genuine and intense Paul's concern is about the possibility of divine eschatological judgment that is integral to this apocalyptic attitude toward the demonic powers behind idolatry and apostasy. After extensive examination of Hellenistic-Jewish *gnosis* of the One God and of the nothingness of idols, it is clear that not all early Christian preaching of the One God (was) at the same time eschatological proclamation, preaching of the impending judgment of the world.[54] But, whereas that was not true of the Corinthians' *gnosis* of the One God, it certainly was of Paul's gospel, as can be seen in 1 Thess 1:9–10:

> how you turned to God from idols, to serve a living and true God, and to wait for his Son from heaven, whom he raised from the dead, Jesus who delivers us from the wrath to come.

It is just this apocalyptic perspective in Paul that makes his transformation of the Corinthians' formula in 8:6 intelligible. As Koester has pointed out, it was Paul and not the Corinthian *teleioi* who identified Sophia with Christ in 1 Cor 1:24 (30). In his attempt to counter the Corinthians' obsession with Sophia in 1 Cor 1–2, Paul emphasizes that the true *sophia* of God is the crucified Christ. This is also the emphasis where Paul uses *sophia* in the sense of the apocalyptic *mysterion*, the focus of which is the crucifixion of the "Lord of glory" (2:6–8). Then in 1 Cor 8, where Paul is attempting to counter the Corinthians' *gnosis*, which is the specification or doctrinal content of Sophia, he again in effect identifies Christ with Sophia.[55] In 8:6 he transforms the Corinthian theological formula by replacing Sophia with Christ the Lord, thus letting what had been predications of Sophia as the agent of creation apply now to Christ. Paul's focus has now shifted from the crucified Christ to the exalted Lord (cf. 1 Thess 1:10 and 1 Cor 15:20–25). As in 1 Cor 3:21–23, and 10:4 and

---

54. Bultmann, *Theology*, 1:74.

55. Feuillet, *Le Christ*, 82–85, who does not analyze 1 Corinthians in terms of a polemical context, suggests that when Paul implicitly identifies Christ with Wisdom in 1 Cor 8:6 it may be the first place such an identification is made.

15:25, 27, Paul is concerned to assert the Lordship of Christ in a context where some apparently viewed Christ (merely) as a spokesman or revealer of Sophia.[56] In 1 Cor 8:6 he does this by having the exalted Christ take over what were the functions of Sophia, according to the *gnosis* of the Corinthians. Paul thus makes what for him was an unprecedented assertion, that Christ was the agent of creation as well as of salvation.

In the face of mounting skepticism that the *gnosis* in Corinth can intelligibly be labeled "Gnosticism" the Corinthians are now being called, somewhat vaguely, "proto-Gnostics."[57] But we can be more precise about the nature of the Corinthians' *gnosis*. It has emerged from a Hellenistic-Jewish *gnosis* that it closely resembles in every discernible respect. In his critique of traditional assumptions regarding "heresy" and "orthodoxy" in early Christianity, Koester has pointed out that "everyone in the first generation of Christianity was a Jewish-Christian anyway," and that Jewish traditions influenced almost all developments of early Christian theology.[58] However, there was a great diversity among Jews. Especially striking, for example, is the considerable dissimilarity between apocalyptic Judaism (located primarily in Palestine) and the Hellenistic-Jewish religion focused on Sophia (Logos). The differences between them can be discerned precisely in the divergent ways in which they have developed a traditional Jewish teaching such as the polemic against idols. The conflict that comes to light in 1 Corinthians is rooted in just such a diversity of Jewish religious viewpoints. In a pattern of religiosity very similar to that expressed in Wisdom and Philo, some of the Corinthians are caught up into an exalted spiritual status through possession of *sophia*. Their *gnosis* is the theological content (and goal) of this mystical faith. Paul, on the other hand, with his Pharisaic training, maintains an apocalyptic perspective. Yet in his attempt to counter the Corinthians' *gnosis*—for example, by applying to Christ predications that originally belonged to Sophia in Hellenistic Judaism—we can see the syncretistic process by which the religious movement eventually known as Christianity developed.

---

56. Koester, review of Wilckens, 594; and idem, "Structure," 222–23.
57. Conzelmann, *1 Corinthians*, 15.
58. Koester, "GNOMAI DIAPHOROI," 280.

5

The Confessional Formula in 1 Corinthians 8:6

Although the formula of confession in 1 Cor 8:6 became an important basis for the development of the Christian creed and subsequent Christological doctrine, it does not have a Pauline ring to it. As Conzelmann and others have pointed out, "the phrasing has not been chosen by Paul ad hoc. The content is not 'Pauline'; and it reaches far beyond the context."[1] What seems most unusual for Paul's theology and Christology are the formal, prepositional predications:

ἐξ οὗ τὰ πάντα καὶ ἡμεῖς εἰς αὐτόν . . .
δι' οὗ τὰ πάντα καὶ ἡμεῖς δι' αὐτοῦ

from whom are all things and for whom we exist, ...
through whom are all things and through whom we exist

Norden's discussion of "a Stoic doxology in Paul"[2] and Peterson's and others' study of the Hellenistic-Jewish confession of "One God"[3] have provided the basic categories for analysis of 1 Cor 8:6. Despite considerable recent examination of Jewish wisdom speculation[4] that is potentially pertinent to 1 Cor 8, interpretation of the predications in 8:6 still relies primarily on these two basic categories.[5] Although what lies be-

---

1. Conzelmann, *1 Corinthians*, 144.
2. Norden, *Agnostos Theos*, 240–50; further discussion of same material by Dupont, *Gnosis*, 335–41.
3. Peterson, *Eis Theos*, 251–56; cf. Cohen, "Unity of God."
4. For example, Hegermann, *Die Vorstellung*, 93–99, 110–12; Feuillet, *Le Christ*, 69–85.
5. So, apparently, Barrett, *First Corinthians*, 144–45. Similarly Kerst, "1 Kor 8.6," as his opening sentence indicates, follows this same division of material and even finds a

hind (the confessional formulation in) 8:6 may well be a principle of the Corinthians' γνῶσις related to the confession "There is One God" (1 Cor 8:1, 4), the formulation in 8:6 is certainly not a further development of his confession (i.e., into a twofold statement). If our alternatives are the "One God" confession or the Stoic doxology, then the latter is preferable. For the unusual form of the predication in 8:6, the sequence of prepositional phrases, bears a striking similarity to the prepositional phrases in the "Stoic doxology." What is more, Paul's use of this doxological "omnipotence formula" in Rom 11:36 shows that he was well-acquainted with the form.

To illustrate this doxology/omnipotence formula Norden and others have gathered from a variety of sources a plethora of texts that display linguistic or conceptual similarities. Further analysis of these texts according to possible differences in form, tradition, and use, however, indicates (1) that this omnipotence formula is not obviously the form that stands behind 1 Cor 8:6, and (2) that there is another particular form, different from (through perhaps related to) the doxological omnipotence formula, which is much closer in form and substance to the predications in 1 Cor 8:6.

1. There can be distinguished in widely diverse sources a doxological form used in personal or formal praise of the Divine. It is set either in the second or the third person, and expresses some personal religious-philosophical relationship with the Divine principle or person, as in Marcus Aurelius, *Med.* 4.23:

> ἐκ σοῦ πάντα, ἐν σοὶ πάντα, εἰς σε πάντα.
>
> From Thee are all things, in Thee are all things, to Thee are all things.

Or Paul in Rom 11:36:

> ὅτι ἐξ αὐτοῦ καὶ δι' αὐτοῦ καὶ εἰς αὐτὸν τὰ πάντα.
>
> For from Him, and through Him, and to Him are all things.

It occurs separately or as part of a more extended prayer, as in *Corp. Herm.* 13.19. It was used to express the unity of all things in one ultimate, divine

---

third category in the syncretism, the Christian cry of "Lord." Neither Kerst nor van Roon, "Relation," 230–33, two of the most recent interpretations of 1 Cor 8:6, considers that there may be more than one Hellenistic "πάντα formula."

principle, i.e. pantheism, as in Berthelot, *Alch. Gr.* 133,[6] or to state that the divine is the source from which all things emanate, as in *Asclepius* 34,[7] or simply to praise the Divine's omnipotence, as to Selene in *PGM* 4.2838–39.[8] Thus the same or a similar form was widely used in a variety of Hellenistic religious and religious-philosophical texts. There is little evidence that this form belonged originally or primarily to "Stoic pantheism," even though it was congenial to a Stoic such as Marcus Aurelius.

While distinguishable from other uses of similar language, this doxological form has connections with certain philosophical traditions. Perhaps the ultimate origin of such a form of speech was the way in which pre-Socratic philosophers spoke of the ἀρχή. Philo witnesses to the general currency of the form (and currency among Hellenistic Jews no less than others) and to its connections with Hellenistic philosophical traditions in the course of his explication of ordinances dealing with sacrifices in *Spec. Leg.* 1.198–211. In explanation of the division of the animal into its parts (Lev 1:6), which means either that *all things are one* or that *all things are from one and to one*, he rejects the related doctrine of Heraclitus and the doctrine of the Stoics (ἐκπύρωσις καὶ διακόσμησις) preferring his own explanation that God is the Maker and Begetter of the universe and its Savior and Benefactor as well. That is, when Hellenistic Jews reflected on this "doxology" they rejected its apparent doctrinal implications.

All of the principal texts introduced by Norden and others focus on the *one* divine principle of the unity of all things. Indeed, this is precisely the way Paul uses the doxology in Rom 11.[9] It is conceivable that Paul broke apart this formula (as he knew it) and applied the (instrumental) middle predication to Christ (while leaving the other two with God). But if Paul in 1 Cor 8:4–6 is agreeing with the (Jewish) confession of "One

---

6. See also Zosimus, in Berthelot, *Collection*, 143, cited in Norden, *Agnostos Theos*, 249.

7. Nock, *Corp. Herm.*, 2:344, lines 22–26.

8. Preisendanz, *Papyri*, 1:162.

9. Rom 11:36 is simply a religious doxology of confessional-liturgical style. As Norden's material indicates, such doxologies must have been used frequently in diverse religious and religious-philosophical contexts, including Hellenistic-Jewish communities. Aristobulus, in Eusebius, *Praep. Ev.* 666A, corresponds in substance: ἀρχὴν αὐτὸς ἔχων, καὶ μέσσατον, ἠδὲ τελευτήν. Neither in Rom 11:36 (the climax of Paul's argument, Rom 9–11) nor its context is there any concern with Sophia or Christ as mediator of creation or means of redemption.

God" (so Conzelmann) and developing or qualifying it by means of this doxology that focuses on the single divine principle of unity, why does he not just write here in 1 Cor 8:6 what he writes in Rom 11:36? In a letter in which he has taken pains to emphasize the foolishness and humility of the *crucified* Christ over against the Corinthians' focus on Sophia and the exalted spiritual status she provides, why does he then speak of Christ as the divine mediator of creation?

2. Thus, although it is conceivable, it is unlikely that in 1 Cor 8:6 Paul is adapting the omnipotence formula—especially since there is another formula much closer to the form of predication in 1 Cor 8:6, a form that deals not with the *one* principle of the unity of all things but with the different principles that are involved in the constitution of the universe. This other formula appears in another group of texts that are less doxological and more speculative in form and function, largely the products of Platonic (school) philosophy. Sometime prior to Philo, since he already presupposes this philosophical formula, a revived interest in metaphysical speculation must have stimulated the development of stock forms for reflection about the ἀρχαί ("causes" or *primal principles*) of the universe.[10] Seneca (*Ep.* 65.4.8) and Porphyry (in Simplicius, *Phys.* 3.16) provide good examples of the same set of technical terminology from philosophical traditions about the ἀρχαί. Aristotle thought of four, Plato of one or two more; thus:[11]

id ex quo / materia	id a quo / opifex	id in quo / forma	id propter quod / propositum
τὸ ἐξ οὗ / ὕλη	τὸ ὑφ' οὗ / τὸ ποιοῦϋν	τὸ καθ' ὅ / τὸ εἶδος	τὸ δι' ὅ / τὸ τέλος

Plato has in addition:

	τὸ δι' οὗ / τὸ ὀργανικόν		τὸ πρὸς ὅ / τὸ παράδειγμα

---

10. For a presentation of this material within an exposition of its context in "middle Platonic" philosophy, see Theiler, *Die Vorbereitung*, 21–25.

11. Texts and translations, unless otherwise indicated, are from the editions in the Loeb Classical Library. I have usually adapted Colson's and Whittaker's translations of Philo for more consistent English equivalents.

The "middle-Platonist" Albinus, without recounting the difference between Plato and Aristotle, simply produces four: ἐξ οὗ, ὑφ' οὗ, πρὸς ὅ, δι' ὅ.[12]

Perhaps one reason scholars have not distinguished this form, i.e., the more "philosophical" set of prepositional phrases used in speculation about the ἀρχαί, from the more "religious" doxological form, is that the two forms were closely related both in the history of philosophy from which they arose and in the philosophical and religious contexts in which they were used. Thus, for example, in the language patterns of a religious philosopher such as Philo these forms become somewhat mixed. That is, his devotional statements concerning the Logos/Sophia include terminology from the philosophical speculation concerning "causes"; and, as noted already, he reflects philosophically about the implications of the predications in the doxology.

In fact, the most prominent use of the formula concerning the "causes" in ancient literature comes in the Hellenistic-Jewish tradition represented by Philo. The way in which Philo frequently witnesses to this philosophical formula is in reference to one or two of the primal principles, particularly in speculation on the Logos/Sophia. But he does repeat the whole set of principles at points. In *Q.G.* 1.58 and *Cher.* 125–27, for example, it serves his standard argument that Eve (= νοῦς) was mistaken in saying "I have made a man through God." She is mistaken because among the four principles requisite for the genesis of anything (τὸ ὑφ' οὗ, τὸ ἐξ οὗ, τὸ δι' οὗ, τὸ δι' ὅ) God must be the *cause* (αἴτιος) and not the instrument. Then, contemplating the universe, Philo repeats what, with variations in a few terms (e.g., νοῦς instead of λόγος), must have been the doctrine shared by contemporary Platonist philosophers:

> The cause (of the universe) God, by whom it has come into being (αἴτιος ... ὑφ' οὗ), its material the four elements from which it was compounded (ὕλη ἐξ ὧν), the instrument is the Logos of God through which it was made (ὄργανον ... δι' οὗ), and the (final) cause of its creation is the goodness of the Maker (αἰτία).[13] *Cher.* 127

---

12. Albinus, *Didaskalikos* 12 (edited by Hermann, Stuttgart, 1853 and reprints); see further Witt, *Albinus*, 77.

13. To the last point, cf. Plato, *Tim.* 29E.

Most interesting, especially for its relation to Hellenistic-Jewish speculation about the ontological position and role of Sophia/Logos, is the differentiation that has taken place with regard to the "efficient cause." This development occurred before the time of Philo, for he presupposes that both the ὑφ' οὗ and the δι' οὗ are stock terms. Hellenistic philosophers who were reviving Platonic patterns of thought, in attempting to maintain the transcendence of the deity, *by which* . . . , found it necessary to conceive of an ὀργανικόν principle, *through which* . . . . In the Platonic philosophical tradition that Philo presupposes, the principle *through which* (the ὄργανον) is identical with the principle *after* or *according to which* (the παράδειγμα, i.e., the ἰδέα or νοῦς of God).

Philo and his Jewish precursors had appropriated this speculation from Hellenistic philosophy. For they found the predications made of the νοῦς/ἰδέα/λόγος as the pattern and/or instrument of creation (in distinction from the transcendent Deity) to be of special affinity and utility in connection with their own traditional speculation about Sophia. The conception of Sophia as the instrument of creation (and redemption) expressed in Wis 7:20–29 and 9:1–2 reveals how close the Jewish speculation had become to the predications in the Platonic "causes" formula. In Philo, and in at least that Jewish theological tradition in which he stands, there is a whole complex of terms and phrases used interchangeably to express the status and role of Sophia/Logos as the instrument and pattern of creation, including its relation to God.

> The 'shadow' of God is His Logos, by which, as an instrument (ὄργανον), He made the world. This shadow is the archetype (ἀρχέτυπον) the Image (εἰκών) the Pattern (παράδειγμα). (*Leg.* 3.96; cf. *Op. Mund.* 24–25)

> The immortal soul (of the priest) was made after the Image of Him who Is. And the Image of God is the Logos, through whom (δι' οὗ) the whole universe was made. (*Spec. Leg.* 1.81)

> . . . Accord a father's honor to Him who created the world, and a mother's honor to Sophia, through whom (δι' ἧς) the universe was brought to completion. (*Det.* 54; cf. *Fug.* 190)

As can be seen in these and many other passages (such as *Quod Deus* 57; *Her.* 199; *Ebr.* 30–31; *Sacr.* 8; *Leg.* 2.49) the philosophical predications concerning the primal principles, especially those of the "efficient" and the "formal" causes, have became central and standard language for

Sophia/Logos in Philo and his tradition, whether mentioned in connection with God or independently.

Most important for possible elucidation of 1 Cor 8:6 is the occurrence here in Hellenistic-Jewish theological speculation of a formula linking Sophia/Logos, as the instrumental principle *through which* all things were created, with God (or His goodness), as both the ultimate and the "final" principles *by* or *from which* and *because of* or *toward which* all things were created. The actual prepositions vary somewhat from text to text in Philo, just as they do in the extant philosophical texts which attest this formula. But these Philonic texts point to the use, in Hellenistic-Jewish speculation on God and Sophia, of the philosophical formula about the "causes" of creation, a formula that appears strikingly similar to the forms of predication about God and Christ in 1 Cor 8:6. That is, if we leave the formula in 1 Cor 8:6 in its integrity and do not split it into a confession of "One God" followed by a confession of "Lord," then the prepositional predications in 1 Cor 8:6 most resemble not the "Stoic doxology" but certain texts in Philo that express the distinction between, and the respective dignity and roles of, God and Sophia/Logos.

Besides the close similarity in form there is also similarity in substance. Just as the formulation in 1 Cor 8:6 includes the soteriological role of God and Christ as well as the creative role, so also the Philo texts link the redemptive role of God and Logos/Sophia with the creative:

> But he (Moses) is translated 'through the *Word*' (ῥῆμα) of the Cause, *through which* also the *whole world* was formed. This is in order that you may learn that God values the wise person as the world, for by the same Logos he makes the universe and leads the perfect person from earthly matters to himself. (*Sacr.* 8)

Pertinent here also is Philo's concluding statement in *Cher.* 130 in connection with his explicit use of the Platonic formula concerning the "causes": "Not through God, but from Him as Cause does salvation come." For in this Hellenistic-Jewish theology Sophia/Logos is the divine instrument *through which*, in salvation as well as in creation.[14]

Conzelmann suggests that, in effect, 1 Cor 8:6 is the result of the juxtaposition of "the type of λόγος/εἰκών/σοφία Christology" onto the Stoic doxology. Kerst finds in 1 Cor 8:6 a syncretistic combination of the

---

14. On the redemptive role of Sophia, pertinent to 1 Cor 8:6 and probably also to 10:1–4, see esp. Wis 9:17–18 and 10:15–21.

Hellenistic-Jewish propaganda formula of "One God," the Christian cry of "Lord," and the Stoic formula.[15] It would seem more likely, however, that the confessional formula in 1 Cor 8:6 is a Christian adaptation of Hellenistic-Jewish forms of predication regarding the respective creative and soteriological roles of God and Sophia/Logos, which in turn was an adaptation of a Platonic philosophical formula concerning the primal principles of the universe.

---

15. Conzelmann, *1 Corinthians*; and Kerst, "1 Cor 8:6."

6

Consciousness and Freedom

"Modern Christianity might ask whether I have the inner freedom from idols, for eating, whether my conscience agrees. The norm in that case would be my conviction. But this would avoid the real ethical question."[1] Ironically enough, it was apparently precisely such inner freedom based on one's spiritual conviction that some of the ancient Corinthians were asserting over 1900 years ago. Perhaps "modern Christianity" has either not understood or not heeded Paul's attempt in 1 Cor 8–10 to clarify "the real ethical issue," for outstanding theologians such as Conzelmann do not discern that "the freedom of conscience" is the problem Paul deals with in 1 Cor 8–10, not the solution he offers.[2]

The Background of the Polemical Situation in the Corinthian Community

It is generally recognized that ἔξεστιν (lawful/possible), ἐξουσία (authority), and γνῶσις (knowledge) were catchwords of (some of) the Corinthians[3] and that we thus face a polemical situation behind 1 Corinthians. It would seem, therefore, that a clearer understanding of "the real ethical issue" depends on a more precise determination of the religious viewpoint of those Corinthians who claimed to possess ἐξουσία and γνῶσις. In dealing with the Corinthians' principles of γνῶσις, in-

---

1. Von Soden, "Sakrament und Ethik," as paraphrased in Conzelmann, *Outline*, 183.

2. Conzelmann, *Outline*, 183. On the literary integrity of 1 Cor 8–10, see von Soden, "Sakrament und Ethik," and Hurd, *Origins*, 126–42.

3. E.g., Dupont, *Gnosis*, 282–90; Bultmann, review of Dupont, *Gnosis*, esp. 18–20; Conzelmann, *1 Corinthians*, 108, 140.

terpreters such as Conzelmann tend to look to Greek "enlightenment philosophy" or Gnosticism for elucidation. When dealing with ἐξουσία they tend to look, more particularly, to Stoic and Cynic comparative material.[4]

However, it is becoming increasingly clear that the Hellenistic-Jewish theology represented by Philo of Alexandria and the Wisdom of Solomon offers the most convincing background and most helpful elucidation for the Corinthian situation that Paul addressed in 1 Corinthians. It has already been demonstrated that the Corinthians' understanding of Sophia and the spiritual status attained through intimacy with her (as discerned through 1 Cor 1–4) is analogous to the understanding of Sophia expressed in Philo's treatises and Wisdom.[5] Similarly, it has long been observed that Philo provides the most helpful elucidation for the contrast between the heavenly humanity and the earthly humanity addressed by Paul in 1 Cor 15.

This same particular tradition of Hellenistic Judaism provides the most convincing background for the Corinthians' γνῶσις addressed by Paul in 1 Cor 8. The principles of the Corinthians' γνῶσις certainly do display the style of Hellenistic enlightenment philosophy. But this enlightenment philosophy had long since been assimilated by Hellenistic Jews such as Philo, Aristobulus, and Pseudo-Solomon.[6] Γνῶσις in this tradition, is understood as given by God or his consort Sophia to people who thereby attain an exalted spiritual status as wise or righteous (Wis 7:17; 10:10). The spiritual content thus imparted appears as a doctrinal specification of, and is often almost identical with, Sophia. This knowledge provides divine power and immortality to the individual soul (Wis 15:2–3). Philo writes that the σοφός dwelling in Sophia possesses "knowledge of the One" (ἐπιγνῶσις τοῦ θεοῦ, Leg. 3.46–48), and pictures the goal of the perfect royal way, which is Sophia, as "knowledge and understanding of God" (γνῶσις καὶ επιστήμε θεοῦ, Quod Deus 143; cf. Leg. 3.126).

---

4. E.g., Conzelmann, *1 Corinthians*, 142, 108–9; Niederwimmer, *Freiheit*, 28–68, 196–212.

5. Koester, "GNOMAI DIAPHOROI," 149–50; Pearson, *Pneumatikos–Psychikos*, chapter 2; Hamerton-Kelly, *Pre-existence*, 112–23; Horsley, "Wisdom of Words," chap. 2 above; and idem, "Spiritual Status," chap. 1 above

6. Conzelmann (*1 Corinthians*, 142) points this out, but makes nothing of it in his interpretation of 1 Cor 8.

Similarly Philo and the tradition he represents provide the most elucidating background for the principles of the Corinthians' γνῶσις cited by Paul in 1 Cor 8:4: "There is no God but One," and "an idol is nothing in the world." The Jewish confession that "God is One"[7] is the immediate background to the first of these principles. "That God is One . . ." is the lesson Moses continually teaches in the Laws (e.g., *Spec. Leg.* 1.30), and is the second major principle in a five-part summary of doctrine (*Op.* 170–72; cf. *Conf.* 170–71). Correspondingly, Wisdom and Philo concentrate their extensive critique of false gods and idols[8] around an absolute antithesis between ignorance and knowledge of God. Ignorance of God is synonymous with supposing that idols and heavenly bodies are gods. Knowledge of God means knowing that other gods do not exist, that idols are mere foolishness (Wis 13:1; 14:22; 15:2–3; Philo, *Dec.* 7–8, etc.).

The understanding of knowledge of the One true God vs. the false gods in this particular tradition of Hellenistic Judaism is thus highly pertinent to the mission context constituted by the nascent church in Corinth. In Philo, for example, it is precisely by learning doctrine (principles of γνῶσις!) about God vs. false idols that the conversion from ignorance to knowledge takes place (*Spec. Leg.* 1.15–30). Moreover, Philo's description of this transformation in Abraham displays connections with some aspects of the Corinthians' self-understanding discerned through 1 Cor 1–4. When he reaches knowledge of the One God, Abraham also is inspired by the divine Spirit, possesses eloquence, is regarded as a king, and becomes the standard of nobility (εὐγένεια) for all proselytes (*Virt.* 212–19; cf. 1 Cor 2:10–13; 2:1–5; 4:8; 1:26).

Although it is generally recognized that the "strong" Corinthians' freedom to eat meat offered to idols is related to their possession of γνῶσις, the way in which γνῶσις actually leads to the eating of idol meat has remained somewhat vague. Conzelmann states simply that the Corinthians' conduct is grounded on a freedom principle (1 Cor 6:12; 10:23) that, in turn, rests upon "knowledge."[9] But this formulation leaves out the crucial connecting link by which γνῶσις (σοφία) effects the

---

7. See the general discussion by Cohen, "Unity of God."

8. See esp. Wis 13–15 and Philo, *Dec.* 52–82; *Vita Cont.* 3–9; *Spec. Leg.* 1.15–30; I have discussed their extensive critique of false gods in relation to the Corinthians' γνῶσις in "Gnosis in Corinth," chap. 4 above.

9. Conzelmann, *1 Corinthians*, 14.

freedom/authority vis-à-vis idols: that is, consciousness. This chain of connection (knowledge—consciousness—authority/freedom) is barely evident just under the surface of Paul's argument in 1 Cor 8:1–9. But it can be much more clearly discerned in some of the treatises of Philo. To be sure, Philo nowhere makes an explicit connection with eating idol-meat. But he does portray quite clearly how Sophia (or the equivalent, Logos or γνῶσις) convicts one's consciousness (or mind) with such strength that one enjoys almost absolute spiritual freedom and authority. Starting with the "strong" Corinthians' sense of liberty to eat idol-meat we can trace more precisely how this is related to their possession of γνῶσις and their intimacy with Sophia.

The Corinthians' Understanding of Their Eating of Idol-Meat (1 Cor 8:8a)

Evaluation of the Corinthians' "authority" (8:9) depends considerably on what one imagines the Corinthians' own understanding of their behavior to have been in eating food offered to idols. First Corinthians 8:8a is likely the key to their self-understanding in this matter. Three alternative readings of 1 Cor 8:8 have been suggested by various scholars.

1. The judgment that 8:8 represents Paul's positive correction or even rejection of the Corinthian's view presupposes that "Gnostics" or "fanatics" were purposely eating idol-meat in order to demonstrate their new γνῶσις and freedom.[10] This judgment is based on an analogy with the audacious flaunting of traditional religious and ethical customs by later Gnostic libertines. It is fairly clear from chapter 8 and 10:23–24 that the Corinthians primarily addressed here felt free to eat meat offered to an idol, for by their γνῶσις an idol was "non-existent" and they themselves were above such absurdities. There is no evidence, however, that they were driven by some compulsion to eat idol-food.[11]

---

10. Weiss, *Der erste Brief,* 174.; Lietzmann, *Korinther,* 38; Conzelmann, *1 Corinthians,* 148.

11. I.e., in order to achieve thereby some sort of credit with God, which Paul supposedly rejects as an attempt at justification by works, according to Conzelmann, *1 Corinthians,* 148.

2. The view that in 8:8 as a whole Paul is again, as in 8:1a and 4, quoting or paraphrasing the Corinthians' position, agreeing with it in principle, but qualifying it in practice, is supported by linguistic arguments, the change of person ("we" in 8:8—cf. 8:1, 4, 6; vs. "you" in 8:9-12), and the abrupt shift to a warning style in 8:9.[12] However, this view presupposes that the "strong" felt free to eat any foods in any setting—and probably did, ignoring the anxieties thus created among their weaker brethren. Such a position would be merely a rather extreme instance of the general tendency in the Hellenistic period, expressed also in most Jewish literature, to spiritualize the ritual prohibitions and practices of traditional religion.[13]

3. A third alternative cuts midway between the other two. Barrett views the first clause of 8:8 as a Corinthian slogan, but sees Paul beginning his response in the second two clauses.[14] Paul does this by subtly twisting around the connected slogans of the strong Corinthians, which had been: "we are no worse off if we do eat, and we are no better off if we do not eat." This view, like the second, also presupposes an enlightened superiority complex in some of the Corinthians.

Of the three alternatives, the first rests on a questionable assumption regarding the Corinthians' behavior. Moreover, the whole discussion, chapters 8-10, makes sense only if (Paul thought that) it was the "weak" for whom the eating or abstinence would make some difference. Thus the first clause of 8:8 would appear to represent the position of the "strong" Corinthians who felt free to eat idol-food because they knew that an idol was a non-entity. Of course there are no decisive criteria for deciding whether the "neither . . . nor" clauses represent the Corinthians' position directly or twist it around. But Barrett's reading makes 8:8 intelligible both in the course of Paul's dialectical argument and, prior to Paul's reformulation, as the objection of "enlightened" ones to the scruples of their weaker or stricter brethren. The "strong" Corinthians, in their eating of idol-meat, thus appear neither as a case of compulsive (Gnostic) libertinism

---

12. Jeremias, "Zur Gedankenführung," 273-74.
13. Wenschkewitz, "Die Spiritualisierung."
14. Barrett, *First Epistle*, 195.

nor as a case merely of the general Hellenistic spiritualization of religious practices. They most resemble a type of enlightened Hellenistic Jews (or proselytes) who have discerned the implications of their knowledge that the gods supposedly represented by idols have no real existence.

The statement in 1 Cor 6:13a that "food is meant for the stomach and the stomach for food," which must be viewed as another Corinthian slogan related to that repeated in 6:12,[15] may also help elucidate the Corinthian attitude reflected in 8:8. This slogan would seem to express a self-understanding that has assigned body and soul to separate spheres of life. This is indicated by Paul's response to what he sees as Corinthian immorality. He is at pains to stress the importance of the body soteriologically. "The body is meant not for immorality but for the Lord." "Your bodies are members of Christ." "Your body is a temple of the Holy Spirit within you." Were the Corinthians consigning the body and its functions to a realm unconnected with the Divine, unconnected with the salvation of the soul or true self? Whereas Paul asserts that the body is the temple of the Holy Spirit, Philo holds that the soul, or the mind or reason, is the temple or house of God (*Som.* 1.149; 2.250–53; *Virt.* 188; *Praem.* 123). If this distinction between the divine and the mundane were sufficiently sharp and exclusive, the soul belonging on the one side and the body on the other, human life would be conducted on two mutually exclusive levels. Not only is the soul in its σοφία or γνῶσις independent of the burdensome body, but the body is left to its own devices in its own proper sphere. Hence: "food is for the stomach and the stomach for food" (6:13a) and, of course, "food will not commend us to God" (8:8a). For the salvation of the soul possessed of γνῶσις it would make absolutely no difference whether or not one ate food offered to idols.[16] And, since "all things are possible" and "an idol is nothing in the world," why not eat such food?

---

15. Conzelmann, *1 Corinthians*, 110.

16. At points Philo even speaks as though rules and customs hinder rather than aid the soul's spiritual life; compare, for example, *Sac.* 15. To 1 Cor 6:13a in particular and the question of foods and purity generally, cf. Mark 7:14–19. Perrin *Rediscovering*, 150) pointed out that Mark 7:17–23 and par. show how the early churches struggled to comprehend the significance of so radical a statement as Mark 7:15, "and reached the mundane, although correct, conclusion that this makes all food 'clean' and human sins the means of defilement." It is easy to understand how a denial of the distinction between clean and unclean food could be readily appropriated by the enlightened Corinthians.

The "Liberty" and "Authority" of the Corinthians

There are further aspects of the enlightened Corinthians' attitude discernible in the immediate context. Paul's use of the term ἐξουσία (authority) in 8:9 and 9:4-6, 12, 18 is quite distinctive in comparison with his other usage.[17] Here in 1 Cor 8-9 the term means "authority" in the sense of personal "right" and "liberty," and its use in this sense is confined to 1 Corinthians. Clearly it should be read in close connection with the Corinthian slogan "all things are possible/permissible (ἔξεστιν) for me" in 6:12 and 10:23. This "authority" is obviously a key term for the Corinthians who possess knowledge. The closely related term "freedom" (ἐλευθερία) is also surely a Corinthian catchword, for its use here in the absolute sense is distinctive to 1 Corinthians among the genuine letters of Paul, indeed to this section of the letter (9:1, 19; 10:29).[18] Paul's autobiographical argument concerning "freedom" in chapter 9, in which he further explains his instruction of 8:13, is aimed directly at this "freedom" and "authority" of the enlightened Corinthians.

Conzelmann declares that only the Stoics and Cynics provide material for comparison to the language in 6:12 and related texts (ἐξουσία, etc.).[19] Indeed Stoic-Cynic material is so rich in apt comparisons as to become seductive for an approach that looks primarily for terminological parallels. One need hardly look beyond Diogenes Laertius 7.121: "(The Stoics say that the wise man) alone is free (ἐλεύθερον) and bad men are slaves; freedom (ἐλευθερία) is the power (ἐξουσία) of autonomous action, and slavery the lack of autonomous action." Among several comparable passages in Epictetus, 2.1.23 is especially striking:[20] "Now is freedom (ἐλευθερία) anything other than the right (ἐξεῖναι) to live as we wish?" The inclusion of "consciousness" along with "freedom" and "authority" in the search for comparative material makes Epictetus seem even more

17. 1 Cor 15:24; 2 Cor 10:8; 13:10; Rom 13:1-3. See Foerster, "ἔξεστιν, ἐξουσία, κτλ.," 560-61; Dupont, *Gnosis*, 282-90.

18. The argument in Romans and the situation and issues in Galatia—where "do not surrender your freedom" is Paul's own plea—were different. The use in 2 Cor 3:17 is surely related closely to, perhaps an allusion to, the polemical situation behind 1 Corinthians.

19. Conzelmann, *I Corinthians*, 108-9.

20. Cf. further Epictetus, 1.1.26; 12.9; 17.28; 2.16.37; 4.1.1; and 4.1.151-68. The Corinthians addressed in 1 Cor 5-6, 8-10, however, do not appear very similar to the Stoic σόφοι; for the Stoics freedom meant not the satisfaction but the destruction of desire, as in Epictetus 4.1.175.

attractive: "for the Cynic, . . . his consciousness (συνείδος) provides him this power" (ἐξουσία 3.22.94).

Now Philo's treatises are mines frequently worked by scholars searching for Stoic material.[21] For comparative material on "freedom" the most obvious point of departure would be the most "Stoic" of his treatises, and one with a rather suggestive title: "Every Good Man is Free"! Indeed, for the religious and theological background of the language in 1 Cor 6:12; 8:7-13, etc., just as for the background in 8:1-4, a close analogy can be found in several Philonic passages: *Prob.* 13-14, 20-22, 29-30, 41-46, 57-62; *Det.* 22-24, 146; *Leg.* 3.42-48; *Fug.* 116-18; *Praem.* 162-63.

In *Prob.*, Philo expounds at length as basic Jewish religious teaching a favorite theme of the Stoics: that only the wise (or good) person is free, and this freedom consists in the power to do as one wishes (cf. esp. *Prob.* 21-22, 41, 59-61). Moreover, the language in his argument is even closer to the Corinthian slogan of 6:12 and 10:23 than are the parallels from Epictetus and other Stoics:

> ἐξουσίαν σχήσει πάντα δρᾶν καὶ ζῆν, ὡς βούλεται.
> ᾧ δὲ ταῦτ᾽ ἔξεστιν ἐλεύθερος ἄν εἴν. (*Prob.* 59)

> (The wise or good man) will have the power to do anything and to live as he wishes; the one for whom these things are lawful/possible must be free.

Of course, this idea (along with its terminology) may have been Stoic-Cynic in its origin and style. But Philo and the Hellenistic-Jewish tradition he represents had long since (critically) assimilated this and other ideas of "Greek enlightenment philosophy," and understood them as expressions of the true (Jewish) relation to God, as taught in the sacred writings of Moses (as in *Prob.* 20-22, 29-30, 41-46, 57, etc.).

The Strong Consciousness: The Soteriological Link Between Sophia / Gnosis and Authority

"Consciousness" (συνείδησις) is yet another crucial facet of the enlightened Corinthians' religiosity closely related to their sense of "authority." From the context and usage here and most other occurrences in Paul,

---

21. Note how frequently Philo is the source for "Stoic fragments" in von Arnim, *Stoicorum Veterum Fragmenta*. See also Pohlenz, *Die Stoa*, 2 (frequent references); and cf. Pohlenz's discussion of Philo's relation to Stoicism in *Philon*, 5.

συνείδησις clearly means one's inner consciousness or awareness, and not "conscience" in the modern sense of the English word.[22] Considering its use in Rom 2:15 and 13:5 in a sense closer to "conscience," it is conceivable that the term also belonged to Paul's religious vocabulary prior to the Corinthian conflict. But considering:

1. the heavy concentration (8 of the 14 occurrences) of the term in 1 Cor 8:7–12 and 10:25–27 (in close connection with ἐξουσία and ἐλευθερία);
2. the likelihood that the other occurrences in the sense of one's "consciousness" (1 Cor 4:4; 2 Cor 1:12; 4:2; 5:11; Rom 9:1) are all dependent on or subsequent to the Corinthian conflict; and
3. that Paul does not use the term in the parallel discussion of the same issue in Rom 14,

it is certain that "consciousness" was another theme of the Corinthians that Paul refers to in his arguments for voluntary restraint of one's liberty.[23]

This judgment is confirmed, moreover, by the highly unusual application to "consciousness" of the attribution "weak" in 1 Cor 8:7. In cautioning the enlightened Corinthians Paul is concerned for those who may have a "weak consciousness." First Corinthians 8:7 indicates that weak consciousness is connected with lack of γνῶσις. The implication is that those who possess γνῶσις, i.e. the "strong," have a "strong consciousness." What, then, for the supposedly "strong" Corinthians, would be the relation between "consciousness" and their γνῶσις, such that they are so secure and self-assured?

Again it may be possible to approach the Corinthians' position through analogy from Philonic material. Philo uses συνείδησις, the synonym, συνείδος, and especially the near synonym, ἔλεγχος, "the convictor," in the moral sense of a consciousness (not clearly differentiated from one's reason or mind) that convicts the self of having acted unjustly or

---

22. Maurer ("σύνοιδα," 914) suggests "percipient and active self-awareness" ("das erkennende and handelnde Selbstbewusstsein"). To translate συνείδησις (etc.) with the English word "conscience" would more obscure than elucidate the meaning and issue in 1 Cor 8 and 10. Broader discussion of the meaning and function of *syneidesis* and related terms in Pierce, *Conscience*; Stelzenberger, *Syneidesis*; and esp. in Maurer, "σύνοιδα."

23. Maurer, "σύνοιδα," 914; Pierce, *Conscience*, 64–65.

sinfully.²⁴ This is the same notion presupposed in 1 Cor 8 and 10 and in most other uses of συνείδησις and synonymous terms. According to Philo this convicting consciousness is part of the nature of the soul as created by God (see *Dec.* 87). Its function is to prevent the soul from wrong and/or to accuse and "convict" the soul of having acted unjustly. As Schnackenburg points out, Philo "adapted it to suit his belief in revelation and his personal concept of God."²⁵

It would seem logical, then, that the strong consciousness would be strong in convicting the soul of wrongdoing and the weak consciousness correspondingly less effective in convicting the soul. But this logical pattern does not fit the language usage in 1 Cor 8:7-12 and 10:25-27 at all, where the weak consciousness is the one both susceptible of injury and apt to accuse its owner of wrongdoing.

A closer approach to the significance of the strong consciousness in 1 Corinthians might be attained through the notion of the "good" or "pure" or "upright" consciousness. The latter means, in effect, consciousness with no awareness of wrongdoing.²⁶ The strong consciousness, like the "good consciousness," would thus be the reverse side of the pure mind, i.e., the lack of awareness of unrighteousness.

However, a far more helpful understanding of the "consciousness" that can be strong (in some) or weak (in others) and of the intimate relation between "consciousness" and the possession of γνῶσις can be attained from Philo's portrayal of "the convictor."²⁷ The ἔλεγχος has no mean status or role in the soul, according to Philo. This is clear from the ways in which he characterizes this inner consciousness or convictor: as "the true man" or simply "man," the reasonable mind in each soul (e.g., *Det.* 22-23); as an "angel" of God (*Fug.* 6, 203); and as the

---

24. Philo uses the participial form *to* συνειδός more frequently than *syneidesis*, and uses both usually in connection with *elenchos*, e.g., as in the phrase "the convictor/conviction of one's consciousness." See *Op.* 128; *Det.* 146; *Ebr.* 125; *Spec. Leg.* 4.6, 40; and *Prob.* 149. The following discussion presupposes Maurer's basic treatment in "σύνοιδα," 10-12. See also Brehier, *Les idées*, 295-302.

25. Schnackenburg, *Moral Teaching*, 288.

26. See esp. Pierce, *Conscience*, 36-39.

27. Maurer ("σύνοιδα," 911-12) points out the importance of Jewish wisdom literature as the religious background of Philo's understanding of ἔλεγχος; for example, ἐλεγχειν is conceived as an educational, converting, nurturing function in Sir 18:13; Wis 1:6-8; etc.

divine λόγος, the true priest that enters the soul like a purest ray of light (i.e., "consciousness," as opposed to "ignorance" of our own true interest, *Quod Deus* 134–35). At one point, *Quod Deus* 182, the ἔλεγχος is virtually identified with the divine λόγος, as an angel that guides and removes obstacles along the royal way. To explain the status and role of the convicting consciousness in the soul is, for Philo, almost another way of stating the operations of Logos/Sophia in the enlightened soul in its attainment of knowledge.

If the ἔλεγχος is able to function in the way it was created to function, then it renders the soul free of wrongdoing or unrighteousness. It allows nothing censurable to enter the soul; it naturally hates evil and loves virtue; if sufficiently strong it persuades the soul, if not capable of that, it resorts to attacks and wounds (*Dec.* 87). In Philo the sense of need for reproof for wrongdoing still balances the consciousness of possessing the divine *Logos* in one's mind along with the accompanying salvific benefits (as, e.g., in *Det.* 146). However, in those texts where Philo concentrates on the salvific possession of Sophia/Logos to the exclusion of any sense of sin, there is a closer analogy to the self-assured attitude of the strong Corinthians.

> For as long as this most holy Logos lives and is present in the soul, an unintentional offense cannot enter into it. For the Logos by nature cannot share in or partake of any sin.... For the convictor, the undefiled High Priest, cannot by nature admit any uncertainty of judgment into himself. (*Fug.* 117–18)

A soul thus possessed of the divine Sophia or Logos, and thus convicted of its sinlessness would indeed have a self-confident sense of its spiritual authority.

Philo's comments in *Praem.* 162–63 illustrate further how this notion could be connected with the whole complex of the enlightened Corinthians' ideas that have been discerned through 1 Cor 8. He declares that those (apparently apostate Jews) who return from *polytheistic opinions* and acknowledge the nature of *the One, the highest God* (cf. 1 Cor 8:4) *to whom* alone those who follow truth instead of myths *belong* (cf. 1 Cor 8:6a), and thus have their mind so purified that their *consciousness* (συνείδος) is true and untainted (cf. the *strong consciousness* vs. the weak, 1 Cor 8:7, 10, 12), find favor with merciful God, the Savior, who had granted men the greatest gift, kinship with His *Logos, from whom as an archetype,* the human mind *was created* (cf. 1 Cor 8:6b).[28]

The further connection of these ideas with facets of the Corinthians' self-understanding behind 1 Cor 1–4 should be apparent by analogy with *Leg.* 3.44–48:

> But all these (voices of the senses) cease when the mind finds in God the spring and aim of its own doings and intents. For truly the doings of the wise person will be weighty and immovable and not easily shaken.[29] Accordingly they are steadied by Aaron, the Word, and Hor, which is 'Light,' for the end of the Word is Truth. . . . Mark you not, that when he had received from God (Exod 33:7) the Tent, namely, Sophia, in which the wise person tabernacles and dwells, he fixed and made it fast and strongly established, not in the body, but outside it.[30] . . . And it was called 'the tent of testimony,' Sophia testified to by God. Yes, for 'everyone that sought the Lord went out to it!' Right finely is this said, For if thou art seeking God, o mind, go out from thyself and seek diligently. . . . Thus it is said that while the bad man, who shuns virtue and hides himself from God, takes refuge in his own mind, a sorry resource, the good man, on the other hand, who runs away from himself, returns to the apprehension of the One, thus winning a noble race and proving victor in this grandest of all contests.

Not only does this passage demonstrate how closely Logos/Sophia and the σοφός (and the "*mind*") are associated in this soteriological pattern, but along with the previous passage, *Praem.* 162–63, it illustrates how the Corinthians' extremely self-confident "consciousness" can be rooted in, almost identical with, the absorption of the wise man's mind in divine Sophia. Moreover, the distinction made in the last sentence cited could easily slip off into a distinction between *strong* and *weak* consciousnesses, i.e., those whose consciousness is filled with or identified with divine

---

28. For a more complete explanation of the Hellenistic-Jewish background (in Wisdom and Philo) of 1 Cor 8:6, see chap. 5 above, "Confessional Formula."

29. Note the same interpretation of Exod 17:12 in *Prob.* 29, in the context of one of the key Philonic texts cited above.

30. Note also the mutually exclusive spheres of mind/soul and body similar to what was discerned in the Corinthians' mentality through their slogan, "Food is meant for the stomach, and the stomach for food" (1 Cor 6:13a).

Sophia (or Logos or γνῶσις) vs. those who lack this "perfection" and must still rely on their own weak mind or consciousness.

A final illustration from the Philonic analogy for the whole pattern of the Corinthian self-understanding behind 1 Cor 8-9 etc., can be adduced from the "Stoic" treatise, *Quod omnis Probus Liber sit* (*Every Good Man Is Free*). For we find the same "soteriological" pattern in *Prob.* (esp. 41-47, 59-61) as in *Leg.* 3.44-48, *Fug.* 116-18 and *Praem.* 162-63, even though it is expressed mostly in "Stoic" language. The example from "the legislator of the Jews"—that of Moses' own pursuit of naked philosophy such that, possessed by divine love and worshipping the Only Self-Existent, he was no longer man, but god, a god to men—vividly illustrates the soteriological significance of the wise person's liberty. It is more important for the analogy here, however, to realize that obedience to the *Nomos* or the *Orthos Logos* is for Philo virtually the same as dwelling in Sophia or receiving knowledge of the One God (or being nourished by Sophia or the Logos, etc.). Hence, whether it be expressed as the realization that *Orthos Logos* is imprinted incorruptly in one's immortal mind or as the reception of Sophia, the concomitant result is that the wise person is free (again, cf. *Prob.* 41-47, 59-61).

From these Philo passages it should be clear that at least the Hellenistic-Jewish theology represented by Philo had absorbed Stoic language and doctrines into a complex of ideas including the "freedom" and "authority" of the wise to do as they will and the role of the "consciousness" in providing such autonomous "authority." These texts also document the possibility that such "liberty"—e.g., expressed in a slogan such as "all things are lawful for me" or in the eating of idol-meat—is the expression of a mind or consciousness filled with and made indelible by divine Sophia or Logos. Finally, it should be clear that a self-confident "liberty" such as that behind 1 Cor 8 could be the expression of a consciousness made secure and strong by γνῶσις of the one true God as creator, which simultaneously means that idols are ridiculous nothings. The crucial link between γνῶσις and the liberty to eat idol-meat is thus the strong consciousness convicted by Sophia/Logos.

Freedom of Consciousness and Paul's Ethical Response

Much of the interpretation written about the concept of "conscience" in Paul does not adequately take into account the situation of conflict behind 1 Cor 8–10, in which Paul's usage of *syneidesis* is largely concentrated. The inevitable result is a good deal of commentary that has little to do either with the significance of συνείδησις in earliest Corinthian Christianity or with Paul's response.

The "freedom of conscience" (or rather "consciousness"), far from being Paul's solution, was the real problem in the ethical difficulties created by the eating of idol-meat in Corinth. Apparently Paul does not have a concept of "conscience" already worked out, as he confronts the conflict in Corinth. To all appearances, if our analysis of the polemical situation is correct, he picks up the terminology of συνείδησις from the enlightened Corinthians who were eating the idol-meat. Moreover, the "consciousness" of the Corinthians seems to work in a way contrary to how we conceive of "conscience" working. For it convicts the mind of its authority or freedom to act in a quite autonomous way, completely transcending any ethical issue and oblivious to the interpersonal level of existence. Συνείδησις, as Paul finds it in Corinth, is indeed the slogan of a "religion of consciousness," and the very basis of the freedom of the subject who makes his decisions autonomously according to the divine voice within.[31] Consciousness may be given with humanity as such, but it becomes "strong" and truly capable of "authority" with the enlightenment of the mind with revelation. Moreover, contrary to what is sometimes said of the "conscience" of some people in Corinth, that it was weak and therefore errant,[32] the weak "consciousness" of some of the Corinthians was merely less secure in its *gnosis*, and therefore lacking in spiritual authority.

In his response to the problem posed by the "freedom of consciousness" Paul insists on the "real ethical question" at the interpersonal level. Both the structure and the substance of Paul's response makes the effect of one's behavior on others the criterion of ethics. Paul's framing of the argument both in 8:7 and 13 and in 10:23–24 and 32–33 refers to those who would exercise their new-found spiritual freedom to their fellow members in the community. Substantively Paul calls the attention of the

---

31. Once the polemical situation behind 1 Corinthians is recognized, some of the standard observations (e.g., by Conzelmann, *Outline*, 182–83) about the meaning of "conscience" in Paul do *not* turn out to be true of the meaning of "consciousness" for the "strong" Christians in Corinth.

32. Contra Conzelmann, *1 Corinthians*, 148; and *Outline*, 183.

"strong" to those who, lacking the *gnosis* of the enlightened, have weak consciousness. Far from accepting the Corinthians' *gnosis* as such, Paul perceives that its effect in informing the consciousness and freedom of the strong may be to destroy the weak brother (8:9–11).[33] Thus Paul does not ask the "strong" Corinthians to consult their own consciousness or "conscience." In fact, he insists that the liberty to eat any food in any circumstances has nothing to do with "consciousness": go ahead and eat "without raising any question on account of consciousness" (10:25–27).

Moreover, as so often in 1 Corinthians, Paul is here playing with words and coaxing the enlightened Corinthians along by using their own language, only to give it a very different twist or application.[34] In this case he is leading up to a criterion of conduct almost diametrically opposed to that of the "strong" Corinthians (and of the usual understanding of the freedom of conscience): the (weaker) consciousness of the other (10:28–29). If a concept of "conscience" is emerging in 1 Cor 8–10, then its criterion is not inner freedom based on conviction at all, but the situation and self-consciousness of one's neighbor.

Paul's autobiographical illustration in 1 Cor 9 has the same thrust, that is, making the effect on the other into the determinative criterion of one's religious-ethical freedom. Although Paul may also be attempting to defend his status and privilege as an apostle in chap. 9 (cf. 4:3–4), his argument here aims primarily at demonstrating with reference to himself the principle of self-limitation of one's freedom for the sake of the brother just enunciated in 8:13.[35] In 9:16–19 in particular Paul is clearly alluding again to the ἐξουσία of the "strong" Corinthians. For his comments here directly contradict, in effect, the standard contrast of the freedom and authority of the wise with the slavery and coercion of the foolish, a contrast

---

33. Contra Conzelmann, *1 Corinthians*, 149, "the *gnōsis* has a perverse effect" not because it fails to bring "the free individual face to face with the God from whom his freedom comes" (for that is precisely the effect of the *gnosis*), but because it fails to bring the free individuals face to face with their neighbors.

34. Note that in 1 Cor 10:25, 27 Paul does not say "without raising any question in your own consciousness," but rather "on account of consciousness," which in 10:29 turns out to mean "on account of the other's consciousness"!

35. Paul's argument is spontaneous and rhetorical. The arrangement and relative emphasis of the sub-points, references, and particular illustrations should probably not be over-analyzed and over-interpreted. Compare von Campenhausen, *Die Begründung*, 24–25.

found in Philo as well as in the Stoics. With the terminology of "necessity" and "freedom" (ἀνάγκε, ἄκων, ἑκών, etc. 9:16–19) Paul is deliberately using the language of this "Stoic" idea to contrast his own understanding and practice of his freedom in service of the gospel with the Corinthians' understanding of "freedom" in an absolute and individualistic sense. We can compare Epictetus 4.1.128:

> The unhampered (ἀκώλυτος) man for whom things are at hand as he wishes is free, but the man who is hampered or forced by necessity (ἀναγκάσαι) or hindered or unwillingly (ἄκοντα) thrown into something, he is a slave.

A Philo passage already referred to above, *Prob.* 60–61, is still more pertinent:

> One who is neither forced (ἀναγκάσαι) nor hampered (κωλῦσαι) cannot be a slave. The good man is neither forced nor hindered . . . He does acts of virtue not under constraint but willingly (ἑκών) . . . He does nothing unwillingly (ἄκων) nor is he forced by necessity (ἀναγκάζεται); if he were a slave, he would be forced by necessity."

Such could easily have been the authority and freedom of the strong Corinthians.

Paul surely knows what he is doing when, in 9:16–19, he juxtaposes his freedom from all with his self-enslavement to all, his true possession of authority as an apostle with his non-use of his privileges, indeed, with the necessity laid upon him and the unwillingness involved in being entrusted with a commission. In addressing the strong Corinthians Paul uses their language, but twists it around through a seemingly contradictory juxtaposition to express the principle that he is asking them to heed. As for the substance of the argument, Paul adds the service of a purpose to the focus on the neighbor. From his own service in the eschatological commission of preaching the gospel he illustrates how, under the "necessity" of divine and/or self-limitation, freedom can be liberation for purposive activity and more than just individualistic liberation from burdensome constraints.

It is important, finally, to look briefly at Paul's subsequent treatment of virtually the same issue in a non-polemical context, Rom 14. The principle theme is the same as in 1 Cor 8–9 and 10:23–31: do nothing that might cause your brother to stumble. And there are several points at which Paul's formulations in Rom 14 are directly dependent on his previous arguments in 1 Corinthians.[36] But Paul now completely avoids the use of the term "consciousness" as well as "authority" and "freedom." There is even a brief reference to what seems like "conscience" in 14:22, but without explicit use of any term for it. Instead, the whole discussion is framed with the terminology of "faith": the concern is for the brother who is weak in faith and the criterion of ethical action is stated as faith. But this does not mean that "the freedom of conscience is the freedom of faith." In fact, in Romans 14 neither "conscience" nor "freedom" is under discussion. As in 1 Cor 8–10 the ethical principle is again the concern for the neighbor, as Paul admonishes divisive mutual criticism and encourages mutual edification.

By determining more precisely the Hellenistic-Jewish background of the polemical situation in Corinth it is possible to discern that the crucial link between the *gnosis* of certain Corinthians and their freedom to eat idol-meat was their "strong consciousness." For the Corinthians the eating of idol-meat and other issues were dealt with entirely in one's consciousness. Like the third level of conscience by a modern existentialist theologian, the Corinthians' consciousness was a "very fundamental mode of self-awareness—the awareness of 'how it is with oneself' . . ." Here is one of "those deeper levels of conscience that will sometimes sit in judgment on the pronouncements of a person's own society or social group."[37] The Corinthian's conviction by his own consciousness must have had an effect similar to that suggested in another recent discussion of conscience: "The morally mature man is at one with himself, with God, and with the universe . . . At this point of convergence he is beyond conflict, for in pursuing his true self he is pursuing God and in pursuing God he is pursuing all things."[38] Through his γνῶσις the "wise" Corinthian also understood himself as "mature" (τέλειος) and believed that by virtue of his possession of divine Sophia "all things were his" (1 Cor 2:6 and 3:21). Having thus transcended all conflict in his strong consciousness, he believed that "all things are possible" (1 Cor 6:12 and 10:23).

36. Conzelmann, *1 Corinthians*, 5, 137.
37. Macquarrie, "Struggle of Conscience," 111, 113.
38. Cousins, "Mature Conscience," 372.

For the Corinthians, therefore, the eating of idol-meat and other matters were issues only in an internal personal sense, for one's individual consciousness, and not in a truly ethical, i.e. relational, sense. For Paul, on the other hand, who does not approach the Corinthian situation with any concept of conscience, such issues are ethical, that is, matters of relationships between people, not of one's own inner consciousness.

7

Ecstatic Prophecy in Corinth

In 1 Cor 12–14 Paul addresses the "spiritual things" (πνευματικά) received or possessed by the "spiritual" people (πνευματικοί). This term must be the spirituals' own designation, since Paul's preferred, more inclusive term is χαρίσματα (12:4). As in the previous arguments in the letter, Paul is again addressing questions about which the Corinthians had inquired in a letter to him ("now concerning [the matters about which you wrote]," 7:1; 8:1; 12:1). He begins his argument somewhat generally (12:4–30), then offers an uncharacteristic paean of praise to the abstract quality of love in contrast with an over-evaluation of γλῶσσαι ("tongues") and γνῶσις ("knowledge") (12:31—13:13), and finally argues for intelligible prophecy that builds up the community as opposed to "(speaking in) tongues" that does not (14:1–40).

It becomes clear in chapter 14 that his real concern is with what he terms "(speaking in) tongues," which he is at pains to denigrate in favor of "prophecy" (προφητεία; 14:1–19), and then insists on being interpreted and regulated at meetings of the assembly (14:20–33). "Tongues" is the only gift included in all of the lists in the overall argument (12:8–10, 28, 29–30; 13:1–3, 8; 14:6, 26), and "tongues" is pointedly placed at the end of the lists in chapter 12. The earlier steps in the argument readily make sense as attempts to counter what he considers an overemphasis on "tongues."

But in what does "(speaking in) tongues" consist? Discussion of "tongues" in New Testament literature is confined to 1 Cor 12–14. What has subsequently been called *glossolalia* may well have been a neologism resulting from Paul's phrase "speaking in tongues" (a phrase, not a single word). The speaking at the giving of the Spirit at Pentecost (Acts 2:4,

6, 8, 11) refers to different national languages. References in the Dead Sea Scrolls indicate that some in the Qumran community were specially interested in the prophecy about speaking in strange tongues in Isa 28:11–13a, which Paul also cites (1 Cor 14:21). Other Judean communities were familiar with paranormal experiences of prayer-like or human-like speech uttered to God in superhuman language similar to the transcendent experience of "speaking with the tongues of angels" (1 Cor 13:1) that Paul seems to refer to. The *Testament of Job* mentions that Job's daughter, Hemera "received another heart, no longer to mind the things of earth, but uttered a hymn [to God] in the angelic language" (48:2–3a; 49:2; 50:1–2; 51:4; 52:7).

As in the other sections of 1 Corinthians, it may be possible to find clues to the phenomenon that Paul refers to as "(speaking in) tongues" by attending closely to key terms that he objects to or qualifies in the course of his argument. In 1 Cor 14 he makes four representations of "tongues": (1) it is speech or prayer to/with God (and not to/with other people, 14:2; cf. "speaking with the tongues of angels" that Paul contrasts with love in 13:1, which is interpersonal); (2) it is like the indistinct sound of a flute or harp (lyre; 14:7); (3) it is prayer in the spirit but without the mind (14:14–15); and (4) it will appear to outsiders as madness (14:23). As with most of the other favorite terms and slogans of the Corinthian spirituals, these are characteristics that appear in the discussion of ecstatic prophecy—or more appropriately prophetic ecstasy—by Philo of Alexandria.

Prophetic Ecstasy in Philo

Philo's understanding of the wise as occasionally experiencing ecstatic prophecy was surely a development of a tradition cultivated by earlier Judean sages and Hellenistic-Jewish devotion to heavenly Sophia.[1] Jesus ben Sira's portrayal of the scribe's curriculum and competence indicates that second temple Judean sages understood themselves as having inherited a certain prophetic function (39:1–11). They were occasionally filled with the spirit of understanding and poured forth words of wisdom (39:6; 24:33). In a significant step toward Philo's more elaborate description of ecstatic prophecy, the praise of transcendent Sophia in Wisdom of Solomon declares that "in every generation She passes into holy souls and makes them friends of God and prophets" (7:27; see further the char-

---

1. See Hengel, *Judaism and Hellenism*, 1:255–61; and for the social-political context, see Tcherikover, *Hellenistic Civilization and the Jews*, 253–65.

acterization of the spirit of Sophia in 7:22–23). This tradition of wisdom theology that has closely identified Sophia with the Spirit, which is usually associated with prophecy in the Judean scriptures is the matrix of Philo's understanding of prophecy as an experience of the wise. "Thus may the divine Spirit of Sophia not lightly shift its dwelling and be gone, but long abide with us, since it did thus abide with Moses the wise" (*Gig.* 47; cf. *Quod Deus* 1–3).

Philo's sense that a divine ecstasy was the highest form of prophecy was rooted in the Platonic philosophical tradition. In a key passage in the *Timaeus* (71E; cf. *Ion* 53B), Plato had states that

> No man achieves true and inspired divination when in his rational mind (ἐννούς μαντικῆς ἔνθεου καὶ ἀληθούς), but only when the power of his intelligence is fettered in sleep or when it is distraught by disease or by some divine inspiration (ἐνθουσιασμός).

Plato, however, had continued the discussion.[2] When back in his right mind a man should recollect and ponder the things spoken and seen in the "enthusiastic" dream or vision. It was the prophet's function to examine and interpret the inspired divinations and apparitions of those who had undergone the frenzy. That Hellenistic philosophers were aware of this distinction between unintelligible ecstatic "enthusiasm" and a manticism that retained its rationality is indicated by Plutarch's comments in *Def. Orac.* 40 (see also, in the Platonic tradition, Lucan, 5.161–218).[3] Plutarch even says at one point (432E) that the best seer is the intelligent man who follows along the way the leading part of the soul that retains its νοῦς along with probability—although he immediately qualifies this, saying that inspiration involves an irrational withdrawal of the soul by the power of the divine mantic spirit and is often diverted or extinguished by mortal intelligence (432D–F). But Philo is far more single-minded about ecstasy, without Plato's and Plutarch's qualification.

Philo's most extensive discussion comes in *Her.* 249–266 (an interpretation of Gen 15:12) regarding the ecstasy that fell upon Abraham. The fact that Philo uses this same philosophical tradition elsewhere (e.g.,

2. Plato and the Platonic tradition, moreover, were ambivalent about whether the poet's or philosopher's mode of inspiration was a form of possession by the divine or an ascension of the soul/mind into the divine. This is typical of mystical religion and spiritual or ecstatic religion. See the discussion in Lewis, *Ecstatic Religion*, chap. 2.

3. Further discussion of the difference between Philo's "prophetic Spirit" from the Hellenistic mantic Spirit in Verbeke, *L'evolution de la doctrine du pneuma*, 250–57.

Q.G. 3.9; *Mos.* 1.274; *Spec. leg.* 1.65; 4.49) as the interpretation of Gen 15:12 and in interpretation of Gen 28:11 (which connects Isaac, who is an example of a prophet [*Her.* 261], with the theme of the sun having set [*Som.* 1.115–19]) suggests that it was standard doctrine inherited from his Jewish predecessors and mentors. Philo first (*Her.* 249) distinguishes four kinds of ecstasy: mad fury (ἡ λύττα μανιώδμς), extreme amazement (ἡ σφόδρα κατάπλεχις), serenity of mind (ἡ ἐρημία διάνοιας), and as the best, the divine possession and frenzy to which the prophets as a class are subject (ἡ ἔνθεος κατακωχή τὲ καὶ μανία, ἡ τὸ προφητικόν γένος χρῆται; cf. *Phaedrus* 244E–245A). After giving examples of the first three kinds (250–57), he presents in interpretation of Gen 15:12 what is really a discussion and exemplification of prophecy ecstasy (258–66). Not only did Abraham, Noah, Isaac, Jacob, and Moses enjoy divine possession, but such prophecy is available to any noble and wise person (though not to a bad person):

> Now with every good man it is the holy Logos which assures him his gift of prophecy. For a prophet utters nothing of his own, but all he utters is from elsewhere, echoes of Another. A bad person may not become the interpreter of God, so that no worthless person is really God-inspired (ἐνθουσιᾷ), but these things fit only the wise person, since he alone is the vocal instrument of God, being plucked and played by Him invisibly. . . . (*Her.* 259)

> "Sun" (Gen 15:12) is what he calls, through a symbol, our mind (τὸν ἡμέτερον νοῦν). . . . When it comes to its setting, naturally ecstasy and divine possession and frenzy fall upon us ... (ἔκστασις καὶ ἡ ἔνθεος κατακωχή καὶ μανία) . . . . This is what regularly befalls the prophetic race. The mind in us is evicted at the arrival of the Divine Spirit (ἐξοικίζεται μὲν γὰρ ἐν ἡμῖν ὁ νοῦς κατὰ την τοῦ θείου πνεύματός ἀφιχιν). Mortal and immortal may not dwell together. (*Her.* 263–65)

Most of the key features in the longer description in *Her.* 259–265 can be seen also in the more compact representation of prophetic ecstasy in *Spec. leg.* 4.49:

> The prophet never pronounces anything which is his own, but rather he is an interpreter prompted by another in everything which he utters, when in ignorance he becomes filled with inspiration, as his reason withdraws and surrenders the citadel of

the soul to a new visitor and tenant, the Divine Spirit which plays upon the vocal organ and raises sounds from it which clearly express its prophetic message.

Both the longer and shorter versions of Philo's description of prophetic ecstasy display other key aspects of his religious orientation focused on the relationship of the wise person with the divine Sophia/Logos/Pneuma. The prophet is the same as the *sophos*, contrasted with others of lesser status. The divine Spirit is synonymous with the divine Logos as the agent of the soul's salvation or transcendence.

While this and other descriptions of prophetic ecstasy in Philo are interpretations of scripture and use a philosophical commonplace, Philo is directly interested in ecstasy. This is indicated by Philo's description of his own experience of divine possession.

> On other occasions I have approached my work empty and suddenly become full, the ideas falling in a shower from above and being sown invisibly, so that under the influence of the Divine possession (ὑπο κατοχῆς ενθέου) I have been filled with corybantic frenzy (κορυβαντιαν) and been unconscious of anything, place, persons present, myself, words spoken, lines written. For I obtained language (ἑρμενείαν), ideas (εὑρεσιν), an enjoyment of light, keenest vision, pellucid distinctness of objects, such as might be received through eyes as the result of clearest showing. (*Migr.* 34–35)

What the Philonic Analogy Suggests about the Corinthians' "Tongues"

Philo's discussions of prophetic ecstasy offer a striking analogy to what Paul calls "(speaking in) tongues," judging from his four principal representations listed above. It is a direct spiritual relation of the soul with the Divine (Spirit/Sophia/Logos), pointedly without any mortal human instrument in mediation (not even the mortal "mind"). What is emitted by the voice, moreover, is vocal but not intelligible. It is more like quasi-musical sounds, as if the human voice were being plucked or played by the Spirit like a harp or lyre. Philo does not even hesitate to offer, as an appropriate description of such ecstatic experience of possession by the divine Spirit that it is madness (μανία), like a corybantic frenzy. Most prominent in Philo's descriptions, however, is the sense that "reason withdraws" or that "the mind is evicted at the arrival of the divine Spirit" (*Her.* 259, 264–65; *Q. G.* 3.9; *Mos.* 22.188–91). The focus though is not on revelation of an intelligible content to be shared with others, but on a personal spiritual experience of the divine. The "prophet" becomes "filled with inspiration" or caught up in "ecstasy, divine possession, and madness." And in a further parallel to the features that Paul objects to in the Corinthian spirituals' "tongues," Philo says that only the "wise" person can be truly "God-inspired" and "plucked and played as the vocal instrument of God." Given these similarities of expressions, it seems clear that what Paul referred to as "(speaking in) tongues" must have closely resembled what Philo discusses as prophetic ecstasy.

Judging from the distinctive language and terms that Paul qualifies in other sections of 1 Corinthians, the Corinthian spirituals' experience of ecstatic prophecy was closely related with other aspects of their spiritual transcendence. This is confirmed again and again by the appearance of parallel language in the Wisdom of Solomon and Philo. It was integrally connected with devotion to heavenly Sophia. In a striking parallel to the image used by Paul for revelatory experience of God, "Sophia, a spotless mirror of the working of God and an image of his goodness, ... passes into holy souls and makes them friends of God and prophets" (Wis 7:26–27). Similarly, according to Philo's account, the Hellenistic-Jewish mystics, the Therapeutae/trides, near Alexandria, regularly worked themselves up into ecstatic prophetic experiences in group meetings. They also had separated from their spouses in the belief that their mortal life had come to an end in their intimate relation with heavenly Sophia (*Vita Cont.* 13, 68).

Paul makes many allusions to other aspects of the Corinthian spirituals' religiosity to which he responded in earlier sections of the letter. Early in his argument he attempts to establish common ground with them by mentioning among the valued spiritual gifts the "word of wisdom" (σοφία) the "word of knowledge" (γνῶσις) on which they were so keen (12:8; in earlier sections his tone had not been so positive: see 1:17–25; 2:1–6; 8:1, 4). The statements that Paul had quoted in 8:4 were almost certainly prime examples of the spirituals' "words of *gnosis*" (as discussed in chapter 4 above).

At a key point in his argument against "tongues," Paul bluntly subverts the "mirror" image, which must also have been central in the spirituals' understanding of prophetic ecstasy. It certainly was central in

Hellenistic-Jewish devotion to heavenly Sophia. For Plato and the platonic philosophical tradition, the mirror symbolized clarity (*Tim.* 72c; Plutarch, *Is. et Os.* 384a; Apuleius, *Apol.* 14). The Hellenistic-Jewish devotion to Sophia that seems to underlie Apollos' teaching and the Corinthian spirituals' transcendence understood Sophia as "a pure emanation of the glory of the Almighty" and "a spotless mirror of the working of God" (Wis 7:25–26). Philo presupposes the same key image in discussion of the vision of God (*Leg.* 3.100–102), and links it with divine prophetic inspiration and Wisdom-possession (*Migr.* 189–91). As Philo explains, knowledge of God by the rational mind alone is only imperfect. Only when the rational mind is expelled by the divine Spirit (=Sophia), in an ecstatic prophetic experience does the full vision of God happen. In their ecstasy, which Paul calls "tongues," the spirituals must have been experiencing a full or perfect knowledge of vision of God, available through Sophia, the very mirror of God and God's workings.

That Philo's discussion of prophetic ecstasy provides a compelling analogy with the Corinthian spirituals' excitement about "tongues" becomes one more key basis for questioning the construction of Paul's Corinthian "opponents" as "already" experiencing eschatological realities, such as resurrection (with appeal typically to the people in 2 Tim 2:18). In German scholarship (particularly that built on Lutheran theological tradition and taken over by some English-speaking interpreters),[4] this is often termed ἐνθυσιασμός. Interpreters seem to have in mind the sort of "enthuasiasm" that was attributed to "fanatical" leaders in the Reformation, such as Thomas Müntzer, i.e., being caught up in the Spirit into revolutionary action. Philo, with his background in Platonic philosophical tradition of the seizure of the soul by the divine in a sort of ecstasy or vision of the divine, which Plato referred to specifically with the term ἐνθυσιασμός (being filled with the divine), was pointing to a private individual spiritual experience that had virtually no discernible social-political implications—other than a sort of quietism. The spiritual ecstasy described by Philo was clearly not operative along a historical-eschatological axis.

By analogy with the prophetic ecstasy described by Philo, the ecstatic prophecy of the Corinthian spirituals (what Paul labels "tongues") thus apparently involved a transcendent ("paranormal" in modern

---

4. See, for example, Schniewind, "Die Leugner," 273; Käsemann, "Primitive Christian Apocalyptic," 118–20; Thiselton, "Realized Eschatology at Corinth."

terms) experience of being taken over/possessed/filled by the Divine Spirit in a way that included hymn-like or prayer-like utterances (to or in the divine). Despite the apparent (possible) loss of self in seizure by the Spirit, the transcendent experience offered a kind of spiritual bliss or security for the ecstatic. The experience of union with the divine presumably meant periodic (even if temporary) transcendence of the troubles of an ordinary and perhaps oppressive and depressing life. Paul may have characterized such ecstatic experiences as "childish" and "madness," and modern psychologists may see them as "regressive." But such "regression" in spiritual or mystical form can lead to an alternative self or life rooted in the child-like creative energies that have become overlaid by oppressive social forms and "reality." A periodic "loss of self" can be the means of establishing a new self above the social realities that diminish or deny it. The Corinthian spirituals' lives could well have been transformed by such experiences. Moreover, while we have descriptions of such transcendent experiences only from the literate elite among Hellenistic Jews, such as Philo, there is no reason to imagine that such experiences would have been confined to the cultural elite.

Studies of what has become, in standard parlance, referred to as "glossolalia" in comparable modern circumstances provide suggestive parallels to the Corinthian spirituals in this connection. The recently rebuilt city of Corinth having been peopled by veterans and "surplus" population from Rome, some of whom were surely freedpersons, many of the residents of Corinth (including members of the assemblies Paul had catalyzed) had probably not been born there. Corinth was full of people with no roots or shallow roots in the city. Parallel to the disruption and displacement of the lives of people in ancient Corinth, none of the people involved in a poor charismatic group in Mexico City had been born there. The experience of glossolalia transformed their lives in a way that was not simply subjective and internal. They no longer participated in certain economic or social behavior normal in the larger society, such as dancing, drinking, smoking, or the cinema, lest they lose their capacity for "tongues." Like the Therapeutae, their mortal life had ended. "Afterward I felt strong, and all my problems were forgotten." "In the world one suffers much, but I am happy." Of special significance is the feeling of security and assurance in receiving manifestations of the Spirit, an assurance of eternal life (immortality).[5]

5. This comparative material is from Goodman, *Speaking in Tongues*, 25–27, 29, 40, 48, 87–89, 94.

Paul's Response: Intelligible Prophecy and Building Up the Community

In response to what he called the Corinthian spirituals' "(speaking in) tongues" Paul focused on the common life of the community. More than any other section of 1 Corinthians his argument about spiritual gifts emphasized social relations in the assembly rather than the vertical relation of people with God. "Manifestations of the Spirit" were a prominent and integral feature of his mission in most places, judging from the frequent references in his letters (e.g., 1 Thess 1:5-6; 5:19-22; Gal 3:2-5; Rom 12:6; 15:19; and 1 Cor 2:4-5). One might even say that the assemblies he helped found were "Pentecostal." He had urged the Thessalonians not to quench the Spirit and not to despise prophesying (1 Thess 5:19-20). Yet if we take seriously his fundamentally political language such as "the common good" and the standard political analogy of the "body," the very purpose of the Spirit's workings were political. "To each is given the manifestation of the Spirit *for the common good*" (1 Cor 12:7). Paul thus insisted that spiritual gifts be used for the "building up" of the assembly. For him that meant that any prophetic gift of the Spirit had to be made intelligible to the whole community.

Anxious that what was apparently the ecstatic prophecy of several members of the assembly be diversionary for the community, Paul attempted to persuade the Corinthians to blunt and transform the spontaneity of the spiritual's ecstatic experiences. It is possible but not clear from his argument that the excitement of the spirituals was leaving other assembly members feeling spiritually inferior (see esp. 14:6). Such is implied in his argument in 1 Cor 1-4, but it may also be only his own construction of the situation in Corinth. We can only say that the spirituals' ecstatic prophecy had been one of the issues about which the Corinthians had inquired in their letter (7:1; 8:1; 12:1). In any case, as a creative device to tame the spirituals' "zeal for the spirits" he invented a new "spiritual manifestation" for the Corinthian assembly: "interpretation of tongues" (12:10; 14:6-19). He did not forbid, indeed did not even discourage, "speaking in tongues." He rather insisted that the ecstatic utterances be transformed into some intelligible message for the assembly, to become more like a "revelation," "prophecy," "teaching," or even one of the spirituals' "statements of *gnosis*" (14:6-19, 26). To check the spontaneity of the spiritual ecstasies he insisted that they limit how many could be entertained in a gathering of the assembly and proceed one at a time, with interpretation (14:27–33). For Paul the general purpose of any communication in the assemblies was mutual exhortation and edification. Thus personal transcendence and even the mutual support of small-group intensity had to yield to the "common good" of the whole assembly. The "greater" gift, the "better way," was to contribute to the mutual caring in the community (ἀγάπη).

Paul's overall argument in response to the spiritual's ecstatic experiences, however, is broader than his attempts to limit and tame their "tongues." In his arguments earlier in 1 Corinthians, especially in chapters 5, 6, 7, and 8–10, he urged the Corinthian assembly, in effect, to form an alternative society over against the established order, attending to their own internal conflicts, not participating in the usual communal "sacrifices" by which society was held together, and limiting their interaction to recruitment. In his argument about "spiritual gifts" he insists that precisely the "manifestations of the Spirit" are what was empowering the assemblies of Christ as a new social-political reality. An international movement of local "assemblies" (note the political term for the new communities) was emerging precisely through the work of apostles, prophets, and teachers as well as through the "gifts of healing," "deeds of power," and various "forms of leadership and assistance" (12:9–10, 28). In the prophesying that would build up the assembly (14:4) Paul thus probably has in mind the kind of "revelation, prophecy," or "teaching" that has helped found and nurture the assemblies. His own ἀποκάλυψις ("revelation") had been the decisive and formative experience and "intelligible" content (gospel) in his own commissioning as an apostle (Gal 1:13–17). In such passages we can see that his conception of his own mission and of the movement of assemblies he was helping catalyze was rooted in the Jewish apocalyptic tradition of "revelations" and "prophecies" through which prophets discerned how God was fulfilling his "plan" (μυστήριον, 1 Cor 1:21; 2:6–8) for history, despite the continuing domination of the Roman empire.

Paul's use of the standard "body" metaphor for the "body-politic" exemplifies the way he envisioned the assemblies of Christ as an alternative society to the established Hellenistic-Roman order. The analogy of the body and its members with the city-state and its people of different standing and function is known particularly from Stoic political philosophy (e.g., Marcus Aurelius, *Med.* 2.1; 7.13; Epictetus, *Diatr.* 2.10.3–4; Seneca, *Ep.* 95.52). The metaphor was used by the aristocracy in Rome and other ancient city-states to manipulate the rebellious ordinary people into cooperation during times of crisis (e.g., Menepius Agrippa [fifth cent. BCE] in Livy, *Hist.* 2.32). By contrast, Paul used it in an argument against what he saw as those who were boasting of exalted spiritual status to relativize and democratize "manifestations of the Spirit." In contrast to the usual construction of the analogy to emphasize unity, Paul construed the metaphor to argue for diversity (within the unity) for the common good. The Corinthian pneumatics may also have been in favor of unity, but if the principle of unity was prophetic ecstasy, it would have been a unity of sameness in a dissolution of embodied difference. Paul advocated embodied difference, an incorporation of diversely gifted and mutually contributing, interdependent, embodied persons. Paul used the body analogy, in direct opposition to the dominant aristocratic values and hierarchical order of society, to advocate egalitarian values. He insisted that the "weaker" and "less honorable" and "less respectable" members of the community be given "greater honor" on the analogy of God's creation of the body (12:22–24). He urged mutual "care for one another" and reciprocal solidarity in suffering as well as in rejoicing (12:25–26)—which he then advocates again in the "hymn."

Paul's "hymn to love" involves an acute contradiction between the form of the hymn and the style with which he expresses it. By suddenly shifting into the lofty encomium on "love" he is mocking aristocratic culture with its focus on etherealized qualities and disembodied virtues abstracted from concrete social relations. But he uses active verbs of relationship to focus the Corinthians on the kind of concrete relations that would build up communal solidarity in the midst of the established order that, while "passing away," still wielded power. The eight verbs indicating what love does not do in 13:4b–6 all refer directly or indirectly to his criticism of their religiosity or behavior in earlier sections of the letter. In the comparison step of the encomium, 13:8–13, Paul contrasts the spirituals' most-valued "spiritual gifts" with love: "tongues," "*gnosis*," and (probably also) "prophecy."

Perhaps Paul's key rhetorical and ideological move in contrasting the spiritual's excitement over ecstatic prophecy with love is his sharp distinction between the present and the future fulfillment. This is fundamental to the way Paul thinks and to his whole gospel and mission, and it points to the basic misunderstanding between Paul and the Corinthian spirituals. The premise and point of Paul's gospel was that in the crucifixion and resurrection of Christ God had inaugurated the fulfillment of history, the delivery of the promise to Abraham of blessings to all peoples. The fulfillment would be completed, of course, only with the *parousia*, the "day of the Lord" and the final full realization of "the kingdom of God" (1 Cor 15:20–28, 50–57; 6:10). As a result of God's acts in Christ, the Spirit was active in various manifestations and Paul himself had become an eager catalyst of prophesying and other effects of the Spirit. The Corinthian spirituals, at least to Paul's mind, were focused heavily if not exclusively on the present realization of the gifts of the Spirit. They thought that they had become "nobly born," "wealthy," and "perfect/mature" (no longer "children") in their high spiritual status (1:26; 2:6—3:4; 4:8–10), and that their knowledge was full (6:12; 8:1, 4; 10:1–4). In the final step of the encomium on love Paul focuses directly on these spiritual gifts of the *pneumatikoi*. Tongues will cease, knowledge will pass away, knowledge and prophecy are imperfect. The perfect is indeed coming, in the future, and when it comes the imperfect things in which they think they have perfection, will pass away.

At the end of his arguments in 1 Cor 12 and 14, however, despite his insistence on egalitarian relations in the Corinthian assembly, Paul once again cannot resist asserting his own authority (see also the end of his argument in 1 Cor 1–4). After giving a purposely unranked list of "manifestations of the Spirit" (12:9–10), he pointedly ranks "apostles, prophets, and teachers" as most important in the "body of Christ" (12:28), leaving no doubt about who is supposed to be the key authority figure in Corinth. More ominously at the end of the whole argument (14:37–38), he places anyone who claims to be a "prophet" or a "spiritual person" on notice that they had better defer to his authority.

Note on 1 Cor 14:34–35

The highly respected rhetorical and feminist critics Elisabeth Schüssler Fiorenza and Antoinette Clark Wire, whose analyses I have followed in most matters, have in recent years argued that the statements in 1 Cor 14:34–35 form part of Paul's argument against "tongues." Text critics, however, have commonly considered them to be interpolations into the original text. These statements silencing women in the assembly that NRSV places in 14:34–35 are found in two different places in the ancient manuscripts (between 14:33 and 14:36 and after 14:40). This is a good indication that they were not originally part of the text. That they ended up in different places in the text is most easily explained by the hypothesis that they were a marginal gloss in an earlier manuscript that was later copied into the text in different places by two different copyists. In any case these sentences ordering women to keep silence intrude into the argument, either as an afterthought unrelated to the argument, if they were after v. 40, or as an interruption of the argument, if between v. 34 and v. 36. They also interrupt the conclusion to the argument in 1 Cor 12–14 that otherwise parallels the conclusion to the argument in 1 Cor 1–4, citing the situation "in all the assemblies" and then pronouncing an ominous threat (cf. 14:33, 36–38; and 4:17–21). Nothing in the intrusive statements has anything to do with the manifestations of the Spirit in the community. The "all" in 14:23–24, 31 and "each one" in 14:26 also assume that women pray and prophesy. It thus seems most likely that these statements were not part of Paul's argument.

8

No Resurrection of the Dead?

Why would some of the Corinthians have denied the resurrection of the dead? Robinson explains this as "the turgid fanaticism of those who have already risen and are living it up in glory."[1] This interpretation, deriving from 2 Tim 2:18 where Hymenaeus and Philetus are attacked for teaching that "resurrection is past already," notes that the same word "already," although lacking in 1 Cor 15:12, is found in 1 Cor 4:8 "with all its heretical overtones." Thus, by approaching the Corinthian situation through 2 Tim 2:18, Robinson and others find that what would appear to be a denial of the resurrection is instead a "fanatical form of belief in the resurrection." The other language and behavior of the Corinthians are then understood as manifestation of this "eschatological enthusiasm" or realized resurrection.

This approach, however, may involve some questionable assumptions. The word "already" in 1 Cor 4:8 may not be the key to the Corinthians' situation. There is nothing in the text of 1 Cor 4:8 to suggest that the "already" belongs to the language of the Corinthians. First Corinthians 4:8 is a sarcastic formulation. The "already" surely represents Paul's perception of the Corinthians' position. It is generally agreed in Pauline scholarship now that Paul thinks in terms of an eschatological reservation, in terms of "already . . . but not yet" (i.e., we have already died with Christ but are not yet raised with him, etc.).[2] There is, however, no reason outside

---

1. Robinson, "Kerygma and History," 33–34; similarly, Käsemann, "On the Topic," 118–20 (German orig., 272–73); both building on earlier work by von Soden and Schniewind. Note the literature cited in Conzelmann, *1 Corinthians*, 261–62 (German orig., 309–10).

2. Käsemann, "On the Topic," 128–33 (German orig., 280–83); Schoeps, *Paul*, chap. 3.

of 2 Tim 2:18 to think that the "already" belongs to the thinking of the Corinthians. Moreover, the Pastorals and the situation they address are fully two generations later than Paul's letter and the Corinthian situation he addressed. Hence it would make more sense to interpret the later text, 2 Tim 2:18, in the light of the earlier text, 1 Cor 15:12 (and 4:8).[3] The interpretation of the Corinthian denial of the resurrection of the dead as an expression of an eschatological fanaticism may, therefore, merit some skepticism, such as that shown by Conzelmann in the most recent major commentary.[4]

We have a good deal of information, however, about the Corinthian situation and the religious language and doctrines of some of the Corinthians precisely through Paul's letter in response, 1 Corinthians.[5] That there was some sort of conflict between Paul and at least some of the Corinthians is clearly indicated by his rejection of certain aspects of their statements and behavior. This is what enables us to reconstruct the Corinthians' position. Paul reacts partly by explicit rejection of, partly by ironic or sarcastic comment on their religious self-expressions. The particular language of these Corinthians can be delineated by noting those aspects to which Paul reacts negatively. The absence or relative insignificance of this language in Paul's other letters confirms that this language is that of the Corinthians—which Paul uses in his arguments against them.

First Corinthians 1–4 and 15 have received the most scholarly attention and provide the best starting point for investigation of the Corinthians' positions. From Paul's argument in 1 Cor 1:10—3:23 it is clear that the divisiveness with which Paul is so concerned is closely connected with an obsession with *sophia*.[6] In the midst of his elaborate word-play rejecting both rhetorical wisdom and soteriological wisdom he opposes *sophia* as a means of salvation in no uncertain terms: "Since,

---

3. Robinson's discussion of the Deutero-Pauline development ("Kerygma and History," 34–35), including the statement "already you have the resurrection" from *de Resurrectione*, demonstrates the plausibility of precisely this reconstruction. See also Käsemann, "On the Topic," 118–20.

4. Conzelmann, *1 Corinthians*, 261–62 (German orig., 309–10).

5. See, for example, Hurd, *Origin*.

6. So Wilckens, *Weisheit und Torheit*. But Wilckens's reconstruction of the Corinthian situation and his exegesis require the corrections of the searching and critical reviews by Koester (1961) and Colpe (1963).

in the wisdom of God, *the world did not know God through wisdom . . .*" (1:21). From Paul's ironic and even sarcastic comments in 1:26-29; 4:8-10; and 3:18 it is possible to discern some of the self-designations of these Corinthians whom Paul sees as arrogant and divisive. They apparently viewed themselves as being *wise, powerful, nobly born, filled, rich, kings* and *glorious,* as opposed to *foolish, weak, dishonored* (i.e., σοφοί, δύνατοι / ἰσχυροί, εὐγενεῖς, κεκορεσμένοι, etc., versus μωροί, ἀσθενεῖς, ἄτιμοι).

Bultmann, Wilckens, and others have suggested that Paul, after rejecting his opponents' language in 1:18—2:5, himself uses the same or similar language in 2:6-16, speaking wisdom among the τέλειοι and πνευματικοί.[7] He is not compromising, however, for he brings them up short in 3:1-4: "But I could not speak to you as πνευματικοί, . . . but only as νήπιοι . . ." We can thus discern two sets of antithetical terms used by the Corinthians: they are themselves πνευματικοί as opposed to ψυχικοί; they must claim to be τέλειοι, as opposed to mere babes, νήπιοι . . . Moreover, *solid food* and *milk* (βρῶμα and γάλα) in 3:2 are the "foods" appropriate to the perfect and babes, respectively, in the same religious language.

The contention that these terms represent the Corinthians' religious language is confirmed by the fact that most of them occur exclusively in 1 Corinthians. The few remaining terms either occur only here with the particular meaning they have here, or else their other use by Paul, in a later letter, apparently derives from his conflict with the Corinthians. Were there merely one or two terms that occurred only in 1 Cor 1-4 it would occasion no surprise. Since Paul addresses specific situations with his letters certain language will occur only in connection with those specific issues. But when a whole set of religious language not used significantly by Paul elsewhere, occurs exclusively in 1 Corinthians, it is especially noteworthy.

The terms πνευματικός, πνευματικά and the contrast πνευματικός / ψυχικός merit special attention since they play an unusually significant role in subsequent sections of 1 Corinthians (i.e. chapters 8-10, 12-14, and 15) where Paul is treating other forms of the Corinthians' religious expression.[8] The πνευματικός / ψυχικός terminology also provides a di-

---

7. Bultmann, "γνώσκω κτλ.," 709; and idem, *Faith and Understanding,* 70-72. Wilckens, *Weisheit und Torheit,* 52ff.

8. On this particular language see Pearson, *Pneumatikos-Psychikos.*

rect connection between the Corinthian views dealt with in 1 Cor 1–4 and those dealt with in 1 Cor 15. In 1 Cor 2:13 and 3:1 πνευματικός, synonymous with τέλειος, 2:6, refers to high spiritual status or ability. In contrast to the πνευματικός stands the ψυχικός, a person of lesser status or ability. This same contrast between πνευματικός and ψυχικός occurs elsewhere in Paul only in 1 Cor 15:44–46, where Paul is clearly countering the Corinthians' views of the priority of "spiritual" over "psychic." In this same context, moreover, are other sets of contrasting terms that fit the same pattern of contrast as that expressed by πνευματικός / ψυχικός and τέλειος / νήπιος, etc., in 1 Cor 1–4—that is, *heavenly/earthly, immortal/mortal, incorruptible/corruptible*. Almost all the key terminology of 1 Cor 15:44–49, 53–54 are pairs of contrasting terms. Now the simple use of contrasting pairs of terms is not unusual for Paul—for example, the basic contrast between living according to the flesh and living according to the Spirit (Gal 5:6–26; Rom 8:4ff.). But the antithetical pairs in 1 Cor 15:44–54 are peculiar to this context, or to this context and 1 Cor 2. There is thus reason to believe that we have here further language of the Corinthians whom Paul is addressing.

Can all this terminology of the Corinthians thus discerned through 1 Cor 1–4 and 15 be understood as an expression of a particular and coherent religious viewpoint? If so, how might this clarify the significance of particular statements such as the Corinthians' denial of the resurrection of the dead? Koester has called for "the most precise definition of the background of Paul's theological vocabulary" in order to delineate precisely the particular differences between Paul and his opponents.[9] In his major commentary on 1 Corinthians, Conzelmann claims that the background of Paul's opponents in 1 Corinthians cannot be established on the basis of the material available. Like previous commentators, however, Conzelmann does not pursue systematically the potential pertinence of the rich and varied comparative literature he cites. The significance of the fact that most of the Corinthians' language and themes in 1 Cor 1:26; 3:21; 4:8–10—plus those which can be discerned in 6:12; 10:23; 8:9; 10:29—can all be found in the *same* Stoic passages and in the *same* passages from Philo thus goes unnoticed.[10] A more systematic and comprehensive approach to relevant comparative material would seem

---

9. Koester, "Paul and Hellenism."

10. Indeed, Conzelmann (*1 Corinthians, passim*) cites some of these same passages at several points in his commentary, but does not draw the connections.

to be appropriate. In fact, although different particular terms of the Corinthians can be paralleled in various "Gnostic" or "Stoic" or Jewish sapiential sources, *all* of the Corinthians' language and principles, except perhaps the *pneumatikos/psychikos* contrast, are extensively paralleled in the writings of Philo of Alexandria and much of it occurs significantly in Wisdom. In Wisdom and in Philo, moreover, these terms and principles occur in close interconnection as expressions of a coherent and distinctive religiosity.

Examination of the meaning and function of this language in Wisdom and Philo, therefore, should be helpful for our understanding of the Corinthians' religious viewpoint. My intent is not necessarily to establish a source for the Corinthians' religion, although the Hellenistic-Jewish theology represented by Philo may actually be such a source, mediated through the eloquent scriptural interpreter Apollos, who taught in the Corinthian community after Paul. I am making rather a systematic comparison. Language (evidently of the Corinthians, qualified by Paul) that appears only fragmentarily in 1 Corinthians is used prominently in Wisdom and extensively in Philo. From the way in which such language is used in the latter literature, from the pattern of meaning it expresses there, we can by analogy determine more completely important facets of the Corinthians' religious viewpoint.

Distinctions in Spiritual Status

Judging from the contrast Paul makes between speaking wisdom among the τέλειοι on the one hand,[11] and the necessity of addressing the Corinthians as νήπιοι, on the other (1 Cor 2:6—3:4), it is clear that this terminology refers to a distinct difference in levels of religious status or achievement. The "solid food" and "milk," as part of this same set of terms, refer to the respective diets appropriate to these different levels.[12] This same set of terms figures prominently in Philo's writings. Although

---

11. In interpreting 1 Cor 2:6-16, Conzelmann (ibid., 60), Wilckens (*Weisheit und Torheit*, 53ff.), and others still follow Reitzenstein's derivation of τέλειος from Hellenistic mysteries, in *Mysterienreligionen*, 338-39. Critique by Pearson, *Pneumatikos-Psychikos*, 27-28. Actually, τέλειος and this whole set of terms, τέλειος / νήπιος etc., were common usage in many philosophical, ethical, and religious contexts (evidence in Delling, "τέλος κτλ.,"), including those of Hellenistic Judaism. Neither Delling nor Bertram ("νήπιος"), however, really covers the τέλειος / νήπιος terminology and the distinction of religious achievement it expresses in Philo.

12. Among NT writings, only Hebrews (5:12-14) uses this same set of terms.

he does not use the individual terms exclusively in this way, he regularly uses this whole set of terminology in various connections to express a fundamental distinction in degrees of religious achievement.[13] These texts take us directly into Philo's basically soteriological orientation, which is individualistic and highly spiritual. His primary concern is with the individual soul or mind and its attainment of perfection.

> And who else could the man in each of us be except the mind, who is to reap the benefits from what is sown or planted? But since food for *babes* is *milk*, and for the *mature (perfect)* is *cake*, there must also be as *milk-like* foods for the soul during its *infancy* the elementary education of school studies, and as foods for the *mature* instruction through *wisdom* and moderation and all virtue. (*Agric.* 8–9)

Such language is sufficiently integral to his repertory of ideas that he can freely vary the particular terms and can mix the τέλειος / νήπιος scheme with other terms of contrast to articulate these same distinctions in religious status. Philo sometimes distinguishes two, sometimes three levels of religious status. He makes a two-fold distinction between the wise and perfect as the highest religious status and the praiseworthy but lower status of the babes (νήπιοι) or practicers (ἀσκήται) or those making progress (οἱ προκόπτοντες). The three-fold distinction situates the babes or practicers in between the two extremes with the possibility of moving either direction. Sometimes Philo also speaks of a process leading toward perfection in terms of a three-stage scheme: beginnings, progress, and perfection (e.g., *Leg.* 3.159; *Agric.* 165). Actually, all of this language of the different levels of spiritual attainment forms part of Philo's more extensive exposition of what might be termed patterns of perfection, following the paradigms of the great patriarchs.[14] The curious distinctions among the τέλειοι in *Agric.* 157–65 indicates that "perfection" was a spiritual status reached and established ever more firmly in the course of

---

13. See esp. *Prob.* 160; *Congr.* 19; *Agric.* 8–9, 157–62; *Migr.* 28–33, 36–40; *Sobr.* 9–10; *Som.* 2.10–11, 234–36; *Leg.* 1.90–94. Philo certainly may have found some precedence for use of this terminology in his scriptural text (see Bertram, "νήπιος κτλ.," 915–16; Delling, "τέλος κτλ.," 72–73). Interestingly enough, however, these passages do not touch off an exposition couched in this language of religious status.

14. See, for example, *Leg.* 3.244; *Congr.* 154; *Q.E.* 3.20. Clear and sympathetic exposition by Goodenough, *By Light, Light*, chapters 5–6, 8; excellent notes in Alexandre, *De Congressu*.

life,[15] and not merely some sort of ideal "heaven" to which the soul would retire after separation from the burdensome body.

Although the τέλειος / νήπιος terminology may designate the stages along the process leading to spiritual perfection, the effect of this and related language is to make sharp distinctions between the abilities and achievements of the two levels. The perfect person is able to transcend the body and achieve perfect freedom from psychic passions, while the person making progress can only check their effects on his higher self (e.g., *Leg.* 3.131-44). The τέλειος receives perfect goods from God without having to "toil," while the child or "ascetic" acquires virtue only through toil but cannot thus reach perfection (e.g., *Leg.* 3.135). The situation of training is clearly of inferior status. The higher religious ideal is to become perfect or wise. This involves leaving behind the merely infantile and milk-like teachings to feed on Sophia herself. In doing this the wise man possesses perfect good and immortality. Indeed, the τέλειος enjoys such exalted position as to be changing ontological status, from corruptible to uncreated nature, whereas the one making progress is merely on the border between the living and the dead (*Som.* 2.234-36). The distinction between these two levels of spiritual achievement is often so sharply made that the τέλειοι and the νήπιοι are divided into two separate groups.

> There are two companies (θίασοι) . . . The noble company led by Isaac . . . absolutely disdaining to make any use of soft and milky food suited to infants and little children, and using only strong nourishment fit for grown men . . . (and) the company which is ready to give in led by Joseph . . . thoughtful for the well-being of the body also and naturally drawn in different directions . . . (*Som.* 2.10-11; cf., *Sobr.* 9-10; *Migr. Abr.* 28)

Such distinctions of spiritual status sound strikingly similar to those in Corinth that Paul blames for divisiveness in that community.

We have determined above that the terms σοφός, εὐγενής, ἔνδοξος, etc., (1 Cor 1:26; 4:8-10) represent related expressions of the Corinthians' self understanding. As with the τέλειος / νήπιος contrast, Philo displays a use of these terms analogous to that of the Corinthians. From

---

15. Philo generally uses τέλειος for the highest status or achievement, for those who enjoy fullness of knowledge and are quite aware of it, such as those who fight with the sophists in this text (*Agric.* 157-62).

this analogous usage we can more closely approach the significance of these Corinthians' self-designations.

Philo uses this same set of terms in two different senses. Noble birth, wealth, ruling, etc., in their natural and social sense he devalues, even to the point of seeing them as a liability.[16] On the other hand, he regularly uses these same terms in the sense of spiritual or true nobility, wealth, honor, kingship, etc.[17] Most of this cluster of terms can be seen together in *Virt.* 174 or *Sobr.* 55-57.

> For the wise is a friend of God rather than a servant . . . But he who has this allotment has passed beyond the bounds of human happiness. He alone is nobly born (μόνος εὐγενῆς) . . . , not only rich, but all-rich (οὐ πλούσιος, ἀλλὰ πάμπλουτος) . . . , not merely of high repute, but glorious (οὐκ ἔνδοξος, ἀλλ᾽ εὐκλεῆς), sole king (μόνος βασιλεῦς) . . . , sole freeman (μόνος ἐλεύθερος) . . .

Such language may well have been Stoic and Cynic in origin,[18] but Philo and the Jewish tradition he represents had thoroughly assimilated it into their religious modes of expression.[19]

Philo uses these terms, separately and together, to characterize the faithful Jew of the highest religious status.[20] Philo thus understands the patriarchs as types of the wise man, as spiritual models for the devout

16. *Abr.* 262-65; *Som.* 1.155.

17. Among the numerous passages, see, for example, *Rer. Div. Her.* 27, 313-14; *Virt.* 8, 174, 187-90, 216-19; *Migr.* 197; *Som.* 2.242-44; *Sacr.* 43-44; *Q.E.* 4.76. Terms in *Virt.* 174 compared with those in 1 Cor 1:26 and 4:8-10:

πλουσιώτατος	—πένηται	ἐπλουτήσατε	
ἐντιμότατος	—ἄδοξοι / ἄτιμοι	ἔνδοξοι	—ἄτιμοι
ἰσχυρότατος		ἰσχυροί / δύνατοι	—ἀσθενεῖς
φρονιμώτατος		φρόνιμοι / σοφοί	—μωροί
λογιώτατος		(1.17; 2.1-5)	
ἐπιστημονικώτατος	— ἀνεπιστήμοναι	σοφοί	

18. Use of this terminology was standard in Stoic and other philosophy; see esp. *S.V.F.* 3.85-89, 150-57; Diogenes Laertius 7.117-25.

19. On Philo's appropriation of Stoic language and ideas, see esp. Turowski, *Die Widerspiegelung*; Pohlenz, *Die Stoa*, 1:369-78; 2:180-84.

20. "Being filled" (κεκορεσμένοι, 1 Cor 4:8) is the only one of these terms that is not used regularly in connection with the others in the Philonic corpus. It sometimes has the literal sense (*Leg. All* 3.155, 183; cf. *Conf.* 154; *Mos.* 1:284), but—a further illustration of our analogy with the Corinthians—Philo uses the term also in a religious sense for becoming satiated with divine, spiritual blessings, as in *Som.* 2.149; cf. *Post.* AC 145 and *Conf.* 7.

to follow. For example, in *Q.E.* 4.76 and in *Virt.* 216-19, he presents Abraham not as an historical figure but as a true king through possession of *sophia,* as the standard of εὐγένεια (for converts!) that is attained through divine inspiration.

Philo's concern throughout these passages is the salvation or spiritual achievement of the individual soul. The wise, nobly-born, or perfect do not belong so much to a social group of people as to a generic type of soul. It is almost always stated or implied that the soul must avoid or escape matters of body and sense-perception in order to attain Sophia and the rank of σοφός or τέλειος. Benefits may accrue to the bodily existence of the σοφός from higher intercourse with the Divine (*Virt.* 216-19; *Her.* 313-15). But true wisdom, nobility, kingship, etc. are attributes of the soul secure in an exalted spiritual existence.

As with τέλειος in the τέλειος / νήπιος distinction, therefore, the designations σοφός, εὐγενῆς, βασιλεῦς, etc., refer to a spiritual elite. The contrast between those who are (spiritually) wise, nobly-born, rich, and the foolish and wicked is usually quite explicit. In many passages, there is also a contrast between the elite who possess wisdom and are thereby rich, well-born, etc., and those merely of lesser religious achievement. The antitheses to rich, honored, wise, i.e., poor, dishonored, ignorant, could be used by one who claimed the highest status in reference, not to the wicked, but to those merely of ordinary status (*Virt,* 174; cf., the Corinthian language borrowed by Paul in 1 Cor 4:10). This same passage also indicates that some of those who characterized themselves as being rich, nobly-born, strong, knowledgeable, appeared arrogant even to one (Philo) who himself valued such characterizations of the σοφός. How much more would they seem arrogant to Paul, who found strength in weakness and wisdom in the crucifixion.

Conzelmann, noting that language of rich and reigning in 1 Cor 4:8 is paralleled in a few sayings of the *Gospel of Thomas,* finds that "we have here a set combination of language and motifs which expresses the self-consciousness of the Gnostic." But these same terms plus others such as "glorious" and "noble birth" also occur prominently as characterizations of the *sophos* in Wisdom (see esp. 6:20; 7:8, 11; 8:3, 5, 10, 14, 18). More significantly still—vs. Conzelmann's and other commentators' atomistic derivation of τέλειος from Hellenistic mysteries, νήπιος from the language of education, "rich" and "reigning" from Gnosticism, etc.—not only two or three terms, but all of the Corinthians' language discerned through 1

Cor 1–4 (with the exception of πνευματικός / ψυχικός) is paralleled in Philo's writings. How much clearer it is, then, that we have here, in the Hellenistic-Jewish tradition represented by Philo, "a set combination of language and motifs which express the self-consciousness" of Hellenistic Jews who had attained the highest spiritual status. Philo and Hellenistic Jews of similar religiosity may well be "proto-Gnostic." But the label is less important than the perception that this language is an expression of an exalted level of spiritual existence—perfection, noble birth, kingship, etc.—attained by the Corinthian elite, as in Philo, through an intimate relationship with Sophia.

Sophia through Sophia

As is perhaps already evident from several of the Philo passages cited in the previous section, all of this language of exalted religious status revolves around the divine figure Sophia, the agent of salvation as well as creation. Thus it is possible to confirm and specify a judgment made a few years ago by Koester that "the first disturbance among the Corinthians arose from a Jewish Hellenist Wisdom teaching."[21] For in both Wisdom and Philo's treatises it is Sophia who provides the glorified spiritual status as perfect, nobly born, rich, etc.

In the development of the Jewish wisdom tradition well before the time of Philo *sophia* had become the focus of Jewish piety and the very content of true religion. Sophia had become personified as a divine figure and, even in that form, was viewed as identical with the substance of the Jewish Law (e.g. Sir 24). The whole section of Wis 6–10 is a poetic panegyric on her as a divine figure, the consort of God. The same passage, however, portrays how Sophia is simultaneously the consort of the *sophos*, the agent of her devotee's immortality as well as true noble birth, kingship, honor, and wealth (see esp. 8:3, 10–18).

Similarly in Philo, Sophia or her equivalent the divine Logos, besides being the mediator of creation, is especially the means and the substance of the soul's salvation. Thus, as expressed in the language of exalted spiritual status, for example, what the paradigmatic *sophos* (Abraham) receives as the substance of the divine promise of land is Sophia (e.g., *Her.* 313–14). It is by virtue of his possession of Sophia (or his possession by the divine Spirit) that Abraham the *sophos*, who has a *kingly* spirit,

---

21. Koester, "GNOMAI DIAPHOROI," 149–50.

is of the highest *nobility*, and in fact is the standard of nobility for all proselytes (e.g., *Virt.* 216–19). In an adaptation of an old Stoic slogan, the wise man is *king*, for the (true) *kingship* is really *sophia*, the learning of which requires a radical separation from the body and other empirical realities (e.g., *Migr.* 197). Similarly, true *wealth* belongs only to truly holy and divinely gifted men, and this wealth is bestowed by Sophia through the doctrines of philosophy that produces the assimilation of the soul to God (e.g., *Virt.* 8).

The way in which this language of exalted spiritual status, all centering around the divine figure Sophia, can be used in soteriological interpretation of the scriptural stories and symbols can be seen again and again throughout Philo's writings. One (abridged) example should suffice to illustrate, an interpretation of Rebecca's offering water to Jacob-Israel (Gen 24:16–20):

> For when would a mind thirsting for wisdom be filled except from Sophia of God, the never-failing spring.... She who is filled with pure *sophia* has no need of a bulky leather vessel. For she who loves bodiless things has learned to strip off the skin, that is the body, completely through the use of reason.... The lover of knowledge, upon seeing that she draws the various forms of knowledge from Sophia, the divine spring, runs.... She immediately offers him the spring of Sophia and exhorts him to take a deep draught, calling him "lord." This is that great doctrine that only the wise man is free and a ruler.... (And) her saying "drink" shows that she was making manifest the divine wealth, which has been poured forth for all to enjoy who are worthy and able to do so. (*Post.* 136–39; cf. the context of 124–39)

This passage along with the parallel in *Fug.* 177–202 also illustrates how Philo repeats the same particular interpretations of given scriptural symbols of stories with slight variations at various points in his writings. This suggests that such passages represent standard religious teachings for Philo and, probably, the particular Hellenistic-Jewish tradition on which he draws. That is, for this tradition of Hellenistic Judaism, salvation or true religion is expressed in terms of the exalted spiritual status (as wealthy, kingly, perfect) provided by heavenly Sophia. It is just such a mode of expression that can illuminate the religiosity of the Corinthians, whose claim to be perfect, nobly born, rich, etc., appears to be connected with their obsession with Sophia.

Other treatments of the Philonic understanding of Sophia, especially as it bears on 1 Corinthians, have tended to focus on one particular image of Sophia. Wilckens, for example, happens to pick the only image, "the royal way," which could possibly fit the scheme of the Wisdom-myth, which is another form of the Gnostic Redeemer-myth in his and others' work.[22] Other treatments have focused on the symbolism of light, Sophia being God's archetypal luminary.[23] These however, are only two among several principal images for Sophia in Philo. And some of these other images are both more prominent in Philo and more relevant perhaps to the Corinthian situation. Sophia is also portrayed as the dwelling place of the wise (*Migr.* 28–30, 45–56; *Her.* 313–15; *Q.G.* 4.46–47 ; *Q.E.* 2.39), and as the divine spring (*Fug.* 177–202; *Post.* 124–39) and a spiritual banquet (*Som.* 1.47–51, 198–200; *Fug.* 137–38, 166, 167; *Congr.* 172–74) from which the *sophoi* or *teleioi* obtain divine nourishment or teaching.

Most important for the light it may shed on the Corinthian situation, however, is the effect of all these various images considered together and in conjunction, as they are actually used by Philo. For Philo, just as in Wisdom, the divine figure Sophia (or its equivalent, the Logos) has rather comprehensive functions. Soteriologically all depends and focuses on Sophia. Sophia is not only the content and goal of salvation, but the means of salvation as well. In all of the principal Philonic symbolism expressing the soteriological relationship, the basic pattern is essentially the same: the *sophos/teleios* knows or possesses *sophia* by means of *sophia*. Philo even states this pattern explicitly in several "by Sophia, Sophia" passages such as *Migr.* 39; *Her.* 98, and *Q.G.* 4.101: thus the wise person who desires wisdom "God has entirely approved and *has made perfect in the knowledge of Sophia by his Sophia.*" In addressing the Corinthians Paul would appear to be rejecting just this understanding of religion centered in Sophia (1 Cor 1:21).

The central and comprehensive soteriological function of Sophia also determines the *difference* in religious status in this Hellenistic-

---

22. Wilckens, *Weisheit und Torheit*, 139–59; cf. his similarly restricted focus in his article "σοφία κτλ."

23. On Sophia as "Light" see esp. Wlosok, *Laktanz*, 77–114; and Klein, *Die Lichtterminologie*, 11–79; but for a more circumspect treatment of Sophia as light in relation to other soteriological images of Sophia, see Goodenough, *By Light, Light*, chapter 4, esp. 157, 161, 170, 173–74; see also the discussion of several of these principal images in Mack, *Logos und Sophia*, part II.

Jewish tradition. For Sophia assumes a relationship to those in lower status distinctly different from her relationship with the wise and perfect. The fools, of course have no relationship with Sophia—that is precisely their problem (*Migr.* 36–40). As for the children, the ascetics who are merely at the elementary stage, Sophia may be the goal soteriologically. But they are incapable of the intimate relationship with Sophia enjoyed by the nobly born and perfect. The children are ready only for the "milk-like" teachings of the "school studies" in contrast with the true knowledge and wisdom enjoyed by the perfect. To shift the image somewhat, for the babes or practicers Sophia (Logos) is only the teacher, whereas the wise and truly rich persons possess or are married to Sophia/Logos (e.g., *Leg.* 3.1ff.; cf. 207). It is quite conceivable that those who claimed to have reached the highest spiritual status, such as apparently the Corinthians Paul addresses in 1:26-27; 2:6—3:4; and 4:8-10, could appear arrogant, and it is clear that their devotion to Sophia could have a seriously divisive effect on the community.

This language of exalted religious status and spiritual perfection provided by Sophia, moreover, cannot be understood as merely allegorical rhetoric. Philo, and apparently the Corinthians as well, were expressing their own religious experience in such language. Indeed Philo sees in the intimate relation with Sophia a profound effect on the soul in both an ethical and soteriological sense. When Sophia/Logos dwells in the soul it is ethically pure, so sinless, in fact, that it will no longer commit even an unintentional offense (*Fug.* 117). Such a soul, being possessed of the pure divine Sophia, no longer encounters the ensnaring pleasures of the body and other "false messengers" (*Migr.* 28-29; *Quod Deus* 1-3). Thus Sophia also produces a firm security. Although harmful and destructive influences on the soul only diminish in the childlike stage of progress, they cease altogether for the perfect (*Som.* 2.236). The cloud of defense and salvation (from Exod 14:20; that is, the Logos) showers on fertile minds drops of *sophia* that is naturally immune from all evil, while it destroys those barren of knowledge with a deluge (*Her.* 203-4). Such is the spiritual security of the true *sophos* that, free of any corrupting mixture and filled with inspiration from heaven above, he enjoys immortality in the possession of Sophia (e.g., *Fug.* 97, 66–168; *Her.* 183–84). One cannot help but think of the Corinthians who, confident in their *sophia* and *gnosis* (1 Cor 8), thought that "all things are possible for me" (6:12; 10:23), the Corinthians whom Paul reminds of their vulnerability (10:1–13) despite their possession of the "spiritual food" and "spiritual drink" and "spiritual Rock."²⁴

Heavenly "Anthropos" vs. Earthly "Anthropos"

It has become a standard observation that Philo's contrast between the οὐράνιος ἄνθρωπος and the γήϊνος ἄνθρωπος is relevant to 1 Cor 15:44-54. Much of this discussion of the relevance of Philo's heavenly "anthropos" to the Corinthian situation has been carried on according to concepts imposed on the material by interpreters influenced by the history of religions approach. Scholars such as Brandenburger have interpreted Philo's heavenly "anthropos" to be a reference to a "Primal Man."²⁵ As Colpe has pointed out, however, the concept of (a Gnostic or proto-Gnostic) *Urmensch* is a scholarly construct used to cover a considerable variety of material; it is historically imprecise, and is inconsistently applied by modern scholars.²⁶ The notion of an *Urmensch* is hardly appropriate to Philo's passages on the heavenly "anthropos"²⁷ and has little interpretative value for any Philonic material, as I have argued elsewhere.²⁸

If we look more carefully at Philo's discussions of the contrast between the heavenly "anthropos" and the earthly "anthropos," however, we find something very similar to the distinction of spiritual status expressed in the τέλειος / νήπιος terminology. Since this hardly fits with

24. The principal symbols from the Exodus narrative—such as the cloud, the manna, the water from the rock, and the rock—are taken as symbols of Sophia throughout Philo's writings; see p. 152 below and the references there.

25. Brandenburger, *Adam und Christus*, 117-31.

26. Colpe, *Die religionsgeschichtliche Schule*, 171ff.; Conzelmann, *1 Corinthians*, 284-86, agrees but continues to use the concept anyway.

27. The article by Wedderburn ("Philo's 'Heavenly Man'") is a lengthy and detailed refutation of Brandenburger's and others' understanding of the "Heavenly Man" in Philo according to the model of the Gnostic Redeemer-Myth. Most of his principal critical points agree basically with the arguments I made in some short sections of my dissertation, "Paul and the *Pneumatikoi*," 11-13, esp. note 30, and 323-29, 333-44. The very Philonic texts, however, which he rightly rejects (310-11) as inappropriate bases for the Redeemer-Myth interpretation are the most relevant to the Corinthian situation. Moreover, in his well-taken critique of synthesizing interpretations of Philo, he is perhaps overly zealous in placing Philonic material and levels of meaning into separate categories—warning us (308-9) not to make precisely the jumps from level to level that Philo himself makes regularly. The problematic nature of the attempt to apply the "Primal Man" conceptuality to Philonic material is, of course, somewhat broader than the scope of Wedderburn's article is designed to cover.

28. See chapter 1 above.

the conceptual apparatus with which the two "anthropoi" contrast in Philo has usually been approached—i.e., the Adam/Christ typology or the *Urmensch*—it would be well to present the case step by step.

1. Philo presents a fundamental and apparently standard distinction between two "anthropoi" or two types of mankind, heavenly and earthly. The distinction is dominated by the contrast between the "anthropos" *made after the Image* of God and the one *moulded* out of *earth*.[29] The basic terminology of the contrast thus can be seen to depend on Philo's scriptural text of Gen 1:26–27 and 2:7 respectively.[30] Apparently Philo and his predecessors had found in the Biblical creation account two distinct types of mankind. These had become standard concepts in Philo's theology and Biblical interpretation. Philo's use of the contrast is not always consistent—one of the principal texts often referred to in relation to 1 Cor 15, *Op.* 134, being a special case, different from his usual usage.[31] But the basic distinction lies between the heavenly "anthropos" who is by nature incorruptible (ἄφθαρτος) and who, being made after the Image of God (i.e., the Logos or Sophia), is altogether without share in corruptible and earthly essence, and the earthly "anthropos" who is by nature mortal (θνητός), being compacted out of matter called clay (χοῦν; see esp., *Leg.* 1.31). In comparison with 1 Cor 15:45–54 we find in these Philonic discussions of the two types of mankind all of the principal terminology paralleled, with the exception of the antithesis of "spiritual" and "psychic"—that is, all of the other pairs of antithesis (corruptible vs. incorruptible, mortal vs. immortal, earthly vs. heavenly) as well as the "image" motif. Moreover, as evident in 1 Cor 15:45, the distinction is based in interpretation of the creation account, Gen 2:7 in particular.

2. It is evident both in 1 Cor 15:46–47 and in Philo that the relative priority of the heavenly "anthropos" and the earthly "anthropos" is a central issue. Commentators usually note that Philo describes the

---

29. See *Op.* 134; *Leg.* 1.31, 53, 88–89, 90–95; 2.4; *Plant.* 44; *Q.G.* 1.4, 8; 2.56; *Q.E.* 2.46; *Her.* 57. The "heavenly" vs. "earthly" occurs in *Leg.* 1.31 and 90–95, and the "two types of man" in *Leg.* 1.31 and 2.4.

30. This distinction, moreover, is used by Philo primarily in interpreting a number of enigmas perceived in the text of Genesis 1 and 2. Philo's writings contain several standard interpretations or uses of (parts of) Gen 1:26–27 and/or 2:7, some of which are discussed by Jervell, *Imago Dei*, 52–70.

31. So also Jervell, *Imago Dei*, 53. To focus on *Op.* 134–35 is not helpful, therefore, either for reconstructing Philo's usual understanding of the contrast or for elucidating the Corinthian situation.

heavenly "anthropos" explicitly as having come into existence *earlier* (πρότερον, *Mund.* 134) and the figure molded from earth as the *second* (ὁ δεύτερος ἄνθρωπος, *Leg.* 2.4-5). Although Conzelmann is more cautious in his recent commentary, Cullmann articulates the more usual exegetical conclusion regarding Paul's polemical statements in 1 Cor 15:46-47: "Philo's order must be just reversed."[32] But to think of 1 Cor 15:46-47 as a matter of Paul *just reversing* Philo's order oversimplifies the Corinthian situation. The very terms that seem so striking, the πρότερον and the δεύτερος ἄνθρωπος, are almost incidental to the more fundamental contrast Philo is making.[33] In the sequence of the narrative the heavenly may have come first and the earthly second. But Philo is concerned to explain a more fundamental sense of priority. Philo is asserting the ontological priority of the heavenly "anthropos" to the earthly "anthropos," the priority in origin and value by nature in the universe ordered by God.[34] This is a different *kind* of priority from the historical-eschatological pattern of thinking that Paul insists upon in 1 Cor 15. For Philo and those who thought similarly, the whole temporal-historical mode of priority was inferior, hence should not be confused with the ontological and soteriological priority of the heavenly type of mankind over the earthly type.[35]

3. Moreover, Philo's expositions of the two-"anthropoi" symbolism indicates that he is interested not so much in the priority of one individual figure over another individual figure, but in the superiority of one type or kind of mankind over another type.[36] In his usual exposition of the heavenly and earthly "anthropoi" Philo understands "anthropos" as

32. Cullmann, *Christology,* 168-69; cf. Conzelmann, *1 Corinthians,* 284-87.

33. In fact, except for *Op.* 134 and *Leg.* 2.4-55, Philo does not use such labels.

34. An explicit statement of Philo's ontologically grounded value priorities appears in *Post.* 62: "Nature wrought soul elder than body, . . . and determines precedence not by time but by worth."

35. Scroggs, (*Last Adam,* 122) perceives that Philo does not emphasize the temporal priority of the heavenly "anthropos" to the earthly "anthropos." But his claim that this temporal priority "would be essential to the argument that Paul is opposing Philo (or a similar position) in 1 Cor. 15:46" is based on the unwarranted assumption that the Corinthians opposed must think along the same lines as Paul, lines of temporal priority.

36. My purpose here, to discern Philo's usual understanding of the "two-men" contrast, is quite different from Wedderburn's enterprise of demonstrating how various Philonic texts do not fit the concept of the Gnostic redeemer or "heavenly anthropos-figure," which forms the determining focus of his article ("Philo's 'Heavenly Man'"), for example 311-12.

referring to "mind" the highest part of the soul.[37] He finds accordingly that the heavenly "anthropos" and the earthly "anthropos" refer to two different kinds of mind: the *mind* existing *after the Image* vs. the *earthborn and body-loving mind* (esp. *Leg.* 1.31-33; 2.4-5; also *Leg.* 1.53ff., 88-89, 90ff.; *Plant.* 441). The earthly mind, clearly inferior in ontological status, is caught in conjunction with earthly and bodily circumstances. It would be hopelessly corruptible (φθαρτός) were it not for God's in-breathing (Gen 2:7b) of the power of real life, which makes the soul intelligent (*Leg.* 1.32).[38] The earthly mind is given the power to win immortality but is also played upon by forces drawing it in the opposite direction (*Plant.* 45).

4. The picture here of the earthly "anthropos" as the mind caught in the middle between immortality and death leads us directly to the primary religious significance of the "two man" concept in Philo, seen best perhaps in *Leg.* 1.53-55 and 90-94. The moulded mind has received only the capacity to apprehend well. But the pure heavenly mind has been additionally endowed with the ability to persevere in virtue and to retain divine teachings. In these passages the distinction between the "anthropos" created after the Image and the moulded "anthropos" is really a qualitative distinction between people of two different levels of religious-ethical ability and achievement.

Indeed, in *Leg.* 1.90-94 Philo expresses the contrast between the heavenly and earthly man in terms of his general distinctions of two and three levels of religious status.[39] Philo interprets the name "Adam" (Gen

---

37. Hamerton-Kelly (*Pre-existence,* 138-39) expresses surprise that Philo speaks of an "earthly mind." But Philo regularly reads ἄνθρωπος as "the true human" in the person or the mind. See the plethora of references in Wedderburn, "Philo's 'Heavenly Man,'" 310 n. 6.

38. This provides only the potential for attaining immortality, however, and only points up the earthly mind's continuing need for divine aid. This passage might appear to contradict Philo's more usual application of the inbreathing by the divine Spirit to the higher type of "anthropos," whereby the inbreathing of the πνεῦμα (Gen 2:7b) is parallel to the creation "after the Image" in Gen 1:26-27. This is not the case. Indeed, when Philo attempts to explain the awkward occurrence of the word "breath" (πνοή) in Gen 2:7b he resorts to the two kinds of "anthropos"—and further clarifies the difference in the endowment of the two types: the mind after the Image partakes of something less substantial (*Leg.* 1.42).

39. For other passages relevant to the substance of Philo's thought here, see, e.g., *Congr.* 128-29; *Her.* 45-57; *Som.* 1.150-52; 2.10-11; cf. *Q.E.* 1.51; 4.157; cf. further, on the three-fold distinction of religious status, *Gig.* 58ff. where the terminology is different

2:16–17) as the moulded man: "Call him 'earth,'"⁴⁰ and thus the earthly and corruptible mind, for the mind after the Image is not earthly but heavenly. In relation to the "command" given Adam comes the following distinction. Prohibitions instead of commands must be given to the wicked. There is of course no need to give either prohibitions or exhortations to the *perfect* man (τέλειος) who is after the Image, who possesses Virtue (= Sophia) innately, being self-learned. The child (νήπιος), however, requires exhortation and teaching, without which he could not come by wisdom. For this reason God commands and exhorts the earthly mind, who is neither bad nor good but neutral. In this passage, Philo merges or identifies the two-men contrast with the standard distinction in levels of religious status. The heavenly "anthropos" and the earthly "anthropos" are the same, respectively, as the τέλειος and the νήπιος.

It thus emerges from a closer examination of Philonic texts that the primary function of the contrast between the heavenly "anthropos" and the earthly "anthropos" is to symbolize the different classes of people, to serve as paradigms or prototypes of two different levels of religious-ethical ability or status. The variations of application and emphasis in Philo's use of this idea all seem to revolve around the basic distinction between the religious type that has transcendent spiritual ability or status and the type of lesser endowment for whom salvation is a struggle against bodily attachment and earthly influence. Throughout Philo's several expositions of the two "anthropoi" he fuses into this one pair of symbols what are often for other thinkers separate questions of ontological origin, moral behavior, and soteriological destiny.

Most significant, finally, for the light it sheds on the Corinthians' language and theology is that this "two-men" symbolism, along with the related sets of antitheses, expresses virtually the same distinction as that articulated in the terminology of different levels of spiritual status, the "perfect vs. children" etc. Far from being evidence of some sort of proto-Gnostic *Urmensch,* the symbolism of the heavenly "anthropos," in the

---

but the basic distinctions and pattern of thinking remain consistent.

40. "Adam," taken by himself, means for Philo ὁ γήινος νοῦς (cf. *Leg.* 1.90ff.; *Plant.* 46; *Her.* 52–53). Adam in connection with Eve means "mind" in distinction from sense-perception or the senses and the "mind" as opposed to the temptations of the senses and pleasure symbolized by the serpent (cf. esp. *Leg.* 3.49–66). When Philo wants to refer to the first-created, empirical human he uses variations of the phrase ὁ πρῶτος καὶ γήγενης ἄνθρωπος . . . (*Op.* 79, 136–56; *Plant.* 34; *Mut. Nom.* 64; etc.).

contrast with the earthly "anthropos," is similar to and really a part of the symbolism and theology of differential religious endowment that is so central in Philo's treatises—and that, as we have seen, Paul addresses in 1 Cor 1–4. It thus also becomes clear what the Corinthians mean by their highly distinctive terminology, the πνευματικός vs. the ψυχικός, and how this terminology can appear parallel both to the contrast between the perfect and the children (1 Cor 2:6—3:4) and to the contrast between the heavenly and earthly types of mankind (1 Cor 15:45–50).[41]

5. A few other Philonic passages, however, enable us to extend the argument a step or two to further elucidate the religious position of the Corinthians that Paul is attempting to counteract. Q.G. 2.56 is yet another illustration of how the language of exalted spiritual status is parallel and synonymous with the symbolism of the paradigmatic "anthropos" after the Image vs. the earthly "anthropos." But more importantly, this passage illustrates the general typological pattern that Philo is following, that is: as the prototype or paradigm, so those who belong to that type or paradigm. This is exhibited, for example, when Philo exhorts the souls of intelligent people to follow the paradigm of the "anthropos" made after the Image. This same typology is attested in other passages as well when the lower prototype, "the earthly mind called Adam," is contrasted with those who belong to the higher type, "the truly alive who have Sophia for their mother" (*Her.* 52–53), or "the people endowed with sight" (*Plant.* 44–46). To state in more complete form the pattern of types and prototypes that Philo articulates in such passages: those who are perfect, endowed with sight, immortal, etc., belong to the heavenly type of mankind that is made after the Image, whereas those who are still subject to corruptible influence of the body and in need of instruction, etc., belong to the earthly type of mankind.

If the Corinthians were thinking similarly to Philo, then the statement in 1 Cor 15:48 taken by itself would appear to be another Corinthian principle (οἷος ὁ χοϊκός, τοιοῦτοι καὶ οἱ χοικοι, καὶ οἷος ὁ ἐπουράνιος τοιοῦτοι καὶ οἱ ἐπουράνιοι) borrowed and qualified by Paul, especially

---

41. The use of Philo as an analogy for the Corinthians becomes more complicated in dealing with this terminology. Since the πνευματικὸς / ψυχικός contrast does not occur in Philo and other contemporary Hellenistic-Jewish literature, the argument must be couched in terms of a similarity of thought-patterns and not in terms of a derivation of these particular words, contra Pearson, *Pneumatikos–Psychikos*, 18–20; cf. Brandenburger, *Fleisch und Geist*, esp. 26–41; this is attempted in Horsley, "Paul and the *Pneumatikoi*"; see also chap. 1 above.

in the immediately following statement that insists on a historical-eschatological difference between two particular men, as opposed to an ontological division between two different kinds of humanity.

6. In at least some passages Philo indicates that the distinction between types of people or levels of spiritual endowment symbolized by the "two man" contrast refers to actual Jewish religious communities. In Q.E. 2.46, for example, he fuses the contrast between the paradigmatic heavenly "anthropos" and earthly "anthropos" with a distinction between the type of prophetic people who, as symbolized by Moses, become initiates into the divine mysteries (cf., *Gig.* 53–55; and 1 Cor 14:37) on the one hand, and the "contemplative race" (cf. Q.E. 2.43) or the faithful adherents of the Jewish religious communities in general, on the other. The latter, the ordinary folk, have indeed a considerable value to God. Their election is compared with the ordering of the world and the creation of the earth-born moulded "anthropos"—to all of which is assigned the symbolic number "6." But the calling above of the prophetic type, the symbol for which, Moses, is fused with the heavenly "anthropos," is declared to be an origin (and destiny) superior to that of the moulded figure's corruptible mixture with the body and earth, and is rather ethereal and incorporeal, in accord with the ever-virginal Hebdomad, i.e., Sophia/Logos.[42]

7. As suggested by this last, numerological symbol, the same passage, Q.E. 2.46, besides its specifications of sociological references, evidences yet another crucial connection within all this religious language, and one highly pertinent to the Corinthian situation. That is, just as those of the higher type in *Her.* 52–53 have "Sophia for their mother" so the "calling above" and the origin of the "prophetic type," the spiritual elite symbolized by the paradigmatic heavenly "anthropos," is in accord with Sophia.

From the more elaborate (and analogous) use of the same paradigmatic symbols and related terminology in Philo, therefore, it is possible to perceive how the Corinthians, in the contrast between the heavenly "anthropos" and the earthly "anthropos," conceived of themselves as enjoying an extraordinary level of spiritual existence. In contrast to the ordinary believers who were still caught in conflict with bodily and earthly influences, according to the prototypical earthly "anthropos," they had attained, through their intimate relation with Sophia, the ulti-

---

42. The symbolism of the Hebdomad was important in Philo and in other Hellenistic Judaism, e.g. Aristobulus in Eusebius, *Praep. Ev.* 9.667a–668b.

mate, ethereal level of immortality, according to the type of incorruptible heavenly "anthropos."

The Naked and the Dead—Denial of the Resurrection

With the further aid of the Philonic analogy it is possible to discern also how the Corinthians' denial of the resurrection of the dead is integrally related to their attainment of exalted spiritual status and their devotion to Sophia. From the material already noted it is clear that the Philonic orientation that divides and values reality according to an opposition between earthly and heavenly, mortal and immortal, corruptible and incorruptible, involves a corresponding dualism in its understanding of human nature. Indeed Philo's anthropology is governed by the dualism of the naked and the dead, that is, the immortal soul and the mortal body.[43] The soul or mind is viewed as the true self, "the true human," the human within the human, the better within the worse, the immortal within the mortal (*Congr.* 97; *Op.* 135). This also entails a negative attitude toward the body and its drives, as expressed repeatedly in the writings of this Hellenistic-Jewish tradition. For the body is by nature

> wicked and a plotter against the soul, it is a corpse and always a dead thing.... When, O soul, will you fully realize yourself to be a corpsebearer? Will it not be when you are perfected (τελειωθῇς)? (*Leg.* 3.69-76; cf., *Som.* 1.148)

In Philo's parlance, "dead" and the body are virtually synonymous.[44] If anything the body is alien and a burden, "weighing down the soul" (Wis 9:15). Such an attitude could hardly be receptive to the notion of the *resurrection* of the *dead*. "For a corpse (νεκρός) may not come into God's presence" (*Fug.* 59).

Indeed, the resurrection of the dead would have little or no point. According to such an orientation "dead" in the literal sense would mean the final separation of the soul from the body (*Leg.* 1.105; cf., Plato,

---

43. See further, Goodenough, "Philo on Immortality"; cf. Wolfson, *Philo* I, 395-413; and Brandenburger, *Fleisch und Geist*, 140-54.

44. In his view of the body, over against the soul or mind, as *dead*, Philo shares the common Hellenistic understanding; concise treatment by Bultmann, "θάνατος κτλ.," 11-13; idem, "νεκρός κτλ." 892.

Phaedo 64C).⁴⁵ Thus, Philo's description of Abraham as *sophos*, especially his "kingship," includes the idea that

> death is not the extinction of the soul but its separation and detachment from the body and its return to the place whence it came. (*Abr.* 255-76)

Philo frequently expresses his doctrine of the soul's immortality (*Som.* 1.181) in terms of the soul, whose proper home is heaven (or *sophia*), dwelling temporarily in bodily, earthly reality.⁴⁶ The *sophos* thus dwells in incorporeal wisdom but only sojourns in the strange, sensible body, and the proper treatment for the body is to alienate oneself from it (see esp. *Conf.* 77-82).⁴⁷ The ideal state of the soul in its immortality is to be *naked* of the body and earthly matters. Indeed, Paul's formulation in 1 Cor 15:53-54 of the mortal "putting on" immortality, etc., can be seen to be a direct contrast with or reversal of this ideal state of the soul according to the kind of Hellenistic-Jewish religiosity represented by Philo. For the latter speaks explicitly of Moses and other scriptural paradigms of soul-nakedness, which is the height of soteriological attainment, as leaving or taking off the body and mortal-corruptible things, in order to attain their pure, *naked* immortality (*Gig.* 53ff.; *Ebr.* 99-101; *Fug.* 58-59).⁴⁸

This anthropological dualism, moreover, as an integral part of fundamental ontological and soteriological contrasts (the contrasts found also in 1 Cor 15:44ff.),⁴⁹ is also used together with the characterization of the exalted spiritual status achieved through intimacy with Sophia discussed above. For example, in *Deus Imm.* 148-51 the soul of every

---

45. Philo, of course, also uses "death" in the figurative sense. When writing figuratively and ethically of death and immortality, however, he is never far from his fundamental cosmological antithesis; in *Leg.* 1.105ff. and *Fug.* 55ff., for example, he gradually reverts to the body-soul, earth-heaven dichotomy.

46. Compare the more extensive discussion of this theme by Brandenburger, *Fleisch und Geist*, 154-71.

47. Note also the language of "dust" and "clay" in *Conf.* 79; cf. 1 Cor 15:47-49. Compare further *Her.* 271-74; *Q.G.* 3.10; *Agric.* 65-66.

48. Philo's treatment of Nadab and Abihu in *Fug.* 58-59 brings out another important aspect of his understanding of death, immortality, etc. He shares with Wis 2:23—3:4 the notion that the wise or righteous only seem to have died. The context in Wisdom is noteworthy because the pattern of thought there is so similar to the Philonic pattern that we have been examining. Philo interprets Cain's fratricide in a similar manner, *Det.* 46-49; cf. *Virt.* 67 and *Q.G.* 1.76; cf. also Wis 10:3.

49. For this terminology and this pattern of thinking see, e.g., *Her.* 239 and *Gig.* 12ff.

disciple of Moses, having learned the basic principles of Sophia, is filled with a vision of genuine and incorruptible values and abandons transient "earthly" things; this concentration on the true wealth, noble birth, and glory manifests a celestial and heavenly soul, which has left the region of the earth and dwells with divine natures. Again, much of this same language found in 1 Cor 15 as well as generally in Philo and in Wis 2–3 is condensed in one sentence, *Her.* 2.76: The good man is represented not as dying, but as departing, in order to show that the type of the fully purified soul is unquenchable and immortal, heavenly in its destiny, and does not undergo dissolution and corruption, which death appears to bring.

Most interesting in possible connection with the alleged arrogance of the Corinthians (see 1 Cor 3:1–3, 18; 4:5, 6, 8–13, 18–19) is Philo's division between the wise and the fools in *Q.G.* 4.74. Here the wise man who is a sojourner in the body, while his own country lies in heaven, cannot live with or be a fellow-citizen with the foolish man, since his sovereign mind does not mix with anything else. Thus the Corinthians' denial of the resurrection of the dead would not only be appropriate to their sense of liberation from bodily and earthly realities but would also be another expression of a spiritual elitism that could have quite divisive effects in a religious community.

Gnosis, The Spiritual Rock, Prophetic Ecstasy

The Corinthians' terms and principles behind other sections of 1 Corinthians are similarly paralleled in Wisdom and Philo, and the analogy between the Corinthians and this particular tradition of Hellenistic Judaism can be extended. In contrast with Sophia and the heavenly "anthropos," this other language of the Corinthians has received less attention and has been subject of fewer hypotheses concerning its religious background. Hence it will suffice, perhaps, merely to sketch the remaining features of the analogy.

1. Paul's strong qualification in 1 Cor 6:12 and again in 10:23 of the same statement indicates that "all things are possible (permissible/lawful) for me" must have been a Corinthians slogan. Stoic material is rich and seductive for an approach that looks only for parallel language. Such Stoic language, however, judging from Philo's writings, had long since worked its way into Hellenistic-Jewish religion. Thus in *Every Good Man Is Free* (*Quod omni Probus Liber sit*), Philo expounds at length on a favorite doc-

trine of the Stoics "that only the wise man is free" (see esp. *Prob.* 21-22, 41, 59-61). Moreover, he produces an argument that is much closer in language to the Corinthians' slogan of 1 Cor 6:12 and 10:23 than are any of the Stoic texts:

> (The wise or good person) will have the power to do anything and to live as he wishes; the one for whom these things are possible must be free (ᾧ δὲ ταῦτ' ἔξεστιν, ἐλεύθερος ἂν εἴη). (*Prob.* 59)

2. Similarly, Paul's strong qualification of "quoted" principles at the beginning of 1 Cor 8 indicate that "we all possess knowledge," "an idol has no real existence," and "there is no God but one" are all theological principles of the Corinthians. Now *gnosis* in Philo and Wisdom is given by God or his consort Sophia to people (souls) who are thereby constituted as wise and possess immortality and a share in divine power (see, e.g., Wis 7:17; 10:10; 15:2-3; *Leg.* 3.46-48, 126; *Quod Deus* 143).[50] *Gnosis* can be understood as the particular religious and theological *content* of *sophia*, i.e., the divine teachings (supposedly derived) from the Scripture (= Sophia). Thus, theological principles similar to those of the Corinthians cited by Paul could be part of the content of the *gnosis*. For Philo, "That God is One . . ." is the lesson Moses continually teaches in the Laws (e.g., *Spec. Leg.* 1.30) and is the second major principle in a five-part summary of doctrine (*Op.* 170-72; cf., *Conf.* 170-71).[51] Knowledge of God means knowing that other gods do not exist, that idols are mere foolishness; knowing God means righteousness and immortality (Wis 13:1; 14:22; *Decal.* 7-8; etc.).[52]

---

50. Since Goodenough's *By Light, Light,* the "subjective element of profound religious knowledge" in Philo's writings has been more adequately acknowledged. See also Jonas, *Gnosis und spätantker Geist,* 99-121; and idem, *Gnostic Religion,* 278-81.

51. See also Josephus, *Ant.* 3.81. There were a number of different traditional Jewish and pagan polemics against idols in the contemporary world. In comparison with the Corinthians' connection of the critique of idols with possession of *gnosis* and the principle that "God is one" it is noteworthy that Philo and Wisdom concentrate their critique of false gods and idols around an absolute antithesis between ignorance of God and *gnosis* of God.

52. Philo provides an interesting comparison with the Corinthians' situation of "conversion" of proselytes into the true religion (wisdom). In Philo the conversion or "transposition" from ignorance to knowledge takes place by learning doctrine about God versus false gods (*Spec. Leg.* 1.15-30; *Virt.* 179-80). As already noted above, as a paradigm of this conversion, Abraham is "the standard of nobility for all proselytes" (*Virt.* 219 [212-19]).

3. Paul's strong reaction in 1 Cor 10:5–13 to the experience of "our fathers" mentioned in 10:1–4 suggests that not only the "spiritual food," the "spiritual drink," and the "spiritual rock" but also the baptism into Moses in the cloud and the sea were some sort of quasi-magical soteriological symbols for the Corinthians being addressed. In interpreting the exodus story for deeper religious meaning Philo was building on a Jewish wisdom tradition that had already identified the "pillar of cloud" as Sophia (Sir 24:4, and esp. Wis 10:17). Philo just assumed, in his interpretations, that the central symbols of the story are really referring to the divine Sophia (Logos). Thus the *cloud* (*Mos.* 1.166; cf., Wis 10:17–18), the *manna* as spiritual food and the *water* (from the rock combined with the waters at Marah and Elim) as spiritual drink (*Sacr.* 86; *Her.* 191, 79; *Fug.* 137–39; *Leg.* 3.162–73), and the *rock* (*Leg.* 2.86; *Det.* 115–17; *Som.* 2.221–22) are all understood as symbolizations of Sophia in her soteriological relation to *the wise*. Such interpretations augment and accord entirely with the symbolization of Sophia as the divine spring and spiritual Banquet that were noted on pp. 137–41 above. It should be recalled, in connection with what Paul says in response to the Corinthians in 1 Cor 10:5–13, that the effect of Sophia on the *sophos* is an ethical purity or sinlessness (e.g., *Fug.* 117).

4. The whole lengthy discussion of "spiritual gifts" in 1 Cor 12–14, in particular of ecstatic prophecy and glossolalia, is peculiar to 1 Corinthians in the Pauline corpus,[53] and it is quite clear that some of the Corinthians were caught up in these ecstatic manifestations, thinking of themselves as "prophets" or "spirituals" (14:37). Prophetic ecstasy is a climactic experience, perhaps the highest spiritual experience in Philo's religion.[54] The ecstasy is inspired by the divine Spirit, which is identical with Sophia or is the Spirit of Sophia (*Quod Deus* 1–3; *Gig.* 47). Thus, for example, the *sophos* reaches a state of "sober-drunkenness" from undiluted draughts of Sophia (spiritual drink! *Fug.* 166; *Q.E.* 2.29). Paul's insistence on the retention of the *mind* in 1 Cor 14:13–19 is directly intelligible if the Corinthian spirituals, like Philo in *Her.* 263–66, were experiencing the eclipse of their reason in their ecstatic possession by the Spirit.

---

53. Of course the much briefer, more general, and less pointed discussion in Rom 12:4–8 is partly derived from Paul's Corinthian conflicts.

54. See esp. *Leg.* 3.100–104; *Migr.* 34ff. (Philo's personal experience); *Her.* 249–266; *Spec. Leg.* 4.49 (allusion to glossolalia?). See further chap. 7 above.

To appreciate the full extent of the "parallel," however, we should note that all of these different terms, symbols, principles, and ideas are found together in a few key passages in Wisdom[55] and especially in numerous passages in Philo. It has already been noted that the heavenly "anthropos" and the earthly "anthropos" correspond to the "perfect" vs. the "babes" as designations of different spiritual status (as in *Leg.* 1.90-94). Similarly, the *sophos* who, by possession of Sophia, possesses all things, including true wealth and kingship, and whose lot is heavenly as opposed to earthly, also possesses knowledge that "God is One alone" (*Plant.* 62-72). Perhaps the most striking passages where all of these terms and ideas come together are *Migr.* 28-40; *Her.* 247-83; *Post.* 124-29; *Abr.* 255-76; *Virt.* 179-80, 212-19; *Q.E.* 2.39-40. The focus, the vortex of this whole pattern of religious thinking is, of course, the divine figure Sophia.

Spiritual Elitism in Corinth

It is clear from the foregoing survey that (with the exception of πνευματικός / ψυχικός) all of the language and ideas of the Corinthians evidenced in Paul's letter are also used in close interconnection in Philo's writings and to a considerable degree also in Wisdom. Systematic analysis of this language thus makes it possible to describe the general background and pattern of the Corinthians' spirituality by analogy with the Hellenistic-Jewish religiosity represented in Philo and Wisdom.

These Corinthians, almost certainly through the ministry of the Alexandrian Jew Apollos, who was eloquent and well versed in the scriptures (Acts 18:24), have been caught up in an enthusiastic devotion to Sophia along the same lines as expressed in Wisdom and Philo. But this appears quite different from a resurrection attained already at baptism whereby "as participators in the cross of Christ, the baptized are at the

---

55. It may be useful to recount just how much of this language is actually present just in Wis 6-10, similarly focused around the divine figure Sophia. Besides being the object of salvation and the means of revelation, including the words or eloquence of wisdom (Wis 8:8-9, 12, 18; 7:7, 21; 9:17-18), Sophia is the mediator of creation (Wis 8:4-6; 7:22, 27; 8:1). Sophia imparts spiritual gifts such as prophecy (Wis 8:8; 7:20-21, 22-24, 27; 9:17) and it is she who accomplishes the (spiritualized) salvation of the Exodus (Wis 10:15-21). She imparts immortality and incorruptibility to the soul (Wis 8:13, 17; 6:19; versus the corruptible body in 9:15), and provides a spiritual status understood in terms of being wise, nobly born, wealthy, kingly, glorious (Wis 8:3, 5, 10, 14, 18; 6:20; 7:8, 11; 9:4).

same time also participators in the resurrection and enthronement of Christ."[56]

The Corinthian spirituals, however, have quite clearly focused their faith on heavenly Sophia and not necessarily on Christ. From all indications in Paul's letter, they were not much interested in the cross of Christ. Moreover, as Koester has pointed out in review of Wilckens, it is Paul who identified Christ with Sophia, not the Corinthians.[57] Furthermore, in thus attempting to replace Sophia with Christ it is Paul who emphasized the exaltation of Christ (1 Cor 3:21–23; 10:4; and in effect, 15:5–11). There is no evidence that the Corinthians' understanding of baptism was even Christo-centric, let alone Christo-morphic. In fact, the evidence such as it is, would point the other way. That is, some saw themselves as baptized into Apollos, or Paul. In fact, the baptism into Moses and the whole spiritual exodus understood as baptism suggest that for the Corinthians this was a baptism of Sophia and not a dying and rising with Christ at all.[58] However much Käsemann's picture of eschatological enthusiasm may describe the hymns and confessions of Colossians and Ephesians and the slogan of the false teachers of 2 Tim 2:18, it does not fit the religion of the Corinthians and its Hellenistic-Jewish background.

Far from being celebrated by the Corinthians as the redeemer whose dying, rising, and enthronement they shared, and far from being "identified" by them with Sophia, Christ—like the apostles Paul, Apollos, and Cephas (1 Cor 1:12)—is regarded as a teacher of divine Sophia, a great mystagogue, perhaps similar to Moses in Philo's writings.[59] By means of the Sophia imparted through Christ, Apollos, etc., these Corinthians are truly *wise, powerful, nobly born, filled, wealthy, kings*. They have reached the highest spiritual status. They are, through possession of Sophia, *perfect* and *spiritual,* and set themselves above those of lesser status, the *babes* and *psychics*—an attitude with obviously divisive implications for a religious community.

---

56. Cf. Käsemann, "On the Topic," 273; Robinson, "Kerygma and History," 123–24

57. Koester's review of Wilckens, 591–92.

58. Meeks, "The Image," 202, has discerned that this was in Corinth a baptism of Sophia; but, not following the implications of Koester's point about the Corinthians' differentiation of Christ and Sophia, he still perceives the Corinthian baptism as Christo-morphic.

59. See Goodenough, *By Light, Light,* chapter 8, esp. 233–34.

No Resurrection of the Dead? 155

Further implications of this spiritual elitism emerge at scattered points in 1 Corinthians. The most obvious empirical manifestation of their transcendent spiritual status was the individual experience of ecstatic prophecy, including glossolalia. Their theological *gnosis* of the Oneness of God and the nonexistence of idols seem innocuous enough. But apparently they believed that this *gnosis* along with their experience of spiritual exodus, spiritual food and drink from the spiritual rock (Sophia), rendered them ethically pure and incapable of sin (implications of 8:7ff.; 10:1–13, 14–22). Insofar as they possessed the divine Sophia they possessed all things, and believed that all things were possible for them.

Their possession of Sophia and perfection also meant that they belonged to the type of the heavenly "anthropos," as opposed to that of the "anthropos" who is still too much attached to earthly and bodily matters. The distinction between two types of human appears to be parallel to if not identical to the distinction in religious status expressed in terms of *perfect vs. children* and the distinctive Corinthian terminology of *pneumatikos/psychikos* is apparently yet another way of expressing the same contrast. Much of the terminology used in making these distinctions presupposes and expresses a fundamental metaphysical and anthropological dualism that contrasts body and soul, earthly and heavenly, mortal and immortal. The real thrust of this religious viewpoint is more soteriological, however, seeking the exalted religious status attained through possession of Sophia. Insofar as it belongs to the heavenly type of mankind, the true self (soul or mind) is secure in its incorruptible spiritual nature, realizing the ontological priority of its origin according to the divine Image (= Sophia). The soul thus realizes liberation from earthly matters and from the body itself. The body is viewed as a burden, a corpse (= "dead") weighing down the soul that desires to reach beyond the infantile or earthly stage, to the naked immortality that transcends all corruptibility in its intimacy with Sophia. Accordingly the Corinthian *teleioi* denied "the resurrection of the dead" (the body). For it would have been the antithesis to their liberation from bodily and earthly realities, a threat to their heavenly immortality, and the loss of their intimate relation with Sophia and the perfection thus attained.

Abbreviations

ANCIENT

Augustine
    Civ.   *De civitatae Dei (City of God)*

2 Bar.   *2 Baruch*

Cicero
    Nat. Deor.   *De natura deorum* (On the Nature of the Gods)

CII   *Corpus Inscriptionum Iudaicarum*

Corp. Herm.   *Corpus Hermeticum,* edited by Arthur Darby Nock, 1945–54

Dio Chrysostom
    Or.   *Orations*

Epictetus
    Diatr.   *Diatribai* (Dissertations)

Eusebius
    Praep. Ev.   *Praeparatio evangelica* (Preparation for the Gospel)

Josephus
    Ant.   *Antiquitates judaicae* (Antiquities of the Judeans)
    Apion   *Contra Apionem* (Against Apion)

Livy
    Hist.   *History of Rome*

Abbreviations

Marcus Aurelius
- *Med.* — *Meditations*

Philo
- *Abr.* — *De Abrahamo* (On the Life of Abraham)
- *Aet.* — *De aeternitate mundi* (On the Eternity of the World)
- *Cher.* — *De cherubim* (On the Cherubim)
- *Conf.* — *De confusione linguarum* (On the Confusion of Languages)
- *Cong.* — *De congressu eruditionis gratia* (On the Preliminary Studies)
- *Decal.* — *De decalogo* (On the Decalogue)
- *Det.* — *Quod deterius potiori insidari soleat* (That the Worse Attacks the Better)
- *Ebr.* — *De ebrietate* (On Drunkenness)
- *Fug.* — *De fuguga et inventione* (On Flight and Finding)
- *Gig.* — *De gigantibus* (On Giants)
- *Her.* — *Quis rerum divinarum heres sit* (Who Is the Heir?)
- *Leg.* — *Legum allegoriae* (Allegorical Interpretation)
- *Mig.* — *De migratione Abrahami* (On the Migration of Abraham)
- *Mos.* — *De vita Mosis* (On the Life of Moses)
- *Mut.* — *De mutatione nominum* (On the Change of Names)
- *Op.* — *De opificio mundi* (On the Creation of the World)
- *Plant.* — *De plantatione* (On Planting)
- *Post.* — *De posteritate Caini* (On the Posterity of Cain)
- *Praem.* — *De praemiis et poenis* (On Rewards and Punishment)
- *Prob.* — *Quod omnis Probus Liber sit* (Every Good Man Is Free)
- *Q.E.* — *Quaestiones et solutions in Exodum* (Questions and Answers on Exodus)
- *Q.G.* — *Quaestiones et solutions in Genesin* (Questions and Answers on Genesis)
- *Quod Deus* — *Quod Deus sit immutabilis* (That God Is Unchangeable)
- *Som.* — *De somniis* (On Dreams)
- *Spec. Leg.* — *De specialibus legibus* (On the Special Laws)
- *Virt.* — *De virtutibus* (On the Virtues)
- *Vita Cont.* — *De vita contemplativa* (On the Contemplative Life)

Plato
  Phraedr.   *Phaedrus*
  Tim.   *Timaeus*

Plutarch
  Def. Orac.   *De defectu oraculorum* (On the Decline of the Oracles)
  Is. et Os.   *De Iside et Osiride* (On Isis and Osiris)
  Placit. philos. *De placita philosophorum* (On Philosophical Maxims)

Seneca
  Ep.   *Epistles*

Simplicius
  Phys.   *On Aristotle's Physics*
  T. Naph.   *Testament of Naphtali*

MODERN

AHAWPHK	Abhandlungen der Heidelberger Akademie der Wissenschaften, Phil.-hist. Klasse
AnBib	Analecta biblica
BHT	Beiträge zur historischen Theologie
Bib	*Biblica*
BZNW	Beihefte zur Zeitschrift für die neutestamentliche Wissenschaft
CBQ	*Catholic Biblical Quarterly*
CRINT	Compendia Rerum Iudaicarum ad Novum Testamentum
EB	Études biblique
FRLANT	Forschungen zur Religion und Literatur des Alten und Neuen Testaments
HR	*History of Religion*
HTR	*Harvard Theological Review*
HUCA	*Hebrew Union College Annual*
JKP	*Jahrbuch für klassische Philologie*
JR	*Journal of Religion*
JTS	*Journal of Theological Studies*
KuD	*Kerygma und Dogma*

LKT	*Lexikon für Theologie und Kirche*
MPT	*Monatschrift für Pastoraltheologie*
NovT	*Novum Testamentum*
NRSV	New Revised Standard Version of the Bible
NTS	*New Testament Studies*
PAAJR	*Proceedings of the American Academy of Jewish Research*
PGM	*Papyri graecae magicae: Die griechischen Zuaberpapyri.* Edited by Karl Prisendanz. Leipzig: Teubner, 1928
*RGG*³	*Die Religion in Geschichte und Gegenwart.* 3d ed. Edited by Kurt Galling, 1957–65
RKAMP	Religion und Kultur der alten Mittelmeerwelt in Parallelforschungen
SGKA	Studien zur Geschichte und Kultur des Altertums
SNTSMS	Society for New Testament Studies Monograph Series
SUNT	Studien zur Umwelt des Neuen Testaments
TDNT	*Theological Dictionary of the New Testament.* Edited by Gerhard Kittel and Gerhard Friedrich, 1964–76
ThBT	Theologische Bibliothek Töpelmann
TU	Texte und Untersuchungen
TWNT	*Theologisches Wörterbuch zum Neuen Testament.* Edited by Gerhard Kittel and Gerhard Friedrich, 1934–79
VC	*Vigilae christianae*
ZNW	*Zeitschrift für die neutestamentliche Wissenschaft*

Bibliography

Albinus. *The Platonic Doctrines of Albinus* [*Didaskalikos*]. Translated by Jeremiah Reedy. Introduction by Jackson P. Hershbell. Grand Rapids: Phanes, 1991.
Alexandre, Monique. *De Congressu Eruditionis*. Les Oeuvres de Philon D'Alexandrie 16. Paris: Cerf, 1967.
Arnim, Hans Friedrich August von. *Stoicorum Veterum Fragmenta*. 4 vols. Leipzig: Teubner, 1903-24.
Barrett, C. K. *The First Epistle to the Corinthians*. New York: Harper, 1968.
Berthelot, M. *Collection des anciens alchemists Grecs*. 3 vols. 1888. Reprinted, London: Holland, 1963.
Bertram, "νήπιος." In *TDNT* 4 (1967) 912-23 = *TWNT* 4 (1942) 913-25.
Bousset, Wilhelm. *Die Religion des Judentums im späthellenistischen Zeitalter*. 4th ed. Edited by Hugo Gressmann. HNT 21. Tübingen: Mohr/Siebeck, 1966.
Brandenburger, Egon. *Adam und Christus*. WMANT 7. Neukirchen-Vluyn: Neukirchener, 1962.
Brehier, Emile. *Les idée philosophiques et religieuses de Philon d'Alexandrie*. 3d ed. Paris: Picard, 1908.
Büchsel, Friedrich. "εἴδωλον κτλ." In *TDNT* 2 (1964) 375-80 = *TWNT* 2 (1935) 373-77.
Bultmann, Rudolf. *Theology of the New Testament*. 2 vols. Translated by Kendrick Grobel. New York: Scribners, 1951-55.
———. Review of *Gnosis* by Jacques Dupont. *JTS* 3 (1952) 10-26.
———. "γνώσκω κτλ." In *TDNT* 1 (1964) 689-719 = *TWNT* 1 (1933) 688-719.
———. "θάνατος κτλ." In *TDNT* 3 (1965) 7-25 = *TWNT* 3 (1938) 7-25.
———. "νεκρός κτλ." In *TDNT* 4 (1967) 892-95 = *TWNT* 4 (1942) 896-99.
———. "πείθω κτλ." In *TDNT* 6 (1968) 1-11 = *TWNT* 6 (1959) 1-12.
———. *Faith and Understanding*. Edited by Robert W. Funk. Translated by Louise Pettibone Smith. 1969. Reprinted, Philadelphia: Fortress, 1987.
Campenhausen, Hans von. *Die Begründung kirchlicher Entscheidungen beim Apostel Paulus: Zur Grundlegung des Kirchenrechts*. Heidelberger Akademie der Wissenschaften. Philosophisch-Historische Klasse. Sitzungsberichte, Jahrg. 1957, Abh. 2. Heidelberg: Winter, 1957.

Cartlidge, David R. "1 Corinthians 7 as a Foundation for a Christian Sex Ethic." *JR* 55 (1975) 220–34.
Chavasse, Claude. *The Bride of Christ: An Enquiry into the Nuptial Element in Early Christianity.* London: Religious Book Club, 1940.
Cohen, Samuel S. "The Unity of God: A Study in Hellenistic and Rabbinic Theology." *HUCA* 26 (1955) 425–79.
Colpe, Carsten. *Die religionsgeschichtliche Schule.* FRLANT 78. Göttingen: Vandenhoeck & Ruprecht, 1961.
———. Review of *Weisheit und Torheit* by Ulrich Wilckens. *MPT* 52 (1963) 487–93.
Colson, F. H. "Philo on Education." *JTS* 18 (1917) 151–62.
Conzelmann, Hans. "Die Mutter der Weisheit." In *Zeit und Geschichte: Dankesgabe an Rudolf Bultmann zum 80. Geburtstag,* edited by Erich Dinkler, 2:225–34. Tübingen: Mohr/Siebeck, 1964. Reprinted as "The Mother of Wisdom." In *The Future of Our Religious Past,* edited by James M. Robinson, 230–43. New York: Harper & Row, 1971
———. "Paulus und die Weisheit." *NTS* 12 (1965–66) 231–44.
———. *An Outline of the Theology of the New Testament.* Translated by John Bowden. New York: Harper & Row, 1969.
———. *1 Corinthians.* Translated by James W. Leitch. Hermeneia. Philadelphia: Fortress, 1975.
Cousins, Ewert. "The Mature Conscience in Theological Perspective." In *Conscience: Its Freedom and Limitations,* edited by William C. Bier. Pastoral Psychology Series 6. New York: Fordham University Press, 1971.
Cullmann, Oscar. *The Christology of the New Testament.* Translated by Shirley C. Guthrie and Charles A. M. Hall. Philadelphia: Westminster, 1959.
Dalbert, Peter. *Die Theologie der hellenistisch-jüdischen Missionsliteratur unter Ausschluss von Philo und Josephus.* Hamburg: Reich, 1954.
Delling, Gerhard. "Josephus und die heidnischen Religionen." *Klio* 43–45 (1965) 263–69.
———. "τέλος κτλ." In *TDNT* 8 (1972) 48–87 = *TWNT* 8 (1969) 48–87.
Dodds, E. R. *Pagan and Christian in an Age of Anxiety: Some Aspects of Religious from Marcus Aurelius to Constantine.* Cambridge: Cambridge University Press, 1963.
———. *The Greeks and the Irrational.* Berkeley: University of California Press, 1951.
Dölger, Franz. "Christus als himmlischer Eros und Seelenbrautigam bei Origenes." *Antike und Christentum* 6 (1950) 273–75.
Dörrie, Heinrich. *Der Königskult des Antiochus von Kommagene.* Abhandlung der Akademie der Wissenschaft Göttingen, Philologisch-historische Klasse 3/60. Göttingen: Vandenhoeck & Ruprecht, 1964.
Dupont, Jacques. *Gnosis: La connaissance religieuse dans les épîtres de Saint Paul.* Leuvain: Nauwelaerts, 1949. 2d ed., 1960.
Eising, H. "Der Weisheitslehrer und die Götterbilder." *Bib* 40 (1959) 373–408.
Eliade, Mircea. *The Sacred and the Profane: The Nature of Religion.* Translated by Willard R. Trask. New York: Harper, 1961.
Eltester, Friedrich-Wilhelm. *Eikon im Neuen Testament.* BZNW 23. Berlin: Töpelmann, 1958.
Festugière, A. J. *Personal Religion among the Greeks.* Berkeley: University of California Press, 1965.

Feuillet, A. *Le Christ, Sagesse de Dieu, d'après les epitres Pauliniennes*. EB. Paris: Gabalda, 1966.
Fichtner, Johannes. *Weisheit Salomos*. Handbuch zum Alten Testament 2/6. Tübingen: Mohr/Siebeck, 1938.
Foerster, Werner. "ἔξεστιν, ἐξουσία, κτλ." In *TDNT* 2 (1964) 560–75 = *TWNT* 2 (1935) 557–72.
Friedlander, M. *Geschichte der jüdischen Apologetik als Vorgeschichte des Christentums*. Zurich: Schmidt, 1903.
Funk, Robert. "Word and Word in 1 Corinthians 2:6-16." In *Language, Hermeneutic and Word of God*. New York: Harper, 1966.
Geffcken, Johannes. *Zwei griechische Apologeten*. Sammlung wissenschaftlicher Kommentare zu griechischen und romischen Schriftstellern. Leipzig: Teubner, 1907.
———. "Bildersteit." In *Zwei Griechische Apologeten*.
Georgi, Dieter. *Die Gegner des Paulus im 2. Korintherbrief*. WMANT 11. Neukirchen-Vluyn: Neukirchener, 1964. ET = *The Opponents of Paul in Second Corinthians: A Study of Religious Propaganda in Late Antiquity*. Philadelphia: Fortress, 1986.
Geyer, John. *The Wisdom of Solomon: Introduction and Commentary*. Torch Bible Commentaries. London: SCM, 1963.
Goodenough, Erwin R. *The Jurisprudence of the Jewish Courts in Egypt: Legal Administrations by the Jews under the Early Roman Empire as Described by Philo Judaeus*. New Haven: Yale University Press, 1929.
———. *By Light, Light: The Mystic Gospel of Hellenistic Judaism*. New Haven: Yale University Press, 1935.
———. "Philo on Immortality." *HTR* 39 (1946) 85–108.
Goodman, Felicitas. *Speaking in Tongues: A Cross-Cultural Study of Glossolalia*. Chicago: University of Chicago Press, 1972.
Gross, H., and F. Mussner. "Brautmystik, biblische." In *LKT* 2 (1958) 660–62.
Grundmann, Walter. "ἐγκράτεια κτλ." In *TDNT* 2 (1964) 339–42 = *TWNT* 2 (1935) 338–40.
Haenchen, Ernst. *The Acts of the Apostles: A Commentary*. Translated by Bernard Noble and Gerald Shinn. Philadelphia: Westminster, 1971.
Hamerton-Kelly, R. G. *Pre-existence, Wisdom, and the Son of Man: A Study of the Idea of Pre-existence in the New Testament*. SNTSMS 21. 1973. Reprinted, Eugene, OR: Wipf & Stock, 2000.
Harnack, Adolf von. *History of Dogma*. 7 vols. Translated by Neil Buchanan. 1894–1900. Reprinted, Eugene, OR: Wipf & Stock, 1997.
Hegermann, Harald. *Die Vorstellung vom Schöpfungsmittler im Hellenistischen Judentum and Urchristentum*. TU 82. Berlin: Akademie, 1961.
Hengel, Martin. *Judaism and Hellenism: Studies in Their Encounter in Palestine during the Early Hellenistic Period*. 2 vols. Translated by John Bowden. Philadelphia: Fortress, 1974.
Hennecke, Edgar, and Wilhelm Schneemelcher, editors. *New Testament Apocrypha*. 2 vols. Translated by A. J. B. Higgins. Philadelphia: Westminster, 1963–65.
Horsley, Richard A. "The Background of the Confessional Formula in I Kor 8:6." *ZNW* 69 (1978) 130–35.

———. *1 Corinthians*. Abingdon New Testament Commentaries. Nashville: Abingdon, 1998.

———. "1 Corinthians: A Case Study of Paul's Assembly as an Alternative Society." In *Paul and Empire: Religion and Power in Roman Imperial Society*, edited by Richard A. Horsley, 242–52. Harrisburg, PA: Trinity, 1997.

———. "How Can Some of You Say that There Is no Resurrection of the Dead?": Spiritual Elitism in Corinth." *NovT* 20 (1978) 203–31.

———, editor. *Paul and Empire: Religion and Power in Roman Imperial Society*. Harrisburg, PA: Trinity, 1997.

———, editor. *Paul and Politics: Essays in Honor of Krister Stendahl*. Harrisburg, PA: Trinity, 2000.

———. "Paul's Assembly in Corinth: An Alternative Society." In *Urban Religion in Roman Corinth: Interdisciplinary Approaches*, edited by Daniel N Schowalter and Steven J. Friesen, 371–95. Cambridge: Harvard University Press, 2005.

———. "*Pneumatikos* vs. *Psychikos*: Distinctions of Spiritual Status among the Corinthians." *HTR* 69 (1976) 269–88.

———. "Rhetoric and Empire—and 1 Corinthians." In *Paul and Politics: Ekklesia, Israel, Imperium, Interpretation*, edited by Richard A. Horsley, 72–102. Harrisburg, PA: Trinity, 2000.

———. "Wisdom of Word and Words of Wisdom in Corinth." *CBQ* 39 (1977) 224–39.

Hurd, John Coolidge. *The Origin of I Corinthians*. 1965. Reprinted, Macon, GA: Mercer University Press, 1983.

Jaeger, Werner. *The Theology of the Early Greek Philosophers*. Oxford: Clarendon, 1947.

Jeremias, Joachim. "Zur Gedankenführung in den Paulinischen Briefen: (3) Die Briefzitate in I. Kor. 8, 1–13." In *Abba*, 273ff. Göttingen: Vandenhoeck & Ruprecht, 1966.

Jervell, Jacob. *Imago Dei*. FRLANT 58. Göttingen: Vandenhoeck & Ruprecht, 1960.

Jonas, Hans. *Gnosis und spätantiker Geist*. 2 vols. 2d ed. FRLANT. Göttingen: Vandenhoeck & Ruprecht, 1966.

———. *The Gnostic Religion*. 3d ed. Boston: Beacon, 2001.

Jong, K. H. E. de. *Das antike Mysterienwesen in religionsgeschichtlicher, ethnologischer und psychologischer Beleuchtung*. Leiden: Brill, 1909.

Käsemann, Ernst. "On the Topic of Primitive Christian Apocalyptic." In *Apocalypticism*, edited by Robert W. Funk, 99–133. New York: Herder & Herder, 1969. German orig. 1962.

Kerst, R. "1 Kor 8.6—ein vorpaulinisches Taufbekenntnis?" *ZNW* 66 (1975) 130–39.

Klein, Franz-Norbert. *Die Lichtterminologie bei Philon von Alexandrien und in den Hermetischen Schriften*. Leiden: Brill, 1962.

Knox, W. L. *St. Paul and the Church of the Gentiles*. Cambridge: Cambridge University Press, 1939.

Koester, Helmut. "GNOMAI DIAPHOROI: The Sources of Diversification in Early Christianity." *HTR* 58 (1965) 279–318. Republished in Robinson and Koester, *Trajectories through Early Christianity*, 114–57. 1971. Reprinted, Eugene, OR: Wipf & Stock, 2006.

———. "Paul and Hellenism." In *The Bible in Modern Scholarship: Papers Read at the 100th Meeting of the Society of Biblical Literature, December 28–30, 1964*, edited by J. Philip Hyatt, 187–95. Nashville: Abingdon, 1965.

———. Review of *Weisheit und Torheit* by Ulrich Wilckens. *Gnomen* 33 (1961) 590-95.
———. "The Structure and Criteria of Early Christian Beliefs." In *Trajectories*, 205-31.
Larcher, C. *Études sur le livre de la Sagesse.* EBib. Paris: Gabalda, 1969.
Leeuw, Gerhardus van der. *Religion in Essence and Manifestation.* 2 vols. Translated by J. E. Turner. New York: Harper, 1963.
Lewis, I. M. *Ecstatic Religion: An Anthropological Study of Spirit Possession and Shamanism.* Baltimore: Penguin, 1971.
Lietzmann, Hans. *An die Korinther.* 5th ed. Handbuch zum Neuen Testament. Mohr/Siebeck, 1969.
Lindsay, Jack, translator. *The Golden Ass.* Bloomington: Indiana University Press, 1932.
Lohse, Bernard. *Askese und Mönchtum in der Antike and in der alten Kirche.* RKAMP 1. Munich: Oldenbourg, 1969.
Luck, Georg. *Der Akademiker Antiochus.* Noctes Romanae 7. Bern: Haupt, 1953.
Lietzmann, Hans. *An die Korinther.* Handbuch zum Neuen Testament 9. Tübingen: Mohr/Siebeck, 1949.
Luck, Georg. *Der akademiker Antiochus.* Noctes Romanae 7. Bern: Haupt, 1953.
Lührmann, Dieter. *Das Offenbarungsverständnis bei Paulus and in den paulinischen Gemeinden.* WMANT 16. Ncukirchen: Neukirchener Verlag, 1965.
Mack, Burton L. *Logos und Sophia: Untersuchungen zur Weisheitstheologie im hellenistischen Judentum.* SUNT 10. Göttingen: Vandenhoeck & Ruprecht, 1973.
Macquarrie, John. "The Struggle of Conscience for Authentic Selfhood." In *Three Issues in Ethics.* New York: Harper & Row, 1970.
Marcus, Ralph. "Divine Names and Attributes in Hellenistic Jewish Literature." *PAAJR* 3 (1931-32) 43-120.
Maurer, Christian. "σύνοιδα." In *TDNT* 7 (1971) 898-919 = *TWNT* 7 (1964) 897-918.
Meeks, Wayne A. "The Image of the Androgyne: Some Uses of a Symbol in Earliest Christianity." *HR* 13 (1974) 165-208.
Merkelbach, Reinhold. *Isisfeste in griechisch-riömischer Zeit: Daten und Riten.* Beiträge zur klassischen Philologie 5. Meisenheim am Glan: Hain, 1963.
Mitchell, Margaret M. *Paul and the Rhetoric of Reconciliation.* Louisville: Westminster John Knox, 1992.
Munck, Johannes. "The Church without Factions: Studies in 1 Corinthians 1-4." In *Paul and the Salvation of Mankind,* 135-67. Translated by Frank Clarke. Richmond: John Knox, 1959.
Neufeld, Vernon H. *The Earliest Christian Confessions.* NTTS 5. Leiden: Brill, 1963.
Niederwimmer, Kurt. "Erkennen und Lieben: Gedanken zum Verhältnis von Gnosis und Agape im ersten Korintherbrief." *KuD* 11 (1965) 75-102.
———. *Der Begriff der Freiheit im Neuen Testament.* ThBT 11. Berlin: Töpelmann, 1966.
———. *Askese und Mysterium: Über Ehe, Ehescheidung und Eheverzicht in den Anfängen des christlichen Glaubens.* FRLANT 113. Göttingen: Vandenhoeck & Ruprecht, 1975.
Nilsson, Martin P. *Geschichte der griechischen Religion.* Vol. 2. 2d ed. Handbuch der Altertumswissenschaft 5. Munich: Beck, 1961.
———. *A History of Greek Religion.* 2d ed. Oxford: Clarendon, 1949.

Nock, Arthur Darby. *Conversion: The Old and the New in Religion from Alexander the Great to Augustine of Hippo.* Oxford: Oxford University Press, 1933.

———. *Corpus Hermeticum,* Translated by A.-J. Festugière. Paris: Les Belles Lettres, 1945–54.

———, Colin Roberts, and T. C. Skeat. "The Guild of Zeus Hypsistos." *HTR* 29 (1936) 39–88.

Norden, E. *Agnostos Theos: Untersuchungen zur Formengeschichte religiöser Rede.* Leipzig: Teubner, 1913.

Pascher, J. H BASILIKH ODOS. SGKA 17. Paderborn: Schoeningh, 1931.

Pearson, Birger. *The Pneumatikos–Psychikos Terminology in I Corinthians.* SBLDS 12. Missoula, MT: Scholars, 1973.

Perrin, Norman. *Rediscovering the Teachings of Jesus.* New York: Harper & Row, 1967.

Peterson, E. *Eis Theos: Epigraphische, formgeschichtliche und religionsgeschichtliche Untersuchungen.* FRLANT 24. Göttingen: Vandenhoeck & Ruprecht, 1926.

Pierce, C. A. *Conscience in the New Testament.* SBT 1/15. Chicago: Allenson, 1955.

Pohlenz, Max. *Philon von Alexandria.* Nachrichten der Akademie der Wissenschaft in Göttingen: Phil.-Hist. Klasse 5. Göttingen: Vandenhoeck &Ruprecht, 1942.

———. *Die Stoa.* 2 vols. Göttingen: Vandenhoeck &Ruprecht, 1949.

Preisendanz, Karl. *Papyri graecae magicae I.* Leipzig: Teubner, 1928–31.

Quasten, Johannes. *Patrology.* 4 vols. Westminster, MD: Newman, 1956–86.

Reese, James M. *Hellenistic Influence on the Book of Wisdom and Its Consequences.* AnBib 41. Rome: Biblical Institute Press, 1970.

Reitzenstein, Richard. *Die hellenistischen Mysterienreligionen.* 3d ed. 1927. Reprinted, Darmstadt: Wissenschaftliche Buchgesellschaft, 1956.

Ricoeur, Paul. *The Symbolism of Evil.* Translated by Emerson Buchanan. Boston: Beacon, 1969.

Robinson, James M. "Kerygma and History in the New Testament." In Robinson and Koester, *Trajectories,* 20–70.

———. "LOGOI SOPHON: On the Gattung of Q." In Robinson and Koester, *Trajectories,* 71–113.

———, and Helmut Koester. *Trajectories in Early Christianity.* 1971. Reprinted, Eugene, OR: Wipf & Stock, 2006.

Roon, A. van. "The Relation between Christ and the Wisdom of God according to Paul." NovT 16 (1975) 207–39.

Rudolph, Kurt. "Urmensch." In *RGG*³ 6:1196.

Rush, Alfred C. "Death as a Spiritual Marriage: Individual and Ecclesial Eschatology." VC 26 (1972) 81–101.

Sampley, J. Paul. *"And the Two Shall Become One Flesh": A Study of Traditions in Ephesians 5:21–33.* SNTSMS 16. 1971. Reprinted, Eugene, OR: Wipf & Stock, 2002.

Schlier, Heinrich. "Excursus on *Hieros Gamos.*" In *Der Brief an die Epheser,* 265–76. 2d ed. Düsseldorf: Patmos, 1958.

Schmid, J. "Brautschaft, heilige." In *RAC* 2 (1954) 546ff.

Schmithals, Walter. *Die Gnosis in Korinth: Eine Untersuchung zum Korintherbriefen.* 3d ed. FRLANT 66. Göttingen: Vandenhoeck & Ruprecht, 1969.

———. *Gnosticism in Corinth: An Investigation of the Letters to the Corinthians.* Translated by John E. Steeley. Nashville: Abingdon, 1971.

Schnackenburg, Rudolf. *The Moral Teaching of the New Testament.* Translated by J. Holland-Smith and W. J. O'Hara. New York: Herder & Herder, 1971.
Schniewind, Julius. "Die Leugner der Auferstehung in Korinth." In *Nachgelassene Reden und Aufsätze.* Edited by Ernst Kähler. ThBT 1. Berlin: Töpelmann, 1952.
Schoeps, Hans-Joachim. *Paul: The Theology of the Apostle in the Light of Jewish Religious History.* Translated by Harold Knight. Philadelphia: Westminster, 1961.
Scholem, Gershom. *On the Kabbalah and Its Symbolism.* Translated by Ralph Manheim. New York: Schocken, 1965.
Schüssler Fiorenza, Elisabeth. "Rhetorical Situation and Historical Reconstruction in 1 Corinthians." NTS 33 (1987) 386–403.
Schweizer, Eduard. "πνεῦμα." In *TDNT* 6 (1968) 389–455 = *TWNT* 6 (1959) 389–455.
Scroggs, Robin M. *The Last Adam: A Study in Pauline Anthropology.* Philadelphia: Fortress, 1966.
Smith, Jonathan Z. "Isis: Review Article." *HR* 11 (1972) 236–49.
Soden, Hans von. "Sakrament und Ethik bei Paulus." In *Rudolf Otto Festgruss*, edited by Heinrich Frick, 1–40. Marburger Theologische Studien. Gotha: Klotz, 1931.
Stelzenberger, Johannes. *Syneidēsis im Neuen Testament.* Abhandlungen zur Moraltheologie 1. Paderborn: Schöningh, 1961.
Stern, Menahem. "The Jewish Diaspora." In *The Jewish People in the First Century*, edited by S. Safrai and M. Stern, ??. CRINT ??. Philadelphia: Fortress, 1974. [AQ: pages and vol. #?]
Taeger, Fritz. *Charisma: Studien zur Geschichte des antiken Herrscherkultes.* Vol. 1. Stuttgart: Kohlhammer, 1957.
Tcherikover, Victor. "Jewish Apologetic Literature Reconsidered." *Eos* 48 (1956) 169–93.
———. *Hellenistic Civilization and the Jews.* Philadelphia: Athenaeum, 1959.
Theiler, Willy. *Die Vorhereitung des Neuplatonismus.* Problemata 1. Berlin: Weidmann, 1930.
Thiselton, Anthony C. "Realized Eschatology at Corinth." *NTS* 24 (1978) 510–26.
Tollinton, R. B. *Selections from the Commentaries and Homilies of Origen.* London: SPCK, 1929.
Turowski, Edmund. *Die Widerspiegelung des stoischen Systems bei Philon von Alexandrien.* Leipzig: Noske, 1927.
Underhill, Evelyn. *Mysticism.* 12th ed. New York: Noonday, 1961.
Verbeke, G. *L'evolution de la doctrine du pneuma: du stoicisme a S. Augustin.* 1945. Reprinted, Greek and Roman Philosophy 43. New York: Garland, 1987.
Vidman, Ladislaus. *Isis and Sarapis bei den Griechen und Römern.* Religionsgeschichtliche Versuche und Vporarbeiten 29. Berlin: de Gruyter, 1970.
Wedderburn, A. J. M. "Philo's 'Heavenly Man.'" *NovT* 15 (1973) 301–26.
Weiss, Johannes. *Der erste Korintherbrief.* Kritisch-exegetischer Kommentar 5. Göttingen: Vandenhoeck & Ruprecht, 1910, 1925.
Wendland, Paul. "Die Therapeuten und die philsophische Schrift vom beschaulichen Leben." *JKP* supp. 22 (1896) 693–722.
———. *Die hellenistisch-römische Kultur in ihren Beziehungen zu Judentum und Christentum.* HNT 1. Tübingen: Mohr/Siebeck, 1912.
Wenschkewitz, H. "Die Spiritualisierung der Kultusbegriffe Tempel, Priester, und Opfer im Neuen Testament." *Angelos* 4 (1932) 70–230.

Wilckens, Ulrich. "σοφία κτλ." In *TDNT* 7 (1971) 465–528 = *TWNT* 7 (1964) 465–529.

———. *Weisheit und Torheit.* BHT 26. Tübingen: Mohr/Siebeck, 1959.

Wilson, R. McL. "How Gnostic Were the Corinthians?" *NTS* 19 (1972–73) 65–74.

Wire, Antoinette Clark. *The Corinthian Women Prophets: A Reconstruction through Paul's Rhetoric.* 1990. Reprinted, Eugene, OR: Wipf & Stock, 2004.

Witt, R. E. *Albinus and the History of Middle Platonism.* Cambridge Classical Studies 3. Cambridge: Cambridge University Press, 1937.

Wlosok, Antonie. *Laktanz und die philosophische Gnosis.* AHAWPHK 1960, 2. Heidelberg: Winter, 1960.

Wolfson, Harry Austryn. *Philo: Foundations of Religious Philosophy in Judaism, Christianity, and Islam.* 3d ed. His Structure and Growth of Philosophic Systems from Plato to Spinoza 2. Cambridge: Harvard University Press, 1962.

Zeitlin, Solomon. "Proselytes and Proselytism during the Second Commonwealth and the Early Tannaitic Period." In *Harry Austryn Wolfson: Jubilee Volume on the Occasion of His Seventy-Fifth Birthday,* 871–81. Jerusalem: Alexander Kohut Memorial Foundation, 1965.

www.ingramcontent.com/pod-product-compliance
Lightning Source LLC
Chambersburg PA
CBHW030112170426
43198CB00009B/598